HISTORY OF THE RENAISSANCE
1350–1550

BOOK IV
LITERATURE and ART

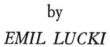

by

EMIL LUCKI

University of Utah Press

Table of Contents

Illustrations

Editor's Note

D<small>R.</small> E<small>MIL</small> L<small>UCKI</small>'s *History of the Renaissance* is the product of many years of study and teaching in the field and of his conviction that in the past some important phases of Renaissance civilization were not given sufficient emphasis in the general histories of the Renaissance. The result quite naturally turned out to be a thorough and a comprehensive manuscript, but too large to be published at today's costs as a single volume; and since printing it in two volumes was precluded by the organization of the work in five parts, the decision was therefore made to conform to the organization of the manuscript and to print it in five quality, but modestly priced, paperbacks. This latter project is now under way with the present Book IV being the last of the series to be printed.

Aside from the obvious virtues of a small and inexpensive book, two other important considerations dictated the decision.

While the series on the Renaissance is labeled "history," the subject matter of each book is of such a nature that the individual books in the series should appeal not only to students of history but also to students in the various other disciplines that are concerned with the study of Western culture. Thus, students of economics and business should find Book I, *Economy and Society*, of much value; and students of religion will discover Book II, *Church and Religion*, equally useful. Book III, *Education, Learning and Thought*, may be expected to appeal to students interested in education, philosophy, and science; while Book V, *Politics and Political Theory*, may serve the needs of those majoring in these fields. Finally, the present book should be welcome to students interested in literature and art. Thus, while the series as a whole can be used as a history textbook on the Renaissance, individual books can be used as collateral and enrichment reading in other courses.

Another reason for publishing the manuscript in several volumes is to make it easily available to the general public. The message and the style of the work are of such a nature that the work should be made available to as wide an audience as possible; and publishing it in one expensive volume or even in two would have defeated the purpose — hence the decision to print it in five handy books.

The University of Utah Press is indeed pleased to have a part in publishing Professor Lucki's *History of the Renaissance*. We believe it is a work which both in its entirety and severally through its parts will leave its mark in the academic world and among the reading public at large.

A. R. MORTENSEN

Preface to the Series

O NE WAY to ascertain the character of a society at a given epoch is to study its economy, religion and church, education and thought, literature and art, and its politics. If the purpose of the inquiry is also to discover in what ways this society differs from that of the preceding age, then a similar examination of the civilization of the earlier period becomes a necessity.

Such are the purposes and nature of this series of five small books on the Renaissance. They will attempt to describe Renaissance civilization and at the same time to discover in what ways this civilization was new and to what extent it was an outgrowth of the Middle Ages.

The purposes of the work naturally determine the chronological limits of the period to be studied. In general, scholars who write about the Renaissance date it approximately from 1350 to 1550. However, while the span of these two centuries may be accepted as the core of the Renaissance period, the dates 1350 and 1550 cannot possibly be regarded as fixed termini. In connection with the history of the church, for example, the date 1517, the year when Luther posted his ninety-five theses, has far more significance as a dividing date than the year 1550. It would be more meaningful, therefore, to stop the survey of church history at 1517 than at 1550. On the other hand, to terminate the survey of astronomy at 1550 would be unjustified, for the Copernican revolution, although made public in 1543, did not gain acceptance until at least a century had elapsed. Similarly, the logical beginning of the study of Renaissance Papacy is not with the events of the year 1350 but with the clash between Boniface VIII and Philip IV of France which occurred some fifty years earlier; and the study of Italian Renaissance painting, not with the works of some painter or painters of the year 1350, but with those of Giotto, whose dates are 1276–1336, or with those of Cimabue who lived even earlier, from about 1240 to 1301. It is clear, therefore, that in any survey of the Renaissance age the beginning and the terminal dates will vary with each aspect of the Renaissance civilization. Dates which may be appropriate for literature may not be appropriate for science, and dates which may hold true for Italy may not apply to Germany.

Aside from the matter of dating the Renaissance, three other factors have influenced the nature and the organization of this work.

One of these additional factors is the secondary purpose of the work, namely, the attempt to discover how the Renaissance civilization was influenced by the preceding age. To answer this crucial question it is necessary to look at the pre-Renaissance century; and so, in general, each phase of the civilization is treated in two stages, the late medieval stage and the Renaissance stage.

A very strong second factor is the desire to provide the reader with an adequate cross-sectional view of each phase of the civilization as well as with its historical, developmental process. If the focus were on the latter alone, then the work would result in a survey of the new developments, in an account, for example, of the growth of a capitalistic economy and not in a picture of the entire economy, or of the decline of the church and not in a view of the church as a whole. Such a treatment would simply reinforce the traditional notion that the Renaissance was a period of innovations, which, while true in part, is certainly in need of revision.

The third factor is the desire to show the several sides to the Renaissance civilization. To accomplish this task, clearly all the major aspects of the civilization need to be examined, and the examination must be comprehensive. Accordingly, some aspects, such as agriculture, economic theory, church organization, educational system, historiography, and diplomacy, are studied at length because to date they have been slighted in histories on the Renaissance; while others, even those which are usually emphasized, such as humanism and art, are treated in considerable detail in order to bring out clearly their dependence on, and deviation from, the medieval civilization.

If this comprehensiveness has resulted, in some places, in a wealth of factual information, the reader is assured that the facts are presented not as ends in themselves, to be learned, but as guides to interpretation. With too few facts at his disposal the reader would have insufficient information upon which to base his judgments, and he would have to depend upon the author's interpretations. While some dependence on the writer is inescapable, it should be reduced to the minimum, as the purpose of any academic discipline is to encourage independence of mind but dependence on evidence. The facts in these books are intended to serve just such a purpose.

EMIL LUCKI

Preface to Book IV

OF THE VARIOUS aspects of Renaissance civilization the two that are usually considered to be most unlike their medieval counterparts are art and literature. Students in general identify Renaissance art with the creations of a Michelangelo or a Titian and Renaissance literature with the works of Shakespeare or a Tasso and conclude that Renaissance art and literature were radically different from medieval art and literature. This approach to the subject and the resulting appraisal are, of course, correct, if it is a comparison of the works of the twelfth century with those of the sixteenth that is desired. But this is not an historical way of treating a subject — to focus on the polar areas and to slight the intervening field. And it is to correct the implication of this comparative approach that this work gives more attention to the developments in art and literature in the course of the slighted centuries than is customary in general histories of the Renaissance.

The study is divided into two parts, literature and art, and each part is opened with an examination of the nature of the works prevailing on the eve of the Renaissance. Then follows a survey of the developments in each field, country by country, care being taken to ascertain what continuities persisted and what changes evolved and with what effects. The result is a picture which presents things in their historical perspective and so becomes a challenge to the popular view that Renaissance literature and art are poles apart from medieval literature and art. Indeed, this approach even discovers that such great artists as Leonardo da Vinci and Tasso retained recognizable medievalisms in their masterpieces.

In a subject as great as this, one would be foolhardy to claim, as Francis Bacon once did, that his findings were all "true, solid, and full of life." Clearly, the task of describing and of analyzing some two hundred years of literature and art and of the myriads of expert works on all the various phases of each subject is beyond the capacity of one person, and occasional errors of fact and judgment may well be discovered by specialists who have devoted their lives to the study of individual writers and artists. Yet it is hoped that much will be found in the book which will pass muster and so render it as a useful corrective to the prevailing conception of Renaissance art and literature.

EMIL LUCKI

I

Development of the Vernacular

I DENTIFYING the Renaissance with humanism, as we generally do, we tend to forget that the enthralment of the Renaissance man with the classics was neither complete nor universal. For, irrespective of its attractiveness, humanism was an exotic, and as such it could not hold all devotees captive indefinitely; sooner or later some of them were bound to free themselves from its fascination. Moreover, there were humanists who always retained some interest in their native literature; while the more lowly folk never forsook their native songs and tales. The rise of vernacular was, therefore, just a matter of time.

While there were some factors, such as, classical literature and printing, which influenced the progress of all the major western vernaculars in much the same way, there were sufficient differences in their respective developments to warrant separate treatments.

Italy

In Italy various dialects appeared even before the dissolution of the Roman empire. With the breakup of the empire, these dialects naturally advanced and a new tongue, the Lombard, came into being. Later in the Middle Ages, partly because of the contacts with southern France and partly as a result of the influx of refugees from the Albigensian Crusade and the subsequent persecutions, the Provençal language also entered. But among these various dialects that of Tuscany remained closest to the original Latin, and this fact contributed to its ascendancy.

The ascendancy began in the later Middle Ages principally because Latin was the language in the schools of that time. Graduates of these grammar schools composing in their respective tongues were inclined to be guided by their knowledge of Latin; and as they incorporated Latin idioms and syntax in their own writings, they brought their own dialects closer to the Tuscan dialect.

Once started, this process of Tuscanization made rapid progress. The superiority of compositions written in the Tuscan dialect, both the lyrical literature before Dante's time and the more celebrated writings of Dante, Petrarch, and Boccaccio, attracted public attention, and so the language in which this literature was written became more widely known. At the same time, this very superiority invited imitation; and since this imitation also included the use of some Tuscan idioms, Tuscanization naturally moved ahead.

In the course of this advance, the humanistic movement appeared in Italy. As is well known, Petrarch and Boccaccio became its ardent promoters and it soon captured the Italian intellectual world. Now, since humanism called for the cultivation of Latin and Greek classics, its rise in popularity might naturally be deemed as a possible obstacle to the advance of the vernacular. Certainly the extensive use of Latin by the Italian writers of the day and their repeated denunciations of the vernacular as boorish and unfit for use in elegant and scholarly works would prompt such an assumption. The fact is, however, that more literature was written in the vernacular during the heyday of humanism than ever before. Clearly, then, the retarding effect of humanism on the evolution of the vernacular was not nearly as great as assumed.

Not only was humanism less of an obstacle than is popularly believed, but it actually contributed to the formation of a common vernacular.[1] As in earlier times, so in the days of humanism, writers in the different dialects found a common teacher in the classics. Indeed, what Christoforo Landino, professor of rhetoric at Florence and a member of the Medicean learned circle, said of Tuscan — "he who wants to be a good Tuscan writer, must first be a Latin scholar" — applied to writers in other dialects. From the classics then most writers absorbed the grammatical and stylistic canons and began to use them in their own native compositions. But by following the same rules of syntax, employing the same spelling, and borrowing the same words and idioms, they not only Latinized and standardized their own respective dialects but actually brought them closer together, so that adoption of one vernacular became a real possibility. What was needed to bring this about was public approbation of the vernacular by the humanists and an agreement among them on the preferred dialect.

Aside from Dante's pre-Renaissance plea for the use of the *vulgare*,[2] which appeared too early and was soon drowned out by the cult of humanism, the first important Renaissance approval came from Leon Battista Alberti, the celebrated architect, scholar, and humanist. Giving up his earlier position that nothing elegant could possibly be written in the vernacular, because, as he said, he "prefer[red] to help many than to please a few," he began to use the vernacular in his own writings — *Della famiglia*, for example. Moreover, to attract more widespread attention of the Italian world to the literary merits of the vernacular, he induced the Medici to sponsor a contest in which poets vied for a crown to be awarded for the best composition in the native tongue. Lorenzo de' Medici added his great prestige in support of the movement. Although an admirer of the classics, Lorenzo, hoping to endear himself to the common folk of Florence, composed lyrics, *laude*, and *sacra rappresentazione* in his native medium. And with Lorenzo leading the way and others following, the vernacular steadily gained in popularity.

The preferred dialect was agreed upon only after a prolonged literary debate among the leading writers. Machiavelli urged the adoption of the contemporary Florentine dialect; Castiglione recommended the living vernacular of the princely courts; the purists and Pietro Bembo, the Venetian cardinal who for a while served as secretary to Leo X (Giulio de' Medici), argued in behalf of the Tuscan dialect as used by Dante and Petrarch.[3] In the end, Bembo's point of view prevailed; and the language of Italy's two greatest poets, refined somewhat in accordance with the standards of humanism, became the accepted language. It was in this language that Ariosto and Tasso produced the crowning glories of Renaissance Italian literature.

France

The rise of the French vernacular was connected with the growth of the royal domain and authority. Like Italy, France had a variety of dialects, and among them was Francien, the dialect used in Isle de France. The extension of the royal domain by the Capetians necessitated the appointment of an increasing number of crown officials as administrators in the acquired lands, and these people naturally carried the language of the court wherever their assignments took them. In the thirteenth century, in the reign of St. Louis (1226–1270), Latin began to yield in administrative documents to the vernacular, and this displacement grew steadily until, in the first half of the sixteenth century, by a series of royal decrees, Latin was actually dropped from all administrative usage. By then the English were driven out of France, and some of the principal feudatories were reduced, so that more French territory was open to the court language. Moreover, this language gained further acceptance from the popularity of the *rhétoriqueur* literature, as many of the prominent *rhétoriqueurs* were court protégés and wrote in the language of the court.

While the vernacular was thus gaining in acceptance, humanism appeared on the scene, with all its attendant influences. As in Italy, humanism at first may have impeded the rise of the vernacular, but with even less success, in view of the upsurge of nationalism in sixteenth-century France. Then, some of the humanists turned defenders of the native tongue and transformed humanism into a chastening influence. Geoffrey of Troy, a humanist engraver and bookseller of Paris, in his *Champ Fleury* (1529), criticized his compatriots for their readiness to resort to Latin and Greek before they knew their own language well. He appealed to their sense of patriotism and offered suggestions for improving the native tongue, at least as to orthography. Estienne Dolet (although a rabid Hellenist and a critic of Erasmus' *Ciceronianus*) in his *Orateur François*, and Joachim du Bellay, in his *La déffence et illustration de la langue Françoyse*,[4] pointed out the literary properties latent in the French vernacular and argued that it could be used as elegantly as Greek and Latin. Simultaneously with these apologies appeared numerous translations of Latin and Greek classics, both prose and poetry, one of the most popular and influential being Amyot's rendering of Plutarch's *Lives*. These translations naturally invited considerable adaptation of the French to the original classical medium. The result was an improvement in the syntax and sentence structure of the native language, increased standardization, and a general elevation of vocabulary and style.

The final step in the rise of the vernacular to primacy was the Protestant movement. To communicate with the bourgeoisie, the class which was most sympathetic to Protestantism and which did not know Latin well, the reformers found it necessary to employ the native tongue in their writings. An excellent example of this was Calvin's translation of his *Institutes*. Originally written in Latin, it was later translated into French, and the clear, concise, persuasive, and dignified style of the translated version helped to elevate the vernacular as a respectable literary medium.

Germany

In Germany the development of the standard modern literary language (*Literatursprache*) was the outcome of four factors.

The first factor was the use of Prague as the capital of the Empire from the time of Charles IV (1346–1378) to that of Sigismund (1410–1437), that is, for almost a century. Prague was so located with reference to Upper (southern) and Middle Germany as to facilitate the blending of the languages of the two regions. The language developed in the imperial chancery was partially adopted by a number of regional chanceries, that of Saxony being one of them. Subsequently, under the Habsburgs and due to their extension of imperial influence in the Empire, the same language came to be employed in imperial communications irrespective of their provenience. The process of nationalization was, therefore, begun.

The second force was that of the printing press. Printers, desirous of profit or solicitous for the religious views they were engaged to disseminate, naturally wanted to reach as many readers as possible and so worked toward standardization. They did so by normalizing the current blend that was already evolving as described above.

The third force was the *Luther Deutsche*, that is, the language Luther used in his translation of the Bible and in his numerous apologetic writings. He employed the language of the Saxon chancery but he vitalized it by infusing it with the language of the ordinary folk and the language of the fourteenth-century German mystical writings, notably that of the *Theologia deutsch*. Naturally, where Lutheranism spread in Germany, his Bible and his writings accompanied it, and the universalization of the Middle German, already promoted by the first two forces, advanced still further.

The fourth factor was the work of the patriotic humanists, Martin Opicz (*Buch von der Deutschen Poeterey*), J. G. Schottelius (*Teutsche Sprachkunst*, 1641), and their followers. As classicists they advocated the purging of the prevailing language of the provincialisms that still clung to it and the acceptance of a uniform standard. Although it took almost two centuries for the language to acquire its modern version, it is with this group that the survey must be terminated. Indeed, even they are more than half a century beyond the chronological limits set for this study.

Spain

In the course of the first millennium and as a result of a series of occupations by various people — Celts, Romans, Suevi and Visigoths, and Arabs — Spain saw a number of related languages arise. Among the principal ones were the Galician of Leon, Castilian, Aragonese, and Mozarabic. Hence to survey the rise of Spanish is to trace the ascendancy of one of these. It proved to be the Castilian tongue.

The ascendancy of Castilian is closely connected with the success of the *reconquista*. But there is no need to trace the whole history of the reconquest. It is enough to recall that by the end of the Middle Ages the Christians recovered most of the peninsula except the territory of Granada in the south, that the major part of the venture was performed by the Castilians, and that the leadership was generally provided by their kings. The reconquest naturally redounded to Castile's prestige and so to the ascendancy of its language.[5]

Fostering this advancement there were two developments in the Castilian language itself. One was the inception of standardization, and the other, the appearance of some influential literature.

The process of standardization might be left to the specialists.[6] But this should be noted: that while some changes in morphology and orthography continued until modern times, fundamentally the Castilian language became the modern Spanish even before the advent of the Renaissance. Entwistle makes the positive assertion that the language in D. Juan Manuel's *Conde Lucanor*, published in 1325, is "virtually the modern literary language."[7]

The literature which helped to fashion and to nationalize the language is indeed the literature which today is studied as the Spanish national literature. The *Cid* appeared in 1140 and represents the epic. The prose was represented by the great works sponsored by King Alfonso the Learned (1252–1284). His *Las siete partidas*, a legal code, served as an exemplar of the preferred Castilian to be used throughout the administration. The *Grande et general estoria, Primera crónica general*, a translation of Latin histories concerning the peninsula, provided a standard for historical composition in the native tongue. In the field of science a like purpose was served by the translations from the Arabic of such works as the *Libros del saber de astronomia* and the famous *Tablas Alfonsiles*. Fiction was served by the *Cabila y Dimna*, a Castilian version of a collection of Hindu moral stories, whose chief characters are the two lynxes Cabila and Dimna. Subsequently, in the field of chivalric romance appeared the *Libro del caballero Cifar*, *Libro de Alixandre*, and *Libro de Apolonio*, and in drama, the incompletely preserved *Misterio de los reyes magos*. Even the lyric, which until the middle of the thirteenth century preferred the Galician (Alfonso the Learned's own 400 religious lyrics, *Cantigas de Santa Maria*, are in this tongue), yielded to the attraction of the Castilian. Juan Ruiz's *Libro de buen amor*, for example, contains several exquisite lyrics. Altogether, these publications served as effective instruments for the standardization and the spread of the Castilian language.

With this wealth of more or less standardized literature the Castilian could begin to eclipse the competing languages. One of the first to yield was the Mozarabic, and it is obvious that the principal reason for its progressive disappearance was the success of the *reconquista*. Then Galician, the literary language of Leon, faded away. We are told that "whereas the grandfather of the famous Marquis of Santillana composed his songs in Galician, the Marquis himself, whose dates are 1398–1458, has only one such experiment, all his other verses being in Castilian."[8] Again the reason is largely political. Leon, after some two centuries of independence interspersed with occasional dynastic unions with Castile, was definitely united to the latter in 1230. Within a century the language yielded to that of Castile.

Next to decline was the Aragonese, but not until the union of Aragon and Castile in 1479. Catalan persisted longer, yet the example of humanist Juan Boscan (1490?–1542), a native of Barcelona, writing his poetry in Castilian may be taken as an indication of the approaching ascendancy of the Castilian literary language even there. The only language, aside from such insignificant — that is, for literary purposes — tongues as the Basque and the dying Arabic, which did not give way to the Castilian, was that of Portugal.

Originally the territory of Portugal was part of the kingdom of Leon. But by the middle of the twelfth century the inhabitants freed themselves (Peace of Zamora, 1143), and to preserve their identity they developed the Galician dialect and guarded it from subversion by the Castilian. By the end of the Middle Ages this cultivation gave rise to a national literature. The lyric was represented by numerous *cancioneiros,* the prose by a series of chronicles and hagiographical works (*Chronica breve de archivo nacional, Chronica de conquista de Algarve, Libros das Linghagens*), and the chivalric romance by a *Historia de Santi Graal*. Although seriously challenged by the Castilian in the late fifteenth and early sixteenth centuries — the ruler Manuel the Fortunate (d. 1525) preferring the Castilian as his court language — the Galician vernacular was saved by the spectacular empire-building and the humanist output of the sixteenth century, Camões contributing his share to both through his distinguished epic, the *Lusiad*. For though the poem is a panegyric in honor of Portugal's favorite hero Vasco da Gama, it clearly is intended as a eulogy of the entire nation. The very title itself, *Os Lusiades* (Sons of Lusus), testifies to this objective as Lusus was the eponymous founder of Lusitania, the Portugal of the future.

England

In medieval England, besides the usual Latin used in the church and schools, there were two competing languages. One was the Norman-French of the court, administration, and aristocracy; the other was English in a number of dialects used by the commonalty. This situation continued until Chaucer's time and is well exemplified by Gower's compositions in French as well as in English. By the end of the fourteenth century, however, French, which had been ruled out of the English courts of law in the years 1356 and 1362,[9] was in rapid decay. In Trevisa's day, for example, according to his own testimony, boys knew "no more French than their left heal," and, worse still, it is reported that English ambassadors to France, as early as 1404, were " 'as ignorant of French as of Hebrew!' "[10] These gibes, of course, cannot be taken seriously, for, Trevisa's boys and the ignorant ambassadors to the contrary notwithstanding, the French language was understood and French literature read. One has only to recall Chaucer's borrowings from French and Caxton's many translations of French chivalric romances to be convinced of this. Yet the fact remains that from Chaucer's day on, French as a literary language in England was rapidly disappearing. The field was left to English alone.

In the establishment of English as the main literary language several factors were very influential. One was the religious lyric, which the clergy, primarily the Franciscans, developed in order to reach the English folk. Religious drama, in use since the middle of the fourteenth century, served the same purpose, as did the various types of didactic literature called forth by the growing importance of the bourgeoisie. Then came the marvelous popularity of Chaucer. His emulators were many, and the diffusion of the language he used correspondingly wide. About the same time Wycliffe's *Bible* and his *Sermons*, in which he called for plain usage, further strengthened the progress of English. Caxton's remarks that the language was fast changing[11] may be taken as evidence of its crystallization as well as of its fluid state in his day. Moreover, he himself partially countered the fluidity by the standardizing influence of the romances which he began printing. Subsequently came the literature connected with the establishment of the Protestant church — the famous Tyndale-Coverdale Bible, Thomas Cranmer's *Book of Common Prayer*, John Foxe's *The Actes and Monuments*, and finally the famous reasoned defense of the Anglican system, *Of the Laws of Ecclesiastical Polity* by Richard Hooker. All of these stimulated further standardization. Simultaneously with this movement went two other movements, the work of the humanist writers seeking to enrich the language and to polish the style, and the effort of Spenser, Ascham, Cheke, and others to save the rugged, masculine English tongue from excessive feminizing borrowings from foreign languages, Latin especially. By the time of Shakespeare the national language was sufficiently well fashioned to become the medium of some of the world's greatest literature.

Summary

From this survey two conclusions are clearly manifest. One is the fact that all the vernaculars matured before the close of the Renaissance period. The other is the fact that these same vernaculars had their beginnings in the Middle Ages. Hence the Renaissance may be said to have brought to fruit the plant which the Middle Ages had raised from a seedling.

1. This relationship is worked out more fully by Kristeller in his essay "The Origin and Development of the Language of Italian Prose," appearing in his *Studies in Renaissance Thought and Letters* (Rome: Edizioni di Storia e Letteratura, 1956), 473–93.

2. See below, p. 31.

3. The views of Castiglione and of Bembo are presented in Castiglione's *The Courtier*. For a summary statement of these views see Ernest Hatch Wilkins, *A History of Italian Literature* (Cambridge: Harvard University Press, 1954), 183, 217–8, 221. Cf. also Charles Sears Baldwin, *Renaissance Literary Theory and Practice* (New York: Columbia University Press, 1939), 27–31.

4. An excellent summary of this famous treatise is to be found in Arthur Tilley's *The Literature of the French Renaissance* (Cambridge: The University Press, 1904), I, 311–4.

5. For a visual picture of this extension see the maps opposite pp. 147 and 161 in William J. Entwistle, *The Spanish Language* (London: Faber and Faber Ltd., 1946).

6. For a concise treatment see Robert K. Spaulding, *How Spanish Grew* (Berkeley: University of California Press, 1948).

7. Entwistle, *op. cit.*, 172.

8. *Ibid.*, 171.

9. The rules, however, were not enforced strictly. On this point see D. S. Bland, "Rhetoric and the Law Student in Sixteenth-Century England," *Studies in Philology*, LIV (1957), 502.

10. Cited from Bennett, *Chaucer and the Fifteenth Century* (Oxford: Clarendon Press, 1947), 114–5.

11. See citation in G. M. Trevelyan, *English Social History* (New York: Longman's Green & Company, 1943), 81–82.

II *Literature on the Eve of the Renaissance*

Renaissance literature like Renaissance art stands out in the public mind as truly superlative. Shakespeare is rated as an incomparable genius, and Ronsard, Tasso, and Cervantes are placed among the greatest. Yet, while an age is to be judged by its finest creations, it must also be judged, if the appraisal is not to be exaggerated, by the rest of its achievements. Works which are not so great or which prepared the way for the masterpieces themselves must also be taken into account. Then and then only can a proper assessment be made. This will be the guiding principle of our survey of Renaissance literature, and this is why the study begins with a consideration of the literature current on the eve of the Renaissance.[1]

The Lyric

Lyric poetry in medieval Europe had attained its finest expression in the love songs of the French troubadours and German *minnesingers*. These are of several types, each with its own suggestive name, but in general they fall into two categories. One type consists of songs of suitors who profess their ardent love, but in vain because the object of their affection is above their station. The other treats of the sweets of mutual love. One example may be cited to illustrate the properties of the second type:

> In orchard where the leaves of hawthorn hide,
> The lady holds a lover to her side,
> Until the watcher in the dawning cried.
> Ah God, ah God, the dawn! it comes how soon.
>
> Ah, would to God that never night must end,
> Nor this my lover far from me should wend,
> Nor watcher day nor dawning ever send!
> Ah God, ah God, the dawn! it comes how soon.

> Come let us kiss, dear lover, you and I,
> Within the meads where pretty song-birds fly;
> We will do all despite the jealous eye:
> Ah God, ah God, the dawn! it comes how soon.
>
> Sweet lover come, renew our lovemaking
> Within the garden where the light bird sings,
> Until the watcher sound the severing.
> Ah God, ah God, the dawn! it comes how soon.
>
> Through the soft breezes that are blown from there,
> From my own lover, courteous, noble and fair,
> From his breath have I drunk a draught most rare.
> Ah God, ah God, the dawn! it comes how soon.
>
> Gracious the lady is, and debonaire,
> For her beauty a many look at her,
> And in her heart is loyal love astir.
> Ah God, ah God, the dawn! it comes how soon.[2]

Here are the thrill of love and the pangs of anticipated parting, a sense of the real and sincere with just a touch of the *courtois* and the senti-mental. It is not a great poem, but it is a lovely poem and represents what the medieval lyricist could accomplish and what was available for transmission to the future.

The date of this selection is unknown; perhaps the late twelfth cen-tury. But it is an established fact that the genre to which it belongs deteriorated after the middle of the thirteenth century. It steadily ad-mitted more and more of the conventional, and in the end yielded to another type of lyric.

The new superseding type has no fixed designation, but it has some identifying features. In general, it is a poetry which sprang from the people, from their festive songs, work songs, and lullabies, but did not long remain true to its humble origin. Striving for social respectability, it turned to the troubadour lyrics as models of propriety and adopted some of their stylistic properties and chivalric airs. The result proved to be of dubious merit. On the one hand, the coarseness of the original was chastened and its style refined; on the other, much of the finished product became an incongruous mixture of earthiness and sophistication, of directness and artificiality, of simplicity and virtuosity. But in either case, what resulted was fashioned poetry, pretty at its best but not inspiring. And the surest evidence of this is the fact that the poets, having become numerous, regarded themselves as artisans and began organizing themselves in gilds, literary gilds that is, in the manner of other craftsmen.

Of course, there were exceptions to this trend toward artificiality. One exception was the religious lyric. Instead of deteriorating, much of it actually developed into warm poetry, principally because of the inspiring Franciscan movement. In the first century of its existence, this movement, still fired with faith, generally stimulated strong pietism which in some instances flamed into inspired devotional songs. Intended for the people and often springing from them, these songs sometimes adapted themselves to the popular secular tunes, but they retained their sincerity, the warmth of the devotion being too real to admit much artificiality.

The other exception was the courtly lyric itself as it developed in Italy. There, instead of deteriorating as described above, it actually approached excellence.

The courtly lyric was popularized in Italy by the Provençal poets who fled from the Albigensian crusaders. Abandoning their harried homeland, the troubadours migrated to northern and central Italy and to the Hohenstaufen court of Frederick II in Sicily. They brought their poetry with them. It soon became fashionable, and in northern Italy even its language was adopted. Thereafter it underwent several modifications which enhanced its popularity still more. One was the adoption of some new verse forms, especially the *terza rima*, the *octave stanza*, and above all, the popular sonnet. Another was the acceptance of the Tuscan dialect whose progressive nationalization naturally increased and extended the popularity of the lyric. The third development was the adaptation of the transported lyric to the tastes of the socially aspiring townsmen, which led either to stylization of theme and language, or to an admixture of enough realism to the *courtois* to make the love themes less idyllic and therefore more acceptable, or to the elevation of love into a transmuting spiritual force. In the end the ultimate result of all these developments was the birth of Dante's *dolce stil nuovo* which in turn led to the Renaissance lyric.

Contributing to this final improvement were several thirteenth-century lyricists of some prominence. Guido Guinizelli of Bologna, credited by Dante with the creation of the *dolce stil nuovo*, exalted love but at the same time abandoned the euphuistic mode of the late Provençal for genuineness; Guido Cavalcanti humanized and psychologized love and achieved mastery over verse forms; the sonneteer Folgare da San Gemignano, in his two sonnet collections *Sonetti de' mesi* and *Sonetti de la semana*, added love of the gay courtly world and depicted this love with deft and delicate language; and Cino da Pistoia multiplied the motifs and the verse forms, in both of which Petrarch subsequently schooled himself.[3]

As an illustration of the two changes which had the greatest influence on the Renaissance lyric, namely, the cultivation of the sonnet form and the exaltation of love as an ennobling spiritual force, we may look to Rossetti's translation of one of Guinizelli's sonnets.

> Yea, let me praise my lady whom I love,
> > Likening her unto the lily and rose:
> > Brighter than morning star her visage glows;
> She is beneath even as her Saint above.
> She is as the air in summer which God wove
> > Of purple and vermilion glorious;
> > As gold and jewels richer than man knows.
> Love's self, being love for her, must holier prove.
> Ever as she walks she hath a sober grace,
> > Making bold men abash'd and good men glad;
> > If she delight thee not, thy heart must err.
> No man dare look on her his thoughts being base:
> > Nay, let me say even more than I have said; —
> > No man could think base thoughts who look'd on her.[4]

If this sonnet is compared with the Provençal song cited earlier, it can be seen what the change amounted to, namely, elevation of sentiment, preciseness of form, and some affectation of language. These certainly make the sonnet a more finished poem; not necessarily a superior work of art, but one in which artistry is more deliberate and more obvious. It is this presence of artistry that characterizes much of the Renaissance poetry; and it is significant to note that the trend had already set in during the last century of the Middle Ages.

Romances

The truly great genre of medieval literature was the chivalric epic and the chivalric romance.[5] Both were products of feudal society, one essentially elemental and overpowering with its heroic qualities, and the other preponderantly *courtois*, rich in knightly and amatory emprise. But with feudalism declining as a social dynamic, no such masterpieces as the *Song of Roland, Tristan and Iseult,* and *Parzival* were possible. Indeed, what was written in the century after the era of Chrétien de Troyes, Wolfram von Eschenbach, and Gottfried von Strasbourg was either in the nature of reaction or mechanical imitation.

In France this decline is manifest in the *Roman de la Rose,*[6] one of the most widely read compositions in the late Middle Ages and the early Renaissance. There are two parts to this long poem. The first 4,058 lines were composed by one Guillaume Lorris (*ca.* 1212–*ca.* 1237), a poet of refined sensibilities. They present a delightful allegory in appropriate courtly spirit on the quest of love. Although the quest is impeded by the interjection of a number of moral abstractions such as Chastity, Shame, and Danger, the spirit of this section nevertheless is buoyant with pleasant hopes of victory and is in keeping with the spirit of courtly love. The second part was added some forty years later by Master Jean de Meun (*ca.* 1237–1305), a learned man of naturalistic inclinations. It is approximately four times longer and is an extended symposium on love and sex, which manages to become a prolix marshaling of knowledge, often in a satirical vein, on all things, from the intractabilities of wives to sensuality and from Creation to Judgment Day and Paradise. Intended as an exposé of courtly idealism, this second part is only formally connected with the first theme. Jean simply leaves the lover waiting at the Portal of Love while he himself engages in ridiculing courtly love or subordinating it to sensuality and reproduction; and only toward the end of the poem is the lover allowed to pluck the Rose, or, to put it more in keeping with Jean's notion, to consumate his purpose. Indeed, even this ending seems like an artistic concession, for women, in Jean's opinion, deserved more of reprobation than of admiration. In Jean's hands, then, romance was made to yield to satire, and the palpitating heart to a realistic tongue and a grating wit.[7] And yet, as was stated at the outset of the paragraph, the work was very popular,[8] a clear indication that the romantic vogue in France was temporarily in disfavor.

The Spanish attitude toward the romance was not much different. The vogue of the *Matière de Rome*, romances woven about such historical or legendary classical heroes as Alexander, Apollonius of Tyre, and Aeneas, was failing, while the national epics (*cantares de gesta*) were almost dead. Ramon Lull (1233–1315), a courtier turned scholar and monk at the age of thirty and a martyr, did write a romance, the *Blanquerna*, but while it concerns itself with knight-errantry, so to speak, its quest is holiness, the conversion of man from things earthly to the service of God, and its weapons are prayer and reason instead of the lance.[9] Nor is the *El Caballero Cifar*, a fourteenth-century "romance of chivalry" which is also classed as the first Spanish novel, much different, for the hero Cifar fulfills his adventures as "the Knight of God," performing every deed according to the canons of religious chivalry and only having one brush with courtly love.[10]

In Germany, the current was considerably stronger, as there were numerous imitators of each of the three leading romantic poets of the Middle Ages, Hartmann von Aue, Wolfram von Eschenbach, and Gottfried von Strassburg. But being imitative, the current was dull and mechanically even. Even the works of the foremost of these imitators, Konrad von Würzburg (*ca.* 1220–1287), were not of high merit. The *Partonopier und Meliur*, in line with the old tradition, was a fair romance; and his *Engelhart*, on a theme of friendship between two courtly members (Dietrich, Engelhart's friend, allows his children to be sacrificed so that with their blood Engelhart could be cured of leprosy), is also quite true to the romance, since its style follows that of Gottfried; but his poem on the Trojan War was both prolix and staid; and his *Die Golden Schmeide*, in praise of the Virgin Mary, was alien to the romantic realism of the genre. Even more oriented in the direction of religion was his contemporary's, Albrecht's, *Jüngere Titurel*, a long and labored treatment of the Graal story, and his enlargement of *Parzival*. Moreover, both suffer from tortured language and pedantry. The only work that saved the stream from monotonous mediocrity was Hadamar von Laber's popular allegory *Die Jagd* (*ca.* 1340); but even this, though occasionally sparkling with freshness of expression and independence of mind, suffered from a naive allegory, the heart in quest of love being represented as a hound (*Herze*) in pursuit of its quarry, the beloved, represented as a doe.[11]

Italy apparently took the romances to heart just as it did the lyric, but the adoption did not stimulate any significant creative work. In the northern part of the peninsula, the Carolingian *matière* was taken over bodily, story, form, and even language. Tuscany showed more independence as to language and form, the French being replaced by the local dialect and the recitative form by one suitable for singing, the *cantare*. But the stories and ideology were for the most part unchanged. The legends of King Arthur and the Round Table were also in circulation.[12] Together these two types had a widespread following, preparing the ground for the great Renaissance outburst under Boiardo, Ariosto, and Tasso.

In England the romantic genre was definitely rising in popularity on the eve of the Renaissance. Prior to 1300, there appeared a number of notable chivalric national epics, with the usual manly characteristics of *chansons de geste*. *King Horn* and *Havelock the Dane*, two of the earliest, drew on the legends of the nation's Viking connections. They were followed by *Bevis of Hampton* and *Guy of Warwick*, two great vehicles for heroic adventure. After 1300, continental themes (the Carolingian cycle: the *Ferumbras* and *Outel* groups; and the *matière de Rome*: Alexander and Troy, for example) made considerable gains. Then came Chaucer and his wide popularization of the romances, which carried the genre as a vogue into the Renaissance period.[13]

By way of summary, then, it can be said that the romance on the eve of the Renaissance, except in England, was decidedly past its prime. As a genre it was of course still alive: the old masterpieces continued to circulate; here and there variants of them appeared; and occasionally religious or satirical versions were prepared. But on the whole the genre lacked vitality and remained in that state until its revival during the Renaissance.

Drama

If the lyric and the chivalric romance were noticeably declining on the eve of the Renaissance, drama on the other hand was just dawning. While some of it, especially in Italy, was little more than minstrelsy in action or classical literature, much of it was already becoming a recognized genre.

The origin is attributed to the inclusion of a brief dialogue, called the trope, in the Mass of Easter and Christmas feasts. As an example the *Quem Quaeritis* trope in the Mass of Easter might be cited. At one point of the service there was interjected the dialogue

> Whom seek ye (*quem quaeritis*) in the sepulchre, O Christians?
> Jesus of Nazareth who was crucified, O Angels.
> He is not here; he has arisen as foretold:
> Go, announce that he has arisen from the grave.

This was sung by two parts of the choir, and with this antiphonal performance medieval drama was born. Once one trope was admitted, other tropes were devised to portray other parts of the Easter service; and what was found valuable for dramatizing the Easter Mass was also employed in the Christmas Mass. As the tropes increased in number and expanded in length, it was ultimately necessary to separate them from the services and to substitute the vernacular for Latin. Simultaneously, the increase in the number of stagings and in the number of actors (impersonators) required transferring the whole performance from the choir to the nave of the church, and from there to the court in front of the church. This transfer invited greater participation by the laity and that in turn led to the admission of some comic and realistic atmosphere, and probably also of such popular semidramatic spectacles as ritual dances and May rites.[14] Thus, for example, the scene depicting Noah's saving of life invited the casting of his wife as a termagant; and that representing the conversion of Mary Magdalene invited casting her first as a worldly woman given to dalliance and cosmetics; and that representing the subsidence of the Flood and the return of life, while obviously of biblical origin, was made to reflect the return of spring. At the same time, the multiplication of settings increased the cost of production and so called for capable financing and management. Normally this was assumed by the gilds of the town; and when this state was reached, medieval drama became a reality.

In the course of its evolution this drama gave rise to three types of plays.

One type was the mystery play, that is a play about some biblical episode or episodes. One of the first of such mysteries was the *Adam,* extant in the Low Countries as early as the twelfth century. It depicted the Fall, Expulsion, the story of Cain and Abel (a lesson on the origin of Evil), and the Prophets. A more expanded dramatization of the Bible history appeared in England, late in the thirteenth century or early in the fourteenth, in what is called the Chester Plays; and the famous York Cycle, numbering close to fifty plays, may have been in existence by 1350, for when they are first mentioned in 1378, they are referred to as "of old time."

The other type was the miracle play, one which depicted the intercessionary powers of a saint. In the thirteenth century, because of the prevalence of Mariolatry, the saint often proved to be the Mother of Christ. The first is exemplified by Jean Bodel's *Jeu de saint Nicolas,* composed sometime before 1205. It treats of the miraculous intercession of St. Nicholas in saving a believer's life, in restoring money stolen from the king's treasury, and in converting a paynim king to Christianity. The second is exemplified by Rutebeuf's *Le miracle de Théophile.* It depicts a disgraced cleric, Theophilus, a kind of early Faust, who, after having first bargained his soul away to Satan, regained it through the help of the Holy Virgin.

The third type was the secular play. Deriving from several sources — the comic elements in religious drama, the dance and song elements in the rituals of primitive religion persisting as part of the folklore, the heritage of classical comedy as taught in some schools, and the mimes of wandering jongleurs — it came to life as an individual genre in the thirteenth century, in the burgeoning Flemish cloth towns. The author who is intimately associated with its crystallization was a citizen of Arras, Adam le Bossu, more commonly known as Master Adam de la Halle, and two of his earliest plays are *Jeu de Feuillée* and *Jeu de Robin et Marion.* The first is a farcical, poetic satire on thirteenth-century society in the form of a somewhat Aristophanic comedy built around the theme of Adam's scheming to resume his schooling and his inability to escape his bothersome wife who suspects him of wanting to return to the bright lights of the city. The second, composed in Italy for the entertainment of the Angevin Court at Naples — Adam had gone there in the company of the Count of Artois who went to the assistance of Charles of Anjou following the Sicilian rebellion of 1282 — is a charming, unpretentious play, pastoral in setting, about Marion's affection for her shepherd swain Robin. Not by Adam, but a secular play deserving notice as a prefigurement of the picaresque novel, was the farce *Le garçon et l'aveugle*. It is a satire, gross in concept and language, on the commercialized begging of the day. A blind man hires a guide to lead him on his begging itinerary; but the guide, alternately impersonating an irate citizen and himself, gets the beggar involved in a tongue-lashing and a beating, and then, after despoiling him of his personal possessions, abandons him to his misfortune![15]

Germany may have been behind the Low Countries, France, and England in the development of drama. If so, it could not have been far behind, for a twelfth-century monk of puritanical inclinations (Gerhoh von Reichersberg, d. 1169) complained that churches were being turned "into theatres and fill[ed] with scenic representations."[16] Although only very few plays or fragments thereof are extant from pre-Renaissance days, they were gaining in popularity, certainly from the fourteenth century when the gilds are known to have become sponsors. One of these was the famous *Play of the Wise and Foolish Virgins*, which portrays Christ as a stern judge refusing to forgive the foolish virgins in spite of the intercession of the Virgin. According to tradition, when the play was being enacted at Erfurt in 1322 before the Landgrave Frederick the Faithless of Thuringia, the scene so affected him that it brought on a stroke and eventual death.[17]

Italy's counterparts were the balladlike *laude*, some two hundred of them, a by-product of the thirteenth-century religious revivalism inspired by the flagellant sects, and the rarer but more accomplished *sacra rappresentazione*, representations dealing with the passion of Christ. Compared with the output of drama in other lands, Spain's medieval drama was relatively poor, although there was more liturgical drama than admitted hitherto[18] and although one of the oldest mystery plays in the vernacular is a Castilian composition, *auto de los reyes magos*.

With the reproduction or imitation of these examples, drama steadily gained in the late Middle Ages and prepared the way for the flowering of the mystery and morality plays in the Renaissance era.

Prose: The Novelle

The subtitle at once brings to mind Boccaccio's *Decameron*; and because Boccaccio himself is regarded as a Renaissance figure, it is customary to associate the short story with the Renaissance also. This association is quite correct provided, of course, it is not carried too far. For here as in many other things the Renaissance appears to have built on what the Middle Ages provided.

Having the properties if not the form of the short story were the French *fabliaux*. Although written in verse, these poems concentrated on the story. A wife consorting with a priest by tricking a stupid or a jealous husband, a woman duping a scholar, a priest being hoaxed into investigating rumors of a talking dog only to find himself the sport of a gang of rough and rowdy pranksters, a courtesan plying her trade among various classes — such are the themes. Intended as satires on the society of the day, they nevertheless became quite popular because of their droll mockery and of the story element in them. They even appealed to the aristocratic circles, although they were directed at the bourgeoisie; and many found their way into such early Renaissance anthologies of stories as the *Decameron*, Chaucer's *Canterbury Tales*, and Poggio's *Facetiae*. A good medieval story, even if vulgar, was not repugnant to a Renaissance humanist.

Another literary genre that served as a precursor of the short story was the fable. Composed in poetic form first in Latin and then in the vernacular, the fables were intended primarily as *exempla*, that is, as lessons in morality. However, the story element in many of them prevailed over the moral content and transformed them, at least insofar as the ordinary folk were concerned, into acceptable short stories. Moreover, the genre as a whole invited imitations involving contemporary situations. Some of these new creations continued to emphasize the moral content, but others stressed the story element. An exemplification of the former may be found in the fables of the thirteenth-century German compiler Stricker; while the latter is nicely represented by the *Wiener Meerfahrt*, a collection of stories about the burghers of Vienna on a sea voyage, whose attractive feature is the depiction of robust conduct on the part of the characters.[19]

But if the classification of the aforementioned types as short stories should be questioned, there can be no question about several collections of stories which anticipated the *Decameron*, some by as much as a century. Omitting the collections that were prepared for purposes of moral edification, such as the Latin composition *Gesta Romanorum* by an unknown Englishman, or the *Edelstein* (*The Jewel*) by the Dominican Ulrich Boner of Bern, we have two compositions which cannot be questioned. One is *Le cento novelle antiche*, otherwise known as the *Novellino*, a large compilation of stories, romantic and other, taken from classical and oriental sources and adapted to the thirteenth-century Italian scene. Although, according to the writer (anonymous) himself, the book "deal[t] with a few beautiful examples of beautiful diction, beautiful courtly acts, beautiful answers, beautiful gifts, which are known to have been accomplished in the past by gallant man,"[20] its strong feature really is its storiology. The other is a Spanish compilation, the *El conde lucanor*, by Don Juan Manuel (1282–1349), a prince and soldier who occasionally retired from his life of intrigue to write books. Though the collection treats of worldly wisdom, the media employed — the moral tale and the fable — are handled in the tradition of storiology. The tale is the thing, the lesson is incidental.[21]

Like drama, then, the short story was coming of age on the eve of the Renaissance. Hence, when we think of the *Decameron*, we should not think of it as a unique composition suddenly blossoming forth, but as one which followed a respectable tradition of story-telling.

Prose: Historical

History in the Middle Ages was for the most part the work of clerics and so was written in Latin. There was an occasional exception to this in the early Middle Ages, such as the famous *Anglo-Saxon Chronicle*, but it was not until the thirteenth century, with the growth of nationalism and of the bourgeois spirit, that the vernacular began to gain in usage.

A review of the steadily increasing number of histories in the vernacular which appeared in the last century of the Middle Ages is more than can be undertaken here. All that is needed is an indication of some of the more reputable works which exemplify the trend.

France produced two outstanding examples. One is Geoffrey de Villehardouin's *Conquête de Constantinople*. From the point of view of history, it is an apologia for the diversion of the Fourth Crusade from the Holy Land to Constantinople; but as a literary composition, it has the merit of directness and simplicity. The other is Jean de Joinville's (1224–1317) *Livre des saintes paroles et des bonnes actions de Saint Louis*. It is a biography of the celebrated French king, St. Louis, and concentrates on the episodes in which the king is the main character. The narrative is a mirror of the man, of his actions, and of his times. Whether one reads of the secret love meetings between Louis and his young wife to escape the watchful eye of his mother, or of Louis' dispensing of justice, or of the physical suffering in the Crusaders' camp in Egypt, one meets with the work of an artist. The image remains always clearly delineated and meaningful. In the Low Countries Jean Bosendale's (1280–1365) chronicle, the *Brabantsche Yeesten*, has won high praise as "le monument le plus caracteristique de l'historiographie laique et populaire dans les Pays-Bas."[22] His contemporary Jean le Bel, more interested in chivalric than in bourgeois activities, produced memoirs which anticipated the later works of Froissart and Chastellian.[23] Germany had no historian who could compare with the above writers. On the other hand, several of its towns had their own chronicles in the native tongue, while the *Sächsiche Weltchronick* (1251) was an attempt at chronicling world history. England's writers of history in the vernacular did not appear until after 1350, but Spain and Italy each had a remarkable representation. In Spain, Alfonso X, the Wise (1252–1284), organized a commission to prepare a national history. The Committee sifted all the available sources, including Latin and Arabic writings and the *Cantares*, and compiled the now-famous *Cronica General,* reportedly the first national history after the old *Anglo-Saxon Chronicle*. Stylistically the *Cronica* is stiff, the prose not having acquired flexibility yet, but its historical merits are high. Italy, Florence especially, developed a strong tradition of vernacular history.[24] There was the *Cronica fiorentina* by the two Malispini which carried the story — a great deal of it legendary — of Florence up to 1286, and the vivid and factual account of thirteenth-century Florence, *Chronicle of Things Taking Place in His own Time,* by Dino Compagni (*ca.* 1266–1324). But the outstanding composition is Giovanni Villani's (*ca.* 1276–1348) *La nuova cronica* begun in 1300. It is a world chronicle of which the latter half is devoted to the history of his native Florence. While still cast in the traditional pattern of a chronicle starting with creation and retaining a good deal of the legendary, the work reveals a bourgeois appreciation of the significance of material forces in history including even some important statistical information. Valuable as histories, these chronicles are also fine examples of vernacular prose in late medieval times, and in both aspects they anticipate the celebrated histories of Florence by Machiavelli and Guicciardini.

Summary

This sketchy survey of literature on the eve of the Renaissance was undertaken to discover the possible relationship between the literature of the Middle Ages and that of the Renaissance. It is quite revealing. It shows that in some types of literature — lyric, short story, history — the trend generally associated with the Renaissance was definitely taking shape in the late Middle Ages. It shows that another type normally associated with the Middle Ages, the religious drama, was just beginning on the eve of the Renaissance and that its fullest development was yet to come. The romance does not fit into either category. It was a medieval genre and was declining in the last century of that age, except in England where it continued strong. In sum, the survey shows that much of what is deemed to be medieval literature belonged to the Renaissance period no less than to the Middle Ages.

1. For a good analysis of medieval literature see W. T. H. Jackson, *The Literature of the Middle Ages* (New York: Columbia University Press, 1960).

2. Cited from Claude Colleer Abbott, *Early Medieval French Lyrics* (London: Constable & Co., Ltd., 1932), 61.

3. For an understanding treatment of these poets cf. Domenico Vittorini, *The Age of Dante* (Syracuse, New York: Syracuse University Press, 1957), 56, 73–81.

4. Quoted from Wilkins, *A History of Italian Literature*, 29.

5. For a valuable treatment of these two genre in the Middle Ages see Jackson, *op. cit.*, 80–215.

6. There is a translation of it in English verse by Harry W. Robbins (New York: E. P. Dutton & Co., Inc., 1962).

7. For a recent study challenging the traditional interpretation of Jean de Meun's addition as a mere bourgeois reaction to the first part, see Alan M. F. Gunn, *The Mirror of Love: A Reinterpretation of "The Romance of the Rose"* (Lubbock, Texas: Texas Technological College Press, 1952). For a shorter treatment see Charles Muscatine, *Chaucer and the French Tradition* (Berkeley: University of California Press, 1957), 71–97.

8. Cf. Charles W. Dunn in his introduction to Robbin's translation of the poem, xxv–xxvii.

9. There is an English translation of the work — *Blanquerna: A Thirteenth Century Romance. Translated from the Catalan of Ramon Lull* by E. Allison Peers (London: Jarrolds Publishers, 1926?). Cf. also Gerald Brenan, *The Literature of the Spanish People from the Roman Times to the Present Day* (Cambridge: University Press, 1951), 104–6, 125.

10. Cf. Otis H. Green, *Spain and the Western Tradition. The Castilian Mind in Literature from El Cid to Calderon* (Madison, Wisconsin: University of Wisconsin Press, 1963), I, 12, 98–99.

11. On romances in Germany after 1250 see M. O'C. Walshe, *Medieval German Literature: A Survey* (Cambridge: Harvard University Press, 1962), 193–210. Hademar is treated on 290–1.

12. This subject is treated in E. Gardner, *Arthurian Legends in Italian Literature* (London: J. M. Dent & Sons, Ltd., 1930).

13. For a succinct treatment of the romantic genre in England see Albert C. Baugh (ed.), *A Literary History of England* (New York: Appleton-Century-Crofts, Inc., 1948), 173–99. Hereinafter this work will be referred to by the editor's name.

14. On this latter point see John Speirs, *Medieval English Poetry. The Non-Chaucerian Tradition* (London: Faber and Faber, 1958), 320–5.

15. For a brief summary of these secular plays and of the other plays written in French see William A. Nitze and E. Preston Dargan, *A History of*

French Literature (3rd ed.; New York: Henry Holt and Co., 1938), 70–71. For a more comprehensive treatment the reader may turn to Gustave Cohen, *Le théatre en France au moyen âge* (Paris: Presses Universitaires de France, 1948), 16–101, or to W. T. H. Jackson, *op. cit.*, 289–93, 306–13.

16. For the complete protest see the translation in Walshe, *op. cit.*, 299–300.

17. *Ibid.*, 300.

18. Its collection and publication has been started by Father Richard B. Donovan. See his *The Liturgical Drama in Medieval Spain*, No. 4 of *Studies and Texts* (Toronto: Pontifical Institute of Mediaeval Studies, 1958). For an informative reference to the work see Ann Freeman's review in *Speculum*, XXXVI (1961), 121–3.

19. Cf. Walshe, *op. cit.*, 207–8, 209.

20. Cited from Vittorini, *op. cit.*, 131. See also Wilkins, *A History of Italian Literature*, 36–37.

21. Cf. Brenan, *op. cit.*, 102–3.

22. Henri Pirenne, *Histoire de Belgique* (Bruxelles: Henri Lamertin, 1908), II, 451.

23. *Ibid.*, II, 456.

24. Cf. Vittorini, *op. cit.*, 137–9.

III *Dante, Juan Ruiz, Petrarch, and Chaucer*

B EFORE undertaking the survey of Renaissance literature, we need to consider four great figures whose prominent role as links between the medieval and Renaissance literature requires individual attention. Two of these, Dante and Juan Ruiz, cap the Middle Ages; and the other two, Petrarch and Chaucer, open the era of the Renaissance. It will be interesting to discover to what extent their compositions prefigure Renaissance literature.

Dante Alighieri (1265–1321)

Although a poet of world acclaim who has been studied exhaustively, Dante the man is not yet completely known.[1] He was born in May 1265 to a Florentine family of ancient lineage, modest in means but high in social pretensions. Little is known about his formal education, except that he studied the art of writing under Brunetto Latini, a celebrated compiler of an encyclopedia called *Livre dou Trésor,* that he learned to love classics, and that he studied philosophy with the Franciscans for some thirty months. During this formative period, in keeping with high society's predilection for the *courtois,* he cultivated the art of poetry after the mode of the troubadours; but being idealistic as well as an aspirant for social recognition, he tried to refine the language and to elevate the themes. Grown of age, he married into one of the more prominent families, registered as a member of the gild of physicians and apothecaries, and entered public life. From 1295 to 1301 he served on several councils of state and held the important office of prior. As a member of these governing bodies, he championed Florentine independence against the encroachments of Boniface VIII who tried to exercise imperial rights during vacancies of the imperial throne. In the ensuing intrigue, his party, known as the "Whites," lost to the opposition, the "Blacks." As was customary for defeated politicians in Renaissance Italy, Dante and some of his political associates were exiled by the government in 1302. From then on, he moved about from one court to another, out of reach of his Florentine enemies, and embittered toward the pope whom he held responsible for his misfortune. Some ten years later, when he learned that Henry VII was planning to come to Italy to revive imperial authority, he entertained hopes of returning to a peaceful Florence. But Henry's enterprise failed, and Dante, having given public support to it, jeopardized his chances of repatriation seemingly beyond repair. And so the balance of his life he spent adrift, proud and bitter, yet hopeful that he might win reinstatement at some future date by publishing a masterpiece which would bring him renown and force the hands of his enemies. This he hoped to accomplish with his *Divine Comedy*. But Florence refused to be impressed, and so he remained an exile to the end of his life in 1321.

If Dante wrote the *Divine Comedy*, his most exalted work, as a reaction to his life's misfortune, it may be taken for granted that the rest of his literary compositions were likewise reflections of his life and passions. Indeed scholars have found that his life fell into three stages, each of which engendered works appropriate to itself.

The first stage occurred in his youth and was conditioned by an unusual love experience and by his aspiration for social recognition. Love came to him when he first espied a little girl in pink, demure and beautiful. He was only nine years old, and she of the same age, but the sentiment that welled in his heart was so beautiful that he called the little girl Beatrice, that is, inspirer of beatitude. This passion was rekindled several years later when he met her once again and she returned his greetings affably. Under its influence everything seemed to turn to beauty and goodness. In the course of this entrancement, and partly because of it — he hoped to be socially worthy of her — he sought to win a place in polite society. Since social acceptability still depended on adherence to the proprieties of chivalric conduct and since one of these was the ability to poetize, Dante took to writing amatory poems. Thus the combination of love and social aspiration led to his first major attempt at literature — his lyric poetry.

Evoked by this dual motive, his lyric poetry bears the earmarks of each. It has signs of artificiality and pretention quite in keeping with the conventions of the courtly lyric, and it has depth of feeling and beauty of language which only true emotions can inspire. Fortunately the latter, even though it does not prevail, appears often enough to irradiate much of his lyrical output.

This poetry he kept writing over a prolonged period, in the course of which Beatrice passed away, while he sought solace in the friendship of another lady, and in active political life. Then one day a great emotion overwhelmed him: to his dismay he realized that he had not been loyal to the chaste love which Beatrice inspired in him. He resolved not to fail again, and as the first act of his resolution he selected some of his best poems and assembled them in a work called the *Vita Nuova*.

The *Vita Nuova* is like Boethius' *Consolation of Philosophy* — it was prompted by Dante's state of adversity. In form it combines verse and prose, the prose being a commentary on the preceding verse and serving to tie the entire work with a theme. In the method of reasoning it is scholastic. In theme it is the glorification of pure love as a transcendent force capable of eliciting the best in man and of preparing him for his noble station here and in the hereafter. The only difference is that whereas Boethius' force is philosophy, namely, wisdom which comes through love of God, Dante's force is beauty and goodness which derive from love of a pure and gracious being, Beatrice.

Imitative of Boethius, utilizing the love poems which had been fashioned earlier in keeping with courtly conventions, and employing the scholastic mode of reasoning, the work has much of the literary past and little of the future in it. What is sometimes regarded as "new" in it are its polished artistry and the sincerity of its passion. But perhaps more important than these probable novelties is the fact that this ardent feeling led him to believe in man's perfectibility. A particularly fine expression of this love and of its influence for good is to be found in the following sonnet:

> My lady carries love within her eyes;
>   All that she looks on is made pleasanter;
>   Upon her path men turn to gaze at her;
> He whom she greeteth feels his heart to rise,
> And droops his troubled visage, full of sighs,
>   And of his evil heart is then aware:
>   Hate loves, and pride becomes a worshipper.

O women, help to praise her in somewise.
Humbleness, and the hope that hopeth well,
By speech of hers into the mind are brought,
And who beholds is blessed oftenwhiles.
The look she hath when she a little smiles
Cannot be said, nor holden in the thought;
'Tis such a new and gracious miracle.

The second stage was prompted by his exile. The *Vita Nuova* and other amatory compositions, he discovered, did not bring him sufficient recognition, for, despite their excellence, they could not be distinguished clearly from the general output of conventional love lyrics produced by his contemporaries. What was needed, he felt, was some work that would elevate him above the crowd of versifiers, a work of more serious purport which would redeem him from the charge of frivolity and reveal him for what he believed he was, a man of deeper understanding. Moreover, such a work might gain him greater respect and more distinguished patrons. This effort at self-defense, so to speak, gave birth to two works, the *Convivio* and the *De Vulgari Eloquentia*.

The *Convivio* (*Banquet*) was to be just that, a banquet, but a banquet of learning.[2] Its course was to consist of "meat and bread," he tells us, the meat being fourteen studies, in poetic form, "on love and virtue," and the bread, his explication of these odes. In a sense the *Convivio* was intended as a kind of panegyric on philosophy and as a demonstration of his acquaintance with it, just as the *Vita Nuova* was a paean to Love and a testimony of his knowledge of it. But while on the surface the *Convivio* might appear to be a repudiation of the *Vita,* in actuality it is but a further development of his notion of man's perfectibility. For just as the *Vita Nuova* explained the transmuting power of a profound love for a lady into love of beauty and goodness, so the *Convivio* taught that the knowledge of philosophy was a gateway to the knowledge of God, the highest end of man.

Dante did not complete the work, finishing only the first four treatises. Apparently he became apprehensive that it might fail in its intended purpose and dropped it for what he believed might have a better chance of accomplishing his objective. But in the part he finished he again revealed himself as a man of the past and of the future. The past is reflected in his adherence to Aristotelianism, in the scholastic method of interpreting texts allegorically, morally, anagogically, as well as literally, and in the acceptance of the premise that reason alone is inadequate for the perfecting of man however noble its formative role might be. The new appears in just this emphasis on man's perfectibility, and in the use of the vernacular in a learned work. Latin was the acknowledged language for works of erudition, but he boldly defied tradition and employed the native tongue and even defended its use, much of the introduction being devoted to the purpose.

This subject he adopted as his theme in the *De Vulgari Eloquentia,* his second major work of this stage. The treatise traces the origin and history of languages; defends the use of the vernacular in works on love, virtue, and salvation; identifies the Italian vernacular as the dialect used by himself and his predecessors Guido Cavalcanti and Cino da Pistoia; and launches into a discussion of the nature and form of what he believed to be "perfect poetry." Like the *Convivio* it was dropped midway, and presumably for the same reason.

The importance of the work is not only in the defense of the vernacular but in the defense of good style. It is evidence of Dante's dedication to poetic artistry. In addition, it reveals Dante's longing for Italian unity.

The third stage is associated with Henry VII's descent into Italy and the hopes for peace and order that the expedition inspired in Dante's bosom. It gave birth to his two concluding works, the *De Monarchia* and the *Divine Comedy.*

The *De Monarchia* is a political treatise and will be examined again in connection with our study of Renaissance political theory. But inasmuch as Dante used it to amplify his notion of man's end, the notion which was incepted in the *Vita Nuova* and advanced in the *Convivio,* it deserves to be considered in conjunction with his literary works.

The thesis is worked out in three propositions: the necessity of temporal authority for the good of society, the providential assumption of this authority by the Roman state, and the derivation of political authority directly from God. All this sounds like an apology for Henry VII's enterprise. And that it was; but it also was an argument for the indispensability of concord if man is to attain temporal well-being and spiritual salvation. If circumstances or institutions arise which disturb or prevent the desired social harmony, then they should be mastered or eliminated — even the church, if by engrossing itself in material interests it neglects its true mission of promoting good will among men. Thus the man whose heart could be purified by transcendent love and whose mind could be illuminated with wisdom until it could approach the knowledge of God is represented as needing social concord in order to attain his destined end. And like the first two, pure love and illuminating wisdom, this social order was also of divine dispensation and was not to be challenged.

This whole process of man's way to God Dante reworked and concluded in his masterpiece, the *Divine Comedy*.[3] This is a powerful epic of man's pilgrimage to his destined end and is symbolically depicted as Dante's journey through Hell, Purgatory, and Heaven. It describes the punishments that the sinners have to undergo and the bliss that awaits the sinless in Heaven. As such it is an extended lesson in morality in conformity with the Catholic teachings of the day, but a searing lesson fired by Dante's outraged conscience, outraged at the disruption of universal justice and order and at the concomitant wrong done him personally. In short, it is a study of what man makes of himself as he goes through life and what he prepares for his soul in afterlife. In Dante's words, the subject taken literally is "the state of souls after death," and taken allegorically, it is "man, as by good or ill deserts, in the exercise of the freedom of his choice, he becomes liable to rewarding or punishing justice."[4]

Through Hell and Purgatory Dante is led by his "first teacher," Vergil, who is here identified with human reason. The road to man's highest goal is thus staked out by his own reason. But reason alone is inadequate, wherefore some men lose themselves forever and suffer without end, while others with less serious sins pay a lesser price and can entertain hopes of subsequently resuming their journey onward to its glorious end. This lesson is brought out by dramatic descriptions of the sufferings of actual personalities and by occasional observations on the doctrine.

On the threshold of Heaven, Vergil leaves Dante, and Beatrice becomes his guide. She represents supernal Love and Revelation and has the same power of ennobling man as she had in the guise of spiritual love on earth in his first poems. She leads him through the first circles of Heaven, ever closer to the abode of the pure and the perfect, and transfers him to St. Bernard who symbolizes Contemplation, the last human intermediary in the ascent. But man alone, even with his reason purified and illuminated by Christian theology, could ascend only so far: grace is necessary for the balance. And so St. Bernard presents the traveler to Mother Mary and entreats her to grant Dante grace to see "the Bliss supreme." This is granted in an indescribable vision, and the journey ends.

As was suggested at the outset, this poem epitomizes Dante's principal ideas and ideals. It labors on his great message, that man's true end is his salvation, and shows how the principles advanced in his earlier works — namely, transcendent love which attunes man to beauty and goodness, knowledge which prepares man for the apprehension of his bliss, social justice and concord which enable man so transformed and illumined to pursue his goal unobstructed — bring man closer to his destined end. What is added here is emphasis on the indispensability of grace and a depiction of the bliss that is man's to gain.

As a synthesis of his previous works, it naturally retains much of the dualism present in them. Like they, it concentrates on man's supernal end, follows Thomistic theology and Aristotelian metaphysics, mingles classical and Christian personalities indiscriminately, and employs the syllogistic method of reasoning and the techniques of symbolism and allegorism. And in these respects it is medieval. On the other hand, its avoidance of asceticism, its sympathetic recognition of the realities of temporal life, its optimism as to man's end, and its artistry reflect its kinship with the Renaissance spirit.

Such are the works of Dante; they mark him as a man who is neither wholly medieval nor wholly Renaissance, but a synthesizer of the former and a harbinger of the latter.

Ruiz (ca. *1280–1353*)

Juan Ruiz is little known, except that he held the office of archpriest at Hita, a village some thirty miles from Alcalá, that he was a writer of jongleuresque verse, that in 1343 he was immured in the prison of the

Archbishop of Toledo where he revised his verse, and that he probably was no more by 1353. Yet this little-known man is rated as a great poet of the later Middle Ages. Indeed some consider him "the equal of Chaucer."[5]

His masterpiece Ruiz calls *The Book of Good Love*. It is an unusual work. Its purpose, he tells us, is to "teach success to one whom women have forsaken."[6] Yet it opens with a prayer to God and the Virgin and a poem on "The Joys of Saint Mary"; contains several poems on the Passion of Christ and on the different sins; and closes with five other songs to the Mother of Christ. It describes his artful seductions of several women, yet from time to time it interrupts these accounts of sexual emprise with homage to chastity and purity. It throbs with lust, yet it is full of moral *exempla* and of fables rich in practical wisdom. It is a strange medley indeed.

This is how the work would appear to the uninitiated. But experts look on it differently.[7] They admit that there is such incongruity and disorganization, but they insist nevertheless that the composition is a careful work of art, and that its contents, structure, and spirit are what they are largely because they have been made to reflect Arabic philosophy of life, and Arabic literary style. The theme, it is said, is not just the joy of carnal love, but the notion that life is an interweave of actuality and idealism. Just as a man who gives himself up to a love of woman experiences both the corruptive and the ennobling powers of the passion, so all life is a continuous spectrum of white and black, alternating, overlapping, and even fusing. Likewise the structure, it is maintained, is the result of design. In order to reflect the theme convincingly Ruiz is assumed to have chosen to alternate scenes of sensuousness with moral *exempla*, scenes of uninhibited realism with vignettes of refined chivalric conduct, scenes of the authentic with others that are fantastic and lyrical. Lastly, Ruiz accommodated the language to the occasion, and there can be no question about the deliberateness of this adaptation. Thus the composition is not a miscellany of uncoordinated anecdotes but a planned work of art.

Enhancing its merits still more, the composition possesses several splendid properties. One is its autobiographic approach. The author represents himself as the subject of the various incidents, and this imparts a greater sense of authenticity to the anecdotes than would be possible if they were depicted impersonally. Moreover, the stories are not narrations but representations of direct experiences, and this makes the work vital. Another fine property is its superb characterization. The characters are not delineated, but are made to reveal themselves through their spontaneous actions and equally spontaneous language. Hence they live and stand out as individuals. The lusting archpriest himself, the high-born Lady Sloe first wrapping herself in decorum and then gradually if reluctantly yielding to the call of love, the artful bawd so frank and proud of her role, and the wary nun wise in the ways of man — all stand out as living personalities, firm and unforgettable. Then there is the language, terse and vigorous and real, befitting the characters and the occasions. It is no limpid warbling, but flows full from a big-chested man, strong and direct. Finally, the spirit of the composition is real enough to be infectious, one of zest for life and robust gaiety. Even its satire is not bitter, but has a Rabelaisian gusto to it.

Such is Ruiz' masterpiece. The question now is to what age it belongs. Among the characteristics that stamp it as a medieval composition several are quite apparent: the jongleuresque handling of the subject, the intermittent moralizing, the use of the fable, and the absence of literariness. On the other hand, its characters are strongly realistic and in that respect they are timeless. Then its organization, despite its episodic quality, essays the unity of a novel, not a prevailing medieval form. Again, the spirit of its satire has some Rabelaisian qualities. Finally, its mood, despite professions of the poem's didactic purpose, is humanistic, giving the impression that the moralizings are mere tags and that the real philosophy is the zest of life.[8]

And thus like Dante, Ruiz is both medieval and not. The former may have adhered to the exalted and the latter to the earthly, yet each in his own field reflected both the past and the future. Neither is just "typically medieval."

Francesco Petrarch (1304–1374)

Petrarch's life is better known.[9] His father was a Florentine notary who had to flee from the Blacks when they seized control of the city's

government. Hence Petrarch was born in exile, in Arezzo, in 1304.
Eight years later the family moved to Avignon where his father secured
employment and Petrarch began his education. His father wanted him
to become a lawyer and sent him for four years to Montpellier and for
another three to the University of Bologna to study law. But Petrarch's
heart was not in the subject. He purposed to be a writer and abandoned
his legal studies when his father died. He returned to Avignon in
1326, attached himself to the influential Colonna family, and, in 1340,
entered the clerical order. His growing literary reputation brought him
a number of benefices which provided the financial independence that
he wanted for the pursuit of letters. His compositions, mostly in Latin,
won him international recognition and the patronage of several princely
houses and governments in Italy. The greatest acclaim came with his
coronation in Rome, in 1341, as poet-laureate.[10] Thereafter he basked in
his literary glory, a man of the world, moving from one place to another,
everywhere welcomed and everywhere honored until death claimed him
in 1374.

With Petrarch as a humanist man of letters we are not here concerned. That has been studied already in Book III, *Education, Learning
and Thought*, and all we need to mention here are the two influences
that his humanism had on his poetry in the vernacular. One was the
love for Italy which his study of the Latin classics set aglow and moved
him to write such fervent patriotic verse as *Italia mia*.[11] The other was
the direct influence of classical poetic art on his own compositions "as
to form and content, figures of speech and comparisons, symbols and
allegories."[12] But it is his poetry in the Italian that commands attention here.

To think of Petrarch's poetry in the vernacular is to think of his
lyrics, the sonnet in particular, and of Laura. The sonnet he borrowed
from his predecessors as a well-established lyrical form. What he did
with it was to fix it as the best poetic genre for the harmonizing of
thought and emotion. Laura he did not borrow, for she was a real person; but, inasmuch as she was to him what Beatrice was to Dante and
what noble ladies were to the troubadours, she too was a tradition. Love
for her, as Dante's love for Beatrice or the troubadour's love for milady,

was a chastening inspiration that evoked exquisite poetry and high idealism.

The high idealism was twofold. One phase of it was the delicacy of his love, human yet sublime, sweet and yet painful,[13] a love that elevates man's feelings and ennobles man's thoughts. It was this, he tells us, that evoked the finest in his verse both in sentiment and in word.[14] The other was the spiritual ideal of salvation. By her purity Laura led him to sublimate his love to a concern for his soul. His own words say this gratefully.

> I thank her soul and her holy device
> That with her face and her sweet anger's bolts
> Bid me in burning think of my salvation.[15]

The exquisiteness of his poetry, an expression of these ideals, derives from the harmony of word and thought, from the sweet flow of his rhythm,[16] from the superb choice of language — in general, from his fine artistry and sensitivity.

But if both the ideal and the artistry are indeed his very own, it cannot be denied that he was merely raising to a higher level the tradition followed by the lyricists of the preceding century. As Symonds says, "the forms he used were not new. The subject matter he handled was given to him," and what he did was to bring "both form and subject closer to the truth," namely, closer to the realities of human emotion.[17] Also "his mastery of limpid diction" he is said to have derived from Cino da Pistoia some fifty years his senior.

Thus where Dante is a medieval poet who promises Renaissance, Petrarch is a Renaissance poet who echoes much that is medieval.

Geoffrey Chaucer (1340–1400)

The last of the great four is the English poet Geoffrey Chaucer. He is often considered as the harbinger of the English literary Renaissance, but this apparently is based more on the general excellence of his poetry than on its properties. Taken as a whole, his work is admittedly superior to anything that came before him, and this may invite placing him in the company of the great writers of the Renaissance period. But examined more closely, this fine poetry reveals a wealth of medieval tradition as to content and attitude and as to style. It is questionable, therefore, if he should be regarded as a Renaissance poet.

What he wrote and how he wrote depended on several powerful factors. Of these the most influential was his membership in the princely houses of the time. For a while he was attached to the court of Lionel, the third son of Edward III, and then, by 1367, he joined the court of the king himself, first as valet, then as squire, and, later still, as a diplomatic representative. Moreover, his wife Philippa was of noble descent and was attached to the Queen's retinue, while her sister was the wife of John of Gaunt. Since Edward and his court were much given to the cultivation of chivalry, Chaucer naturally catered to this interest by composing poetry in the tradition of the medieval romances. Furthermore, since the language of the court was French and since the romantic current flowed from France, Chaucer could not help but draw heavily from the French originals. A second factor was the influence of the early French *rhétoriqueurs*, of Guillaume de Machault and of Eustace Deschamps, those artificers of fashioned verse. From them he borrowed the art of versifying and also their extravagant and pretentious treatment of the courtly ways and ideals. The third influence came from Italy, probably as a result of his diplomatic visits to Genoa, Florence, and Milan, and of his sojourn in Padua where he probably met with Petrarch. From there came his concern for poetic perfection and a goodly supply of stories and themes — Petrarch, whom he honored as "lauriat poete . . . whose rethorike sweete enlumyned al Ytaelle of poetrie," being the principal source of the former, and Boccaccio of the latter.[18] A fourth influence came from the naturalism and realism present in the medieval *fabliaux* and, on a higher, philosophical plane, in Jean de Meun's addition to the *Roman de la Rose*. Chaucer was at home with both, as they were in accord with his own practical, good sense, and made abundant use of them in his poetry, mostly as contrasts to the conventions of the courtly style. Finally, a fifth factor derived from his association with the English folk, the middle class in particular, in his capacity as Comptroller of the Customs and Subsidy of wools, skins, and tanned hides, and of Petty Customs in the busy port of London. It was this contact that familiarized him with the enterprising but unsophisticated Englishmen. At the same time he appears to have known the English countryside, whence he derived his appreciation of nature. All of these influences left their mark on his compositions.

His dependence on the tradition of chivalric romances and on French sources and styles appears throughout his works.[19] His first was a shortened translation of the popular medieval *Roman de la Rose*. His *Book of the Duchess*, an elegy on the death of Duchess Blanche, wife of his patron John of Gaunt, employs the medieval device of the dream and deals with the Duke's love for Blanche in the courtly tradition, with all the mechanics of this tradition. His *Confessio amantis* resembles the *Roman de la Rose* in design and in purpose — "an encyclopedia on the art of love."[20] Many of the tales in his masterpiece, the *Canterbury Tales,* are reworkings of well-known medieval romances, though apparently with the intent of probing the validity of the *courtois* ways. The *Legend of Good Women*, though based on Ovid's *Heroides*, rings true to the mode of courtly love, while the ideas in its prologue are "largely the ideas of the *Roman de la Rose*."[21] Finally, *The Assembly of Fowles* or *Parliament of Birds*, though opened with a summary of Cicero's *Somnium Scipionis* as it appears in Macrobius' commentary and developing into a treatment of the "contradictory variety of men's attitudes toward love" à la the naturalist interpretation of Jean de Meun,[22] does not free itself from the tradition of French romances. Moreover, in all of these compositions he follows the stylistic conventions of the medieval romances. Lyrical settings, elaborate portraiture, aristocratic airs, exaggerated emotionalism, and high language are common, and the pretentiousness of these often ends in sheer artificiality. True, some of this is deliberate art which he employs to capture the atmosphere appropriate to the theme and occasion, and some of this is relieved by the true Chaucerian touch of simplicity, vivacity, and realism; but even these appear to be following Jean de Meun's practice of juxtaposing convention and naturalism for the purpose of exposing the emptiness of the courtly ways and ideals.

The Italian influence, although substantial, is not as pervasive. His *Troilus and Cressid* is a translation of Boccaccio's *Filostrato*, but extended by some 2,700 lines. Also, the story is recast: Boccaccio's autobiographical element is omitted and his violations of the courtly code of *amour* are corrected to conform with the proper conventions of chivalric romances and accepted moral standards. Indeed the romance, however sympathetically it looks at both the human and the courtly love, turns into a tragedy teaching the lesson that "the world of earthly love is vanity fair."[23] Out of the incidental and temporary Chaucer made something which was universal and timeless, and in doing this he returned to the medieval. He tried his hand at the heroic measure in the fashion of Dante, but without success. His *House of Fame*, a poem on how notables acquired their fame, borrows some of Dante's epical mechanics, but fails to exploit them and turns into a tedious comedy of some satire and wit. While *Analeda and Arcite*, begun with epic pretentions, he did not even complete, abandoning it after some three hundred lines. What he acquired from the Italians, other than some themes, is the principle of poetic perfection. Although some of the poems display faults in artistry, in general, where he is at his best, his finish and his choice of words are both proper and superb.

The influence of the medieval naturalism and realism as found in the *fabliaux* and in Jean de Meun and the down-to-earth influence of the English scene are only second to the influence of the romances and are his trade mark. He employs them extensively, but they appear to best advantage in his ever-popular *Canterbury Tales*.

Outwardly the poem is a kind of anthology of stories related one after another by a number of pilgrims on their way to the shrine of Thomas Becket at Canterbury. Probed more deeply and taken together they are really a study on the inadequacy of both the conventional chivalric ideals and the naturalistic ways of men, if not tempered one by the other and both by the higher order of moral values. This provides him with two opportunities. It gives him a chance to regale his contemporaries with a number of romances in the conventional courtly tradition. And he relates these stories so sympathetically that the implied criticism of this tradition often escapes the reader. It also gives him a chance to relate stories depicting the crude, earthy ways of ordinary folk, which he makes convincing by exploiting his knowledge of people of all walks of life, of their environment, and of their idiom. It is here that he reveals his naturalism at its best, seemingly leaving the impression that he favors the natural ways of man above the conventional ways demanded by the courtly tradition. And it is this masterful art and this apparently modern attitude that has persuaded some of his admirers to look upon him as a harbinger of the Renaissance.

Taken by itself this aspect of his work may indeed lead to such an interpretation. But it cannot be taken at its face value, for his treatment here is not primarily reflectional but functional, not something that reveals his personal beliefs and preferences, but something which he finds useful to set off the rawness of uninhibited nature against the pretentiousness of the courtly ways and thereby to reveal the weakness of both. A good case in point, for example, is his treatment of the argument between the clerk and the Wife of Bath concerning the nature of *gentilesse*.[24] Implicit throughout the work is the notion that a higher canon, that of moral idealism, is to be accepted as the real determinant. Just as the real goal of the pilgrimage was not the shrine of Thomas Becket at Canterbury, but what it symbolized, namely, High Jerusalem, that is Heaven, so it is not the earthly ways of men, whether *courtois* or naturalistic, that constitute man's true end. While they cannot be rejected, for they are part of man, they must be subordinated to a higher order of values. Viewed in this light his naturalism is less a part of his philosophy of life than it might appear to be and hardly deep enough to warrant considering him as nonmedieval.

From what has been said of Chaucer it is obvious that he has much in him which is medieval. His stories are mostly borrowed from medieval literature, and the mechanics of his stories — the dream, allegory, visit to the nether world — are equally from the past. His treatment of love is conventional and patterned after that of the chivalric romances. Even the naturalism and realism, so often regarded as uniquely Chaucerian, follow the naturalism and realism of the medieval *fabliaux* and of Jean de Meun, although admittedly his handling of these is more natural and therefore superior.

These, of course, are not the only medieval traits in his works. At least two others are quite noticeable. One is his want of literary perspective. Classical figures are cast in the medieval courtly atmosphere weakening their reality, or thrown pell-mell with medieval characters. The other is his view that poetry should have a didactic rather than aesthetic purpose. In consequence, many of his compositions conclude with a moral lesson; and indeed he even apologized for his "endytinges of worldly vanities" and for " 'The Tales of Canterbury' . . . that gounen into sinne."[25]

But while his poetry is strong in properties identified with medieval literature and with the medieval mind, it is not without some indications pointing to the future. One of these is his successful treatment of characters. Not only does he delineate them realistically, which in itself is quite an achievement, but some of them, like Cressid for example, he develops with the story of the poem, not unlike a modern novelist shapes the character of the principals of his novel. Another is the element of unity in the narrative. In *Troilus and Cressid* the story is sustained despite frequent interruptions by conventions of courtly love. In the *Canterbury Tales* the reader is never permitted to lose sight of the fact that the pilgrimage is the theme, while the occasional dialogues between the travelers by serving as flash backs of the characters help to preserve the unity. Thirdly, there is the ever-present combination of worldly wisdom, liveliness, and humor which inspirits his work with a *joie de vivre* that is agreeable to modern tastes. Although a happy, earthy view of life is not an invention of the postmedieval times, for the goliards and the writers of *fabliaux* certainly reflected this philosophy, still, Chaucer's seems to be more genuine and therefore more convincing.

Chaucer, then, has the past in him and some promise of the future.[26] But if he has the former, it is not that he is behind the times; and if he has the latter, it is not that he is ahead of his time. Rather it is that the times do not change abruptly. Chaucer as a fourteenth-century poet breathes the atmosphere of his age; and heavy-laden with the past and lightly touched with the future, as it is, he cannot help but reflect its close ties with tradition and its glimpse of modernity. On the whole, he constitutes no great break in the history of English literature.

1. Of the multitude of books available on Dante, two are especially recommended as helpful introductory studies: Michele Barbi, *Life of Dante,* trans. and ed. Paul G. Ruggiers (Berkeley: California University Press, 1954), and Umberto Cosmo, *A Handbook of Dante Studies,* trans. David Moore (New York: Barnes and Noble Inc., 1947).

2. A good short treatment of the *Convivio* is to be found in Vittorini, *op. cit.,* 99–102.

3. For a clear analysis cf. *ibid.,* 109–28, and for a philosophical analysis see Erich Auerbach, *Dante, Poet of the Secular World,* trans. Ralph

Manheim (Chicago: University of Chicago Press, 1961), 69–173. The German original appeared in 1929.

4. Dante to Can Grande, cited from *A Translation of the Latin Works of Dante Alighieri* ("Temple Classics"; London: J. M. Dent and Sons, 1940), Epistola x, 348.

5. Brenan, *op. cit.*, 69.

6. Elisha K. Kane, translator, *The Book of Good Love of the Archpriest of Hita, Juan Ruiz* (New York, 1939), 15. This is a privately printed English translation.

7. For a learned analysis of this work and of its dependence on Arabic sources consult Americo Castro, *The Structure of Spanish History*, trans. Edmund L. King (Princeton, New Jersey: Princeton University Press, 1954), 392–465.

8. On this interpretation of the work see Otis H. Green, *op. cit.*, I, chap. II, "Medieval Laughter: The Book of Good Love."

9. There is a delightful biography by the American dean of Petrarchia, Ernest Hatch Wilkins' *Life of Petrarch* (Chicago: University of Chicago Press, 1961).

10. For a detailed description and evaluation of the event see *ibid.*, 24–29.

11. For the translation as well as the original see Anna Maria Armi, *Petrarch — Sonnets and Songs* (New York: Pantheon Books, Inc., 1946), Rime cxxviii, 203–10. Cf. also Theodore E. Mommsen's introduction to this book, xxiii–xxiv.

12. *Ibid.*, xxxviii.

13. For his description of his love cf. his *Triumph of Love* trans. Ernest Hatch Wilkins in *The Triumphs of Petrarch* (Chicago: University of Chicago Press, 1962), 23–37 (end of canto iii).

14. Mommsen, in Armi, *op. cit.*, xxxiv.

15. Armi, *op. cit.*, 411 (Rime cclxxxix). It should be pointed out, however, that a good deal of this sentiment was a literary fiction demanded by the canons of courtly love. He apparently forgot about his soul where other ladies were concerned, for he had two illegitimate children; and, like a "good" medieval monk, he damned woman in general: "Woman . . . is . . . indeed a devil, an enemy of peace, a fountainhead of impatience, a discordant source of strife, whom never to have known is to know tranquility" (*Epistolae seniles*, xiv, 3, as cited in Otis Green, *op. cit.*, I, 73, n. 3).

16. Cf. a contemporary's description: "His rhythms flow so sweetly that not even the gravest people can withstand their declamation and sound" (cited from Mommsen, in Armi, *op. cit.*, xxx).

17. J. A. Symonds, *Renaissance in Italy* (New York: The Modern Library, 1935), I, 894.

18. The Italian influence on Chaucer is treated fully in A. Lytton Sells, *The Italian Influence in English Poetry from Chaucer to Southwell* (Bloomington, Indiana: Indiana University Press, 1955), 19–59.

19. On this see W. P. Ker, *English Literature: Medieval*, no. 45, *Home University Library of Modern Knowledge* (New York: Henry Holt and Co., 1912), 220–35.

20. *Ibid.*, 226.

21. *Ibid.*, 227.

22. Muscatine, *op. cit.*, 116.

23. See Gordon N. Ray (ed.), *Chaucer* ("Masters of British Literature"; Boston: Houghton Mifflin Co., 1958), 7. Cf. also Muscatine, *op. cit.*, 139–41, 157, 165.

24. Cf. Donald C. Baker, "Chaucer's Clerk and the Wife of Bath on the Subject of *Gentilesse*," *Studies in Philology*, LIX (1962), 631–40.

25. John William Hey Atkins, *English Literary Criticism: The Medieval Phase* (New York: The Macmillan Co., 1943), 157.

26. Muscatine would make him wholly medieval. Cf. his concluding statement: "He is not 'modern': nowhere does he assert seriously and as final the primacy of realism in art, or the primacy of matter in the universe. He is medieval" (247).

IV

Literature during the Renaissance: The Lyric

To SYSTEMATIZE the history of lyric poetry during the Renaissance period is a difficult task. The poets are numerous, variations are multiple, and classification is risky. Yet, despite the many exceptions that could be raised to any broad descriptions, some attempt at generalization must be made if mere cataloguing is to be avoided.

"Fashioned" Lyric

The first type of lyric poetry that attained wide prominence during the Renaissance is the "fashioned" genre. It is poetry wrought by skillful makers of verse in accordance with progressively hardening rules of composition. It is poetry that is marked more by dexterity than by true feeling, and by artificiality and imitativeness than by naturalness and individuality.

In France this type of poetry is represented by the *rhétoriqueurs*.[1] It began with Guillaume de Machaut (*ca.* 1300–1377), and lasted until about the middle of the sixteenth century when the influence first of the Marotiques and then of the Pléiade led to its decline. Its early guide was Guillaume de Machaut's disciple Eustache Deschamps (1340–1405) with his *L'art de dictier et fere chansons, balades, virelais et rondeaulx*, a plea for elegant and harmonious verse, and its late teacher was Pierre Fabri with his *Grand et vrai art de pleine rhétorique* (1522), a handbook on the technique of versifying and of proper poetic address to princely society. Its devotees were numerous, some of considerable poetic distinction. Froissart, the famed chronicler of chivalry, naturally carried his devotion to chivalry into his lyrics, but he could also sing of the joys of life with some naturalness.[2] Christine de Pisan wrote fervently in defense of women against her own master's, Eustache Deschamps', anti-feminism. Alain Chartier (1385–1440), canon of Paris and Tours and a bitter critic of French chivalry because of its humiliating defeats at the hands of the English,[3] wrote much elegant and measured verse on courtly love, winning lasting laurels with the familiar *La belle dame sans merci.* Charles of Orleans (1374–1465) who lost his father and later suffered twenty-five years of confinement in an English prison — both because of the decadence of French chivalry — could yet embrace the courtly mode and sing of it with charm and grace, with a note of longing and a touch of intimacy. At the turn of the sixteenth century the outstanding figure was Louis XII's historiographer, Jean Le Maire de Belges (1473–1525). Although susceptible to the influence of humanism, he became, nevertheless, a distinguished *rhétoriqueur*,[4] and it was this reputation of his that influenced Clement Marot (1496–1544) to become one of the finest representatives of the school. At first, Marot was a polished versifier, only occasionally admitting to his poetry some naturalness and directness; but after 1524, in the course of repeated clashes with the church over his flirtation with the Protestant movement, he abandoned the *rhétoriqueur* cult for a personal style that is easy, unaffected, and rich in wit. His finest in this vein are probably his *Epistles.* Marot's difficulties with the church and his departure from traditional poeticizing provoked a literary controversy between the traditionalists and Marot's sympathizers. Occurring in the late thirties, this "battle" between the *rhétoriqueurs* and the *marotiques*, although bringing victory to the new movement, actually testifies to the strong entrenchment of the *rhétoriqueur* tradition throughout most of the Renaissance period.

As in France, so in the Low Countries, the prevailing mode was that of the *rhétoriqueurs*. In the court of Burgundy and in various other urban centers were established *Chambres de rhétorique*, and these imposed the rules of making verse. Aspiring townsmen took to the art, and the result was a multitude of composers. According to the late Professor Pirenne, these numerous devotees cultivated "with greater zeal, determination, and seriousness than with taste and originality, the art of writing or, to put it more aptly, the art of 'rhetorizing' in verse." And he further reports that this art persisted unabated throughout the fifteenth and much of the sixteenth centuries.[5] Only after the Protestant movement broke through did some change occur: Anna Bijns and Van der Noot began to introduce the classical influence.

In Germany this school of versifying was delayed until the fifteenth century. Until then the *minnesong* was still current, its two last noteworthy representatives being the nobles Hugo von Montfort (1357–1423) and Oswald von Wolkenstein (1377–1445), both very active adventurers who sang of their experiences as husbands, lovers, and knights in verses of considerable lyrical talent.[6] However, most of the output lacked spontaneity and so offered an easy transition to the lyricizing of the meistersingers — *meister* (expert craftsman). Like the *rhétoriqueurs* in France and Belgium, these German counterparts were skilled composers of poems on various themes and replete with technical virtuosities. They formed themselves into gilds, most cities in southern and central Germany having one such association, and the members were bound to adhere to the rules adopted by each school. The oldest school was that at Mainz, with the wandering minstrel Meister Heinrich von Meissen (*ca.* 1260–1318), otherwise known as Frauenlob ("extoller of ladies"), as its founder;[7] and the most prolific producer was the cobbler who turned poet, raconteur, and playwright, Hans Sachs (1494–1576) of Nuremberg, with 4,275 songs, some 1,500 poems, and 200 plays to his credit, the most popular one being in praise of Luther's leadership as Reformer, *Die Wittenbergische Nachtigall.*[8] If such a prodigious output cannot speak much for the excellence of this poetry, which suffered from excessive moralizing and from a lack of appropriateness between verse, form, and content, it certainly testifies to its popularity. Moreover, the popularity persisted throughout most of the sixteenth century. In 1571, for example, Adam Puschmann (1532–1600), Hans Sachs's disciple, still considered it worthwhile to publish a handbook on the art of the meistersingers, (*Gründlicher Bericht des deutschen Meistergesangs*).[9] Indeed, the school at Nuremberg lasted until 1770 and that at Ulm until 1839.

Spain was apparently spared a heavy dose of this genre, but enough of it was present to be recognizable as a trend. One of the factors that contributed to its formation was the strict adherence to a verse form known as the *cuaderna via* — a quatrain with a monorhyme — made current in the first part of the thirteenth century by Gonzalvo de Berceo. It was used by Juan Ruiz in his *El Libro de buen amor,* and continued to be accepted as the proper poetic form until the next century. Naturally this constrained composition and promoted preoccupation with mechanics at the expense of poesy. In addition to this "tyranny" of the *cuaderna via*, came the decline of the jongleuresque during Spain's "Century of Troubles" (1368–1474) and the corresponding rise, paralleling the resurgence of feudalism, of fashionable courtly compositions.[10] Both tended to heighten formalism of structure and of language at the expense of genuineness. One has only to turn to the anthology, the *Cancionero de Baena*, which the converted Jew, Juan Alfonso de Baena, compiled from the works of fifty-four poets for the benefit of John II (1445), to see that preoccupation with metrical form and rhetoric is a dominant feature, as prominent as is the strict adherence to the canons of courtly love and the poetic conceits they call for.[11] Even such transitional poets as Micer Francisco Imperial and Íñigo López de Mendoza (1398–1458), the first Marqués de Santillana, contributed somewhat to this trend. The former, attempting to introduce the Italian mode, succumbed to mannered rhetoric and pedantry so that his verse was "dry and labored."[12] The latter, still with some affinity for the style of *Provençal* troubadours, insisted on the aristocratization of poetry and on adherence to form,[13] and so supported the very properties which the *rhétoriqueurs* cultivated. The style was indeed still acceptable as late as the 1520's, as the anthologies (*Cancionero general*) of Hernando del Castillo and of Garcia de Resende are full of such stylized lyrics.

In England the "fashioned" verse is associated far more with the fourteenth- and fifteenth-century romances than with the lyrics. Chaucer had set the mode for the former, and the emulation of his work resulted in compositions that were imitative and artificially constructed. But between the romance and the courtly love lyric there is no great gulf, at least as to atmosphere and environment, and so the artificiality of the one passed into the other. A cursory examination of these lyrics in Miss Robbins' collection reveals this quite plainly. Whether it is of the lady's beauty that the lyric sings, or of her heartlessness, whether of love's sweetness or pain, whether of professions of love or of farewells on parting, its language and its sentiment are of the handbook rather than of the heart. Here is a stanza from *A Lover's Farewell to His Mistress*:

> Ffarewell creature comely of kynde
> ffarewell lanterne lussom of light
> ffarewell mynder most of my mynde
> ffarewell souerain, semely in sight[14]

To be sure this is unusually artificial and so is not quite typical of the rest of this genre.[15] Yet it clearly shows the direction in which the fifteenth-century courtly lyric was inclined — away from sincerity and artlessness and toward superficiality and dexterity: the very trademarks of the *rhétoriqueurs*.

Popular Lyric

Paralleling this courtly versifying was the non-aureate type of lyric. It is generally referred to as the popular lyric; but while much of it is of this genre, some also crosses lines with the courtly.

Much of this poetry is simply the folk song. Songs of dance and drink, songs of work, songs of spring or of love, songs of war or of some other heroic events of the age are among its secular varieties. Hymns to the Virgin, songs of her love for the baby Jesus, her lullabies to him, songs of mortality, songs appropriate to certain religious festivals, and in Protestant lands, evangelical hymns, such as those in Luther's famous hymnbook, the *Geistliche Lieder*, are the religious counterparts. Often these religious carols were but adaptations of the secular songs, the lyrics of the latter simply being replaced by language appropriate to a spiritual theme.

As might be surmised from the preceding statement, one of the principal characteristics of this literary genre was its adaptability to occasion and social stratum. When moving from one locality to another or when passing from the country folk to the court society this poetry adjusted its geographical and social settings correspondingly. Other important properties were its apparent spontaneity and freedom from artfulness. Generally, the language was simple, and sometimes even admitted of grammatical violation. So were the rhythmn (often a slow iambic) and the verse structure (couplets, quatrains, etc.). Another characteristic was its use of the refrain, not infrequently nonsensical at that. On the whole, it was poetry whose tunefulness, lyrics, and sentiment could touch the hearts and lips of many people irrespective of time, place, and social class.

All nations had this type of lyric during the Renaissance, some more and some less. In England and Germany it became rather widespread,[16] probably because the courtly lyric in these lands was for the most part an importation. In France the output was not inconsiderable, and in the works of that Paris Master of Arts and of alley life, François de Moncorbier, better known as Villon, it attained rare poetic excellence,[17] but it was eclipsed by the mass of *rhétoriqueur* works. In Italy its volume was greater than is generally recognized by Renaissance historians. In spite of much Petrarchizing and much denunciation of the *vulgus* by the Italian humanists, the Italian folk kept multiplying its songs, both secular and spiritual, until even the opponents were attracted to them, and occasionally used them as the basis of their own arrangements.[18] In Spain, too, its output and merit are not inconsiderable. Indeed, in one of its forms, the ballad, Spanish popular lyric during the Renaissance was only second to that of England.[19] Drawing on the national events of the past or on the frontier fighting of the time, treating of romance as well as of action, of spiritual themes as well as of secular topics, vulgar or polished, this ballad genre was rich in lyricism and should be included with popular lyric poetry. In addition to this balladry there were the *villancicos*, folk songs that were taken from the soil, polished by courtly poets and set to music.[20] Thus the folk lyric, widespread in Germany and England, and more widespread in the Romance countries than is generally estimated, must be recognized as an important genre of Renaissance lyric poetry.

"Classical" Lyric

The third type of lyric which appeared during the Renaissance was the "classical" lyric. Coming for the most part after the fashioned verse and the folk song, which are often dismissed as medieval relics, this vogue is quite strictly associated with the Renaissance proper. Its dependence on the great lyricists of antiquity, Horace, Catullus, Vergil, Pindar, Theocritus, and Anacreon, has quite appropriately earned it the label "classical." But it also followed the Petrarchan lyric, and so it may well be regarded as a combination of the lyrical mode of antiquity and of Petrarchism. Naturally, it could not detach itself wholly from the immediate past, that is, from the "fashioned" verse, but the carry over, although noticeable, was not great enough to counteract the classical influences.

The characteristics of this "classical" lyric naturally reflected its sources. From the models of antiquity it copied certain form — eclogues, odes, epigrams — purity of style, and refinement of diction. From them also it borrowed themes, especially Ovidian love. Then it appropriated such devices of classical poetics as apostrophes, invocations, and mythological allusions, and often used them to the point of pedantry. Occasionally it captured both the pagan spirit and the freshness of nature. From Petrarch it got form also, particularly the sonnet; but especially it drew on his theme. For every lyricist there was a corresponding Laura, real or imagined, and the love pangs she evoked ranged from sincerest feelings to pretended passion that had to be carried on the wings of affectation and conceit. However, whether it was the first or the latter, limpidity of diction was a necessity, and this gave the lyrics melody and vivacity. From the immediate past, that is from the *rhétoriqueurs*, it unconsciously borrowed the "finely" turned phrase, nor could it escape the influence of the ever-popular romances in which amorous knights thrilled at the sight or sound of their haloed love-mates. Finally, also from the immediate past, from the folk song now, occasionally the Renaissance lyric drew some vigor, in spite of the literary polishing and chastening to which the former was subjected. In sum, the "classical" lyric of the Renaissance was an accomplished product, an exercise in artistic form, graceful words, and idyllic conceits on overtender themes, finished and showy like the rich costumes and tripping manners of the day.

Since one of the integral properties of this lyric poetry was Petrarchism, it stands to reason that the Renaissance lyric must have developed in Italy first. There the number of composers was great, and several attained considerable prominence. Lorenzo de' Medici stands out as the one who rescued the vernacular from the denunciations of the humanists and then set the fashion by using it in his "pretty" *Sonnetti Canzoni* and *Selve d'Amore*. One which reflects Lorenzo's love of idyllic settings and at the same time reveals to what extent poeticizing captured the hearts and the fancy of Italian men of affairs deserves to be cited.

> Let whoso will in courtly show be blest,
>   Or find in splendid edifice his joy —
>   His arts for pleasure or for gold employ,

> The while a thousand cares his soul molest.
> A meadow green, with lovely flowerets drest,
>   A little brook that glides a-murmuring by,
>   A bird that bears its song of love on high —
> More gently these do lull my thoughts to rest.
> The shadowy woods, the rocks, the lofty hills,
>   The darksome caverns and the nimble deer
>   And the swift-fleeting timorous woodland fay —
> Each in my mind some gentle thought instills
>   Of the bright eyes that shine in memory here,
>   But fade 'mid pomp and palaces away.[21]

Angiolo Ambrogini, known better as Poliziano, excelled Lorenzo in artistic refinement, in feeling, and language, and is said to have added "Attic stamp to Italian poetry." The great Petrarchist was Pietro Bembo whose odes and sonnets reveal a very conscious study and emulation of the fourteenth-century style. Jacopo Sannazaro's sonnets and *Canzoni* are superior in their spontaneity, while the lyrical sections of his *Arcadia,* the stylesetter for many other Arcadias even outside Italy, in their artistry and idyllic scenes, reveal a love and a feeling for Vergil and Theocritus. Less polished in finish but really genuine in feeling were the *Rime* of Vittoria Colonna that noble widow whose great heart could never forget her love for her undeserving husband. Lastly, even that mighty-handed sculptor and painter Michelangelo carved some strong sonnets in which he addressed his platonic love for the devout and unresponsive Vittoria.

Besides these selected few, there were a whole host of others, all of whom attempted to turn out compositions in proper form and elegant language but produced artistic pieces laden with conceits and conventions. And by the middle of the sixteenth century, the genre was popular enough to justify publication of anthologies. Some of these contained the verse of early Tuscan lyricists; others consisted of the works of contemporaries. Among these, one of the most comprehensive was Gabriele Giolito's *Rime diverse di molti eccellentissimi autori nuovamente raccolte,* one book of which appeared in 1545 and a second one in 1547. In turn, the circulation of these anthologies further helped to popularize the classical lyric mode and also to "fix" it. Indeed, it was through these anthologies that the Italianate classical lyric spread throughout Europe.

Chronologically Spain was the next land where the classical lyric flowered. Commercial contacts with Italy and the acquisition of Naples by Aragon facilitated the influx of Italian literary influences. Micer Francisco Imperial, a goldsmith from Genoa resident in Seville, introduced Dantesque influence. Santillana, met once before, emulated Petrarch, and his forty-two sonnets followed the latter closely. In the following century, Juan de Mena (1411–1456), fashioner of the popular meter *arte mayor*, enriched the Spanish poetry with classicism. Following these early imitators came the true classical lyricists. Juan Boscan Almogáver publicly argued for the use of the *italico modo* and made the sonnet popular; while Garcilaso de la Vega (1501?–1536), called the "faultless poet," drew heavily on the Petrarchan sonnets for form, theme, and sentiment, and followed the classical practice of polishing his verse until the diction was precise, the movement smooth, and the form correct.[22] Besides the thirty-eight Petrarchan sonnets, Garcilaso also composed three eclogues and two elegies quite in the spirit of Sannazaro and with obvious influences of Horace and Vergil. To the finished artistry of Garcilaso, Fray Luis de Leon (1527–1591), a mystic of the Augustinian order and a humanist professor at Salamanca, added depth of feeling. His lyrics, in which he frequently expresses a longing for the contemplative life, ring with a genuine sentiment and bear their classical learning, including Hebrew, as naturally as do those of Milton.[23] More poignant, even ecstatic, were the lyrics of San Juan de la Cruz (1543–1591). A Carmelite mystic, he wrote of spiritual love, that of the soul searching for its beloved. Quite in the tradition of the classical Italian lyric and emulative of Garcilaso's style, were the platonic love lyrics — mostly sonnets — with which the Andalusian cleric Fernando de Herrera (1534–1597) addressed Dona Leonor de Milán, Countess of Gelves. The sentiment is lofty, the language is refined, and the combination results in elegant but sincere poetry.[24] On the whole, in comparison with the Italian classical lyric, this Spanish poetry has more depth and sincerity. Perhaps this is due to the fact that not one of these poets was a courtly sycophant who traded polished verses for patronage.

In France the classical lyric is associated with the Pléiade, a group of seven poets whose leading lights were Pierre de Ronsard (1525–1585) and Joachim du Bellay (1522–1560). The attitude of this group and of their many followers is represented by Ronsard's memorable statement *Je veux lire en trois jours l'Illiade d'Homere* and by Du Bellay's insistence that the French language is a fit vehicle for poetry (*Deffence et illustration de la langue françayse*) and that poets are trained and not born. Ronsard's statement reflects addiction to the classics, and although it does not refer specifically to classical lyric poetry, we may be sure that it is used comprehensively to denote all classical poetry. At any rate, we know that Ronsard emulated Pindar, Anacreon, and Horace. Du Bellay's essay presupposes that composition of poetry is a form of professional art. Together these men stimulated lyrical poetry refined in sentiment and artistry. A supplementary influence was Petrarchism, direct and as represented by Sannazaro. This added the theme of love, honeyed sentiment, and the rhythmic modes.

Combining all these influences, Ronsard produced, among others, the *Amours de P. Ronsard, Continuation des Amours*, and *Sonnets pour Hélène*, all of them polished expressions of delicate sentiments. Du Bellay contributed the *Olive* and the *Recueil de poésie* in which by actual examples he showed that French lyric poetry need not imitate Petrarch slavishly, and the *Jeux rustiques*, graceful Petrarchisms on the joys of nature. Among the less illustrious followers were Philippe Desportes (1545–1606), a slave to the Italian mode; Maurice Scève, supposed discoverer of Laura's grave; and Guillaume de Salluste (1544–1590), an emulator of Ronsard.

These five and a host of other imitators elevated the classical lyric in France to its height. Their poetry attained great popularity and regained for France the literary pre-eminence which its romances and troubadour lyrics had won for it in the Middle Ages but which the *rhétoriqueurs*, despite their extensive output, had failed to sustain.

Caught between the popularity of the *Meistersang* and the Lutheran literary movement, hymn-writing in particular, Germany did not have an eminent "classical" lyrical movement during the Renaissance. There were reputable composers of lyrics in Latin. Celtis, for example, besides his other humanist achievements, wrote the *Amores*; Eoban Koch, some eclogues; Euricius Cordus, some epigrams; and Petrus Laticius Secundus, some elegies addressed to a haughty Claudia. In the vernacular there was a less distinguished movement, quite Italianate in character, but it boasts of no outstanding poets.

On the other hand, England's "classical" lyric movement was every bit as notable as that of Italy, Spain, or France. It drew heavily on Italian Petrarchism — note the great output of sonnets — and on the French Pléiade, but it was also affected by some native influences. One of these appears to have been the nation's penchant for song as exemplified by such anthologies as William Byrd's and Thomas Morley's *The Triumphs of Oriana* (twenty-five lyric songs in praise of Elizabeth) and Thomas Campion's five books of lyrics, and by the lyricism of some of the medieval-like compositions of Wyatt, Howard, or Sydney.

The lyricists were numerous, and some of them were quite outstanding. Thomas Wyatt (1503–1542), a courtier in Tudor service and known to history as the leader of an unsuccessful anti-Marian rebellion, is sometimes credited with letting "the new Renaissance into English poetry." He "let" Petrarch fashion seventeen of his thirty-two sonnets, which, though "translations" of Petrarch's sonnets, are not really "uninspired works of duty," as Tillyard suggests.[25] For Wyatt personalized them — what Laura was to Petrarch, Anne Boleyn was to Wyatt — and so rendered them more genuine and vigorous, hence less *courtois* and conceited. However, even granted that his humanistic lyrics may deserve higher praise than critics have accorded them, they are inferior to the songs which he composed in the native medieval mode, which also, incidentally, were refashionings, in this case, of the popular love lyrics.[26] Henry Howard, son of the Duke of Norfolk and aristocracy's bad boy — a contemporary referred to him as "the most foolish proud boy that is in England" — and companion of Wyatt's son, likewise paraphrased some of Petrarch's sonnets; but, in general, his compositions excelled Wyatt's in balance and fluency, if not in sincerity.[27] He also fashioned the English sonnet with the three quatrains and the couplet each having its own rhyme scheme and adapted the eleven-syllable unrhymed verse of the Italians to the decasyllabic verse without rhyme in English and thereby "virtually created the metre" which Marlowe and Shakespeare and Milton used so fruitfully.[28] George Turberville is known for his perfection, prolixity, and classical pedantry.

Following these inceptors came the three great poets, Sydney, Spenser, and Shakespeare.

Sir Philip Sydney, called by Spenser "the president of noblesse and chivalry," was the famous Christian knight of the Battle of Zutphen. Dedicated to the cause of refinement, Sydney tried "to fit English poetry to classical meters"[29] and to humanistic literary standards in general. His one hundred and eight elegant love sonnets, published under the title of *Astrophel and Stella* and addressed to Stella, an idealized woman[30] like Petrarch's Laura, are flawless in composition and, except where he follows his Italian models — Petrarch, Pontano, and Tasso[31] — quite genuine in feeling, the sincerity of the latter being enhanced by the clear admission of the natural conflict between flesh and virtue. These properties were undoubtedly due to Sydney's conviction, expressed in his *Defense of Poetry*, that while poetic artistry is not unimportant, true greatness of poetry derives more from spirit than from form and content.

Sydney's friend, Edmund Spenser, is recognized more for his expression of faith in England's great destiny and in chivalry's virtue than he is for his lyrics. Indeed, his diction was purposely patterned after Chaucer and included so many archaisms that later neoclassicists disdained to read him. Yet his lyricism is undeniable. His *Shepherd's Calendar* is in the pastoral mode, following Theocritus and Vergil and their Renaissance imitators, Mantuanus and Marot. If behind the make-believe shepherds and their simple themes lurk contemporary personalities and subjects so that the genuineness is partially vitiated, and if "the prime purpose of the work [was] to rid poetic diction of foreign encumbrance and restore Chaucerian vigor and simplicity,"[32] the several songs in the work, such as the one to Elizabeth in *Eclogue IV*, ring with lyrical melody. More truly lyrical are his *Amoretti*, some eighty sonnets addressed to his future wife Elizabeth, "a sweet country lass" with eyes of "sapphire blue" and hair of "rippling gold." Whether they deal with the pains of unrequited love or with love's sweet joys, they seem to speak in the language of truth and taste. Perhaps even superior to these autobiographical songs are the twenty-three strophes (*Epitha-*

lamion) in which he commemorated his wedding day. Take, for example, the strophe which describes the marriage ceremony:

> Behold, whiles she before the altar stands,
> Hearing the holy priest that to her speakes
> And blesseth her with his two happy hands,
> How the red roses flush up in her cheekes,
> And the pure snow with goodly vermill stayne,
> Like crimsin dyde in grayne;
> That euen th' Angels, which continually
> About the sacred Altare doe remaine,
> Forget their service and about her fly,
> Ofte peeping in her face, that seemes more fayre,
> The more they on it stare.
> But her sad eyes, still fastened on the ground,
> Are governed with goodly modesty,
> That suffers not one looke to glaunce awry,
> Which may let in a little thought unsownd.
> Why blush ye, love, to give to me your hand,
> The pledge of all our band?
> Sing, ye sweet Angels, Alleluya sing,
> That all the woods may answere, and your eccho ring.

And the other strophes are comparable to this. Exalting the marriage ceremony until all nature seems to be embraced in it, they yet retain their human and artistic elements. They remain full of understanding of the human ways and respectful of propriety and of flesh, and at the same time they are charged with rich imagery and word melody. Not even his *Faerie Queene*, that romance on how virtue allied to England's star, the first Elizabeth, would glorify England's role in history, can match this in artistry.

The last and probably the most respected of Renaissance lyricists was none other than the great Shakespeare himself. His sonnets, perhaps autobiographical, carry depth of passion as if it came from his heart rather than from his pen. Although some do yield to artifice and grandiloquence, so characteristic of much Renaissance literature, in general they are not vapid mouthings of an artist skilled in finely turned phrases, but ripe with the fullness of thought. And concordant with this sobriety was the attitude he expressed in these sonnets toward love, one of their prevailing themes: it is not ecstatic, lost, as it were, in its own succulent sweetness, but deep and heavy-winged with resignation.[33] Even more excellent, because they are fresher, more varied, and always completely appropriate to the occasion, are the lyrics interspersed in his plays. The spritely songs of Ariel, or the bits of folk song that escape the lips of broken Ophelia, the improvisations of Amiens and Jacques in *As You Like It*—these, and many others, reveal Shakespeare's ingenuity with the lyric. It is to be noted, however, that, while in many of his dramas he drew bountifully upon "classicisms," in these inserted lyrics he got by without much effusion of Renaissance pedantry.

As stated at the outset of this brief survey of English "classical" lyric in the Renaissance, only the foremost of the composers were considered. Yet to get a true picture of the extreme popularity of this form of poetry it is necessary to add that there were a host of lesser imitators: the prolix Samuel Daniel, religious Robert Southwell, skillful Watson, fluent Giles Fletcher, servile Thomas Lodge, lively Drayton, and others; and numerous anthologies: *Tottle's Miscellany, The Paradise of Dainty Devices, Phoenix Nest, England's Helicon, England's Parnassus*—all of which fed strong the English lyric blaze.

1. For a comprehensive treatment of *rhétoriqueur* poetry in France see Warner Forrest Patterson, *Three Centuries of French Poetic Theory. A Critical History of the Chief Arts of Poetry in France* (1328–1630), vol. XIV, *University of Michigan Publications. Language and Literature* (Ann Arbor, Michigan: University of Michigan Press, 1935), 1–290.

2. Cf. Longfellow's translation of his "On doit le temps ensi prendre qu'il vient."

3. On this see Raymond Lincoln Kilgour, *The Decline of French Chivalry,* no. XII, *Harvard Studies in Romance Languages* (Cambridge: Harvard University Press, 1937), 195–225.

4. Cf. Charles Sears Baldwin, *Renaissance Literary Theory and Practice* (New York: Columbia University Press, 1939), 68–70.

5. H. Pirenne, *Histoire de Belgique*, II, 453; III, 323.

6. For details on these two men see Walshe, *op. cit.*, 279–80.

7. *Ibid.*, 264–9.

8. For a brief but sympathetic treatment of Sachs see J. G. Robertson, *A History of German Literature* (4 ed.; New York: British Book Centre, Inc., 1962), 162–5.

9. For a brief statement of the rules there enjoined, see August Closs, *The Genius of the German Lyric* (London: George Allen & Unvin, Ltd., 1938), 79–80.

10. John II of Castile, himself a poet, is said to have played patron to "over 200 troubadours and poets," Thomas Walsh, *Hispanic Anthology* (New York: G. P. Putnam's Sons, 1920), 70.

11. On this formalism see George Tyler Northup, *An Introduction to Spanish Literature* (3d ed., revised by Nicholson B. Adams; Chicago: University of Chicago Press, 1960), 111; and Otis H. Green, "Courtly Love in the Spanish Cancioneros," *Publications of the Modern Language Association of America*, LXIV (1949), 247–301.

12. Brenan, *op. cit.*, 90.

13. Cf. Northup, *op. cit.*, 112–14.

14. Cited from Robbins, *op. cit.*, 213.

15. But cf. the following:

    by the spectable splendure of hir fulgent face
    my sprete was rauesched, and in my body spent,
    Inflamed was my heart with great solace
    Of the luciant corruscall resplendent

    Cited from Sir Edmund Kerchever Chambers, *English Literature at the Close of the Middle Ages*, in *The Oxford History of English Literature* (Oxford: Clarendon Press, 1945), 116.

16. For a brief survey of the *Volksliede* see J. G. Robertson, *op. cit.*, 140–3. On English carols and ballads consult Chambers, *op. cit.*, chaps. II and III *passim*.

17. On the life of Villon, which is at the same time a treasure-trove of information on fifteenth-century Paris, see D. B. Wyndham Lewis, *François Villon* (New York: The Literary Guild of America, 1938).

18. On its extensiveness see Symonds, *op. cit.*, II, chapters on "Popular Secular Poetry" and "Popular Religious Poetry."

19. Northup, *op. cit.*, 211.

20. For several of these in English translation see Brenan, *op. cit.*, 119–24.

21. Cited from Wilkins, *A History of Italian Literature*, 140.

22. On Boscan and Garcilasso see Ernest Mérimée, *A History of Spanish Literature,* trans. S. Griswold Morley (New York: Henry Holt and Company, 1930), 161–4.

23. See Thomas Walsh's translations of some of them in his *Hispanic Anthology*, 188–211.

24. Cf. Longfellow's renderings in *ibid.*, 226–31.

25. E. M. W. Tillyard, *The English Renaissance, Fact or Fiction* (Baltimore, Maryland: The Johns Hopkins Press, 1952), 50, 55. But cf. Sells, *op. cit.*, 72–74, where Wyatt's dependence on Petrarch is reduced somewhat.

26. This is amply established in H. A. Mason's *Humanism and Poetry in the Early Tudor Period* (New York: Barnes and Noble, Inc., 1960), 143–78.

27. *Ibid.*, 236–54. Mason argues here that Howard was inferior to Wyatt.

28. Sells, *op. cit.*, 77–80.

29. Baugh, *op. cit.*, 473.

30. She has generally been identified with Penelope Devereux, wife of Lord Rich, but apparently incorrectly. On this see Sells, *op. cit.*, 138.

31. Cf. *ibid.*, 139–46.

32. Baugh, *op. cit.*, 484.

33. Douglas Bush, *English Poetry* (New York: Oxford University Press, 1952), 31–32.

V

Literature during the Renaissance: The Romance

Popularity and Changes

As WAS OBSERVED in an earlier section, the romance on the eve of the Renaissance was still a living literary genre. During the Renaissance proper it seems to have grown in popularity. Old romances were multiplied or revised, expanded, and modified. New romances on the old themes were composed; and romances which satirized the standard types were written. The vogue reached such proportions that some of the men of letters became alarmed. Vives, for instance, protested:

> There is a use nowadays worse than among pagans, that books written in our mother tongue, that be made for idele men and women to read, have non other matter than that of war and love.[1]

Erasmus, the universal arbiter of letters, ridiculed them as *fabulae stultae et aniles*.[2] And Ascham charged that the stories "led to no other ende, but only to manslaughter and baudrye."[3] Many others joined in the refrain.[4]

Why the Renaissance age embraced the romance so warmly is not easy to ascertain. But several reasons are highly probable. Vives indirectly provides one when he says that romances were "made for idle men and women." The "idle" were the aristocracy, both the old nobility and the new moneyed class which emulated the aristocratic ways. The age was oriented toward the cult of aristocracy, and interest and fashion dictated that polite society should cultivate aristocratic literature which naturally included the romantic genre. This predilection is well evidenced among other indications by the fact that Caxton "was approached by 'many noble and divers gentlemen' for a printing in English of the History of the Saint greal and of . . . King Arthur."[5] Another reason was the distinction that was attached to this type of literature because it came from the pens of eminent writers. Thus, in England, Chaucer's renown as a poet naturally passed to his works and most of them were romances. To be a Chaucerian was the thing, and to emulate Chaucer was to follow him in the writing of romances. The same reasoning applies to Italy's Boiardo and Ariosto. Still another reason was, of course, the appearance of the printing press and the consequent increase in the number of publications of this type of literature, particularly since cheap editions attracted buyers from among the less wealthy folk, the country squires and townsmen. There is also the reason which induced Malory and Caxton to print them, namely, to revive chivalry which, it was hoped, would help to restore the art of graceful and gallant living. Finally, there is the explanation offered by a late Renaissance Spanish critic of the fad, Fray Luis de Granada, namely, that the romance was a polite form of *erotica* with especial appeal to women, for he charged that

> vain exploits, accompanied many times by an outright licentiousness
> . . . turn[ed] the heads of women readers, causing them to believe
> that they themselves deserve to be the objects of the *service d'amour*
> no less that the fine ladies for whose sake so many exploits and such
> noteworthy feats of arms were accomplished.[6]

Whatever the reasons, the romance became a Renaissance vogue.

The fact that the romance continued strong throughout the entire Renaissance period does not mean that it was as preponderant as in the high Middle Ages, for now it faced competition from the Renaissance lyric and from humanistic literature. Nor does its popularity mean that the genre remained unaltered; it saw some changes. One was the change from poetic to prose form. Whereas formerly it was written in a form suitable for recitation, now it was adapted for private reading. This conversion presently invited the heightening of storiology at the expense of the epical properties. In turn, emphasis on storiology led to the lapse of some of the romances which were weak in that property and to the invention of new and extravagant episodes and so actually to new romances. Another change, a lesser one, but still significant, was the general "chastening" and "academicizing" of the language. If the romance was to help revive chivalric conduct, its language would have to be elegant; and if it was to appeal to the new society given to humanism, it would have to utilize classical properties. Finally, there was the employment of the romance to satirize the genre. This is well represented in poetic romance by Teofilo Folengo's (1496–1544) *Baldus,* a mock epic written in Macaronic form and delineating adventures which land the hero and the author in hell, a not unfriendly place, and in prose romance by Cervantes' *Don Quixote.* Not that the satirizing of the romance was unknown to the medieval period, for the genre of Reynard the Fox certainly throve on such criticism, but the use of the romance itself as an instrument of self-criticism was new.

To characterize this genre during the Renaissance is to overlook such notable differences as exist, say, between *Sir Gawain and the Green Knight, Amadis de Gaula,* and *Orlando Furioso.* But these and other notable compositions aside, the romances in general were monotonously similar. The theme was the constant one of chivalric emprise and love; the atmosphere was that of affectation and sentimentality; and the style "drawn out, clammy and slovenly."[7] Still, if on the whole the genre was not inspiring, it certainly must have been entertaining if its popularity is to be explained.

Romance in the Principal Western Lands

ITALY In Italy the romance proved to be more than just a popular form of literary entertainment. To be sure there were popular versions of the Carolingian *Chanson de geste* and of the Arthurian *matière,* but they did not remain at the ordinary level of vulgar literature. In the hands of skilled artists — and there were four noteworthy ones — they reached the summit of Italian Renaissance poetry.[8]

The first, Luigi Pulci (1432–1484), created the *Morgante Maggiore.* It is an epic of treason dealing with knight-errantry, with the tale of Roncesvalles, and with some additional subjects. Its style is popular, the diction often becoming argot. But its distinction derives from the variability of mood and style, and from the strong if exaggerated characterization of its principals. Renaldo is a fiery lover; Margut is a rogue, something of a forebear of Rabelais' Panurge; and Orlando is "the epitome of chivalric rectitude"; and so on. The poem was written for the amusement of Lorenzo de'Medici's mother, and its amusing properties are to be found in the satire and brusque humor masking behind the argot. It is the work of a worldly bourgeois enjoying himself at the expense of what he considered to be an unrealistic aristocratic social fad.

The next two poets wrote a sequence. Matteo Maria Boiardo (1434–1494), sometimes referred to as the Homer of Chivalry, contributed the *Orlando Innamorato*, and Ludovico Ariosto (1474–1533), the *Orlando Furioso*. Combined, the poems total one hundred thousand lines, and their main theme, although enmeshed with a number of concurrent independent stories concerning some of the principals, is the love and marriage of Ruggiero and Bradamante, the mythical progenitors of the Estensi in whose honor the poems were written. But while in this sense a sequence, the poems differ from each other in mood and style. Boiardo's treatment is quite sincere, chivalry to him still being a respected reality. It allows little of the affectation so common in Renaissance literature, hence it is fresh. Ariosto's part, on the other hand, is studied; indeed, he is said to have spent ten years composing it and another fifteen or sixteen years revising it. Artistry, therefore, is its forte, and chivalry largely a delightful matter for romanticizing. Extravagance is everywhere, and as the title suggests, love becomes insanity. What saves the poem is indeed this artistry, which at times completely overshadows the narrative. Ariosto apparently excelled in seeing the beautiful in the world of nature and of man and in communicating this perception of beauty to the reader. At the same time his fertile imagination filled the poem with a multitude of fanciful scenes rich in charm. And both, the real and the fanciful, he combined with a sensitive expression that enhanced their effect.[9]

The fourth poet was Torquato Tasso (1544–1595) and his work *Jerusalem Delivered*. An artistic genius, with a sensitive soul, an unstable mind, and a timorous heart, Tasso tried to compose an epic which he hoped would reflect the resurgence of Christianity against the Turks and of Catholicism against the Protestants. For the task he employed the heroic theme of the liberation of Jerusalem by the first Crusaders; but while the subject was "big" enough for an epic, he failed to produce an epic. The heavy borrowing from the *Aeneid*, of phrase and picture, injected incompatibility between the intended spirit and expression. The even heavier borrowing from the medieval romance, of knightly deeds and of love, diverted concentration from the central theme to individual episodes. The result became a romance of chivalry, elegant and cultured, interlaced with artistically conceived idylls bathed in pathos. The authenticity of the poem yielded before measured musical rhetoric and sentimentalism.[10] But if it was a failure as an epic, it became a success as a romance.

Pulci, Boiardo, Ariosto, Tasso — Italy's greatest poets between 1450 and 1600 — all attempted to write epics in the tradition of Vergil. But while they drew upon the structure and language of the *Aeneid* and incorporated anecdotes from classical literature, their completed poems failed to attain the status of real epics. Rather they turned out to be romances with epical pretensions, replete with lovely ladies, sweet love, and knightly deeds. There was little of the elemental and of the truly heroic that moved inexorably to the mighty destined goal, but much of the anecdotal and the melodramatic that merely succeeded in charming drawingroom society. This failure is quite revealing, as it testifies to the tenacity of the medieval romantic tradition, and that, in a land which had such great pretensions of rejecting the past.

At the same time as the romantic epic was being attempted by these four poets, a new type of romance, the pastoral romance, was born. Its earliest prototype was Boccaccio's *Ameto*, but this work failed to gain popularity, and it was not until Jacopo Sannazaro of Naples produced his *Arcadia* that the genre won acceptance. Sannazaro had a thorough knowledge of classical literature and mythology, and wrote Latin poetry of considerable distinction. From this mastery of the classics he acquired a predilection for the idyllic type of literature. He was also fascinated by the prevailing cult of romance, and was himself captivated by love in the manner of romantic heroes. All these he combined to produce his style-setting *Arcadia*.

The composition is a combination of twelve sections of prose and twelve poems. The theme is that of unrequited love. It concerns a love-lorn Neopolitan shepherd — Sannazaro himself — who moves from Naples to a pastoral countryside in Greece where he hopes to find surcease from his love pangs. He takes part in the arcadian life of the shepherds for a while, but then, moved by an ominous dream, he returns to Naples only to find his beloved gone. The story is there but, being scarcely traceable, it contributes little to the merits of the poem.

These are to be found in the descriptions of the idyllic settings and the love scenes, in the lyrical language, and in the languid mood. Shepherds and nymphs and beautiful maidens and amorous swains mingle with flocks, disport themselves, and talk of romance while nature smiles benignly on all. It is a world of fancy where the heroic has yielded to the lyrical, and the real to the pictorial and attractive.

Yet much as the composition tries to imitate the tradition of the classical eclogues and idylls, it cannot escape the ideals of love present in the romantic literature of the day. Indeed it was this happy combination of the classical with the romantic that won it popularity. Offering itself as a type of poetic literature of escape, it was warmly welcomed by a society that surrounded itself so much with an air of pretension and a world of illusion.

SPAIN In Spain the history of the romance during the Renaissance conforms to the general pattern outlined at the beginning of this section. The period opened with the continuation of the medieval *chanson de geste*, both as to subject matter — Carolingian and Arthurian cycles; and as to style — caesura, single assonance, direct diction, and emphasis on the dramatic. This continuation also included romances on the national heroes of the past — the *Crónica rimada del Cid* on el Campeador himself, for example. Contemporaneously with this continuation appear the *romanceros*. These were ballads, but many of them were reworkings in ballad form of the old *cantares* and so retained the chivalric themes and the epic mood. Others depicted the frontier warfare (*romances fronterizos*) and the bitter dynastic struggle between Pedro I of Leon and Castile and his illegitimate brother Henry of Trastamara (the Don Pedro Cycle), and so they too reflected some of the qualities of chivalric romances.[11] In the course of time appeared the prose romance, at first translations from French compositions, and later of peninsular origin.[12] The most popular of the latter was the *Amadis de Gaula,* which is believed to have originated in Portugal about 1325, but which did not attain fame until Garci Rodríguez de Montalvo, *regidor* of Medina del Campo, recast it in 1508. Its full title, *Los quatro libros del virtuoso cauallero Amadis de Gaula*, reveals its content, i.e., ideal chivalry; the treatment is often melodramatic, quite in the mode of medieval chivalric romances; and the style is generally florid. However, its treatment of the deep and beautiful love between Amadis and Oriana and of equally deep loyalty of Amadis to his lord King Lisuarte had great attraction, and so the work swept the peninsula and western Europe too, and invited numerous sequels. Of the same variety, but not so widespread in popularity though superior in composition, was the *Palmerín de Inglaterra* and its cycle. Still later appeared the pastoral romance exemplified by the *Diana* of Jorge de Montemajor (*ca.* 1520–1561), a minor official in the households of Philip II's sisters. This composition was both an imitation and an improvement of Sannazaro's *Arcadia*. It retained the latter's idyllic settings and atmosphere, but its love plots were strengthened, making the stories more plausible and the whole more acceptable. The result was widely received, seventeen editions of the work appearing in the sixteenth century alone. Continuing in vogue during most of the sixteenth century, the prose romance finally was undermined by Cervantes' *Don Quixote*, a droll and satirical treatment of the dawning of disillusionment with the chivalric dreamworld. It was further weakened by the development of the picaresque novel, a "romance," as it were, of "low" life. The "errantry" of a Lazarillo was enough to shock the romance of chivalry unto death.

FRANCE Romance in Renaissance France did not attain the literary level that it reached in Italy or Spain. It could claim no Ariosto and no Garci Rodríguez de Montalvo. But it could draw on a rich fund of medieval romances or on some interesting foreign creations. Thus during the fifteenth century, some sixty of the old romances were in full circulation; in the following century the number was still quite high, about thirty. The press naturally increased the circulation. *Fierebras,* which dealt with Charlemagne's conquest in Spain, printed for the first time in 1478, went through six editions before the end of the century; *Tristan* went through several new printings after its publication in 1489, and *Lancelot du Lac* continued to be republished until 1591. Moreover, some of these new printings were cheaper editions and this increased the clientele. To this native output were added translations of a number of Spanish romances, either directly from Spanish or from Italian versions of the Spanish originals. The most celebrated translation was that of *Amadis* by Herberay des Essars. He prepared eight volumes (1540–1548), and these were followed by translations of six more and by additions of another seven and the whole went through several editions before the century was over. Translations of other romances, mostly of those with dolorous endings, added to the trend, namely, those of *Palmerin d'olive; Le judgment d'amour, translaté de Espaignol en Françays; L'Amant mal traicte de s'amye*. And together they helped to sustain the people's interest in the romance throughout the Renaissance and beyond it.[13]

GERMANY Falling below the standards and the popularity attained in Italy, Spain, and France, the romance in Renaissance Germany is said to have "dragged out a wretched existence."[14] The national epic was represented by several collections of earlier works — for example, Ulrich Füetrer's *Buch der Abenteuer* of Arthuriana, and the *Ambraser Heldenbuch* compiled at the request of Emperor Maximilian[15] — and several new compositions, among which were the *Lied von Hürnen Siegfried* and the *Jüngere Hildebrandslied*; but neither of these has any distinction except as evidence of the continuation of the once-vigorous genre. There were also a number of free prose renderings from the French romances, *Loher and Maller* (adventures of Charles the Great's illegitimate son Lothar) and the *Hug Schapeler* (Hugh Capet's love adventures) by Countess Elisabeth of Nassau-Saarbrücken, and also the *Fierebras, Tristan and Iseult,* and *Amadis de Gaula.*[16] The last, appearing after 1596 under the title *Amadis aus Frankreich,* commanded considerable popularity. The truly native composition was the *Teuerdank* (1517) which Melchior Pfintzing prepared at the request of Emperor Maximilian I, sometimes titled, but obviously incorrectly, as the "last of the knights."[17] This tells the story of the hero Teuerdank (Maximilian) combating various agents of the Evil One (vices) which opposed his suit for the hand of the fair queen Ehrenreich (Mary of Burgundy). The romance, although it included such unchivalric feats as ascending a broken stair or crossing on a rotten piece of scaffolding, gained some popularity, as it was republished in 1553 by Burkard Waldis. The fact that Waldis was a converted Protestant while Maximilian was a Catholic and a symbol of the pro-Catholic stand of the imperial office bespeaks the tenacity if not the excellence of the romance in Germany.

While some German authors sought to preserve the romance in one form or another, there were those who poked fun at it or tried to adapt it to unknightly social strata. One telling example of the former was Heinrich Wittenweiler's *Der Ring*. In it peasants replace knights, and the whole becomes a grotesque parody of chivalry and its preoccupations. More serious and therefore more incongruous were the works (*Der Goldtfaden Knabenspiegel*, and others) of Jorg Wickram of Colmar. Although inclining toward the novel, marginally they are still romances. However, they are concerned with the advantages of domestic life, of marriage, and of rearing a family — rather unchivalric themes in the traditional romances. On the whole, therefore, the romance in Renaissance Germany was a fading genre.

ENGLAND But if the romance was not strong in Renaissance Germany, it was a veritable vogue in England. Chaucer's predilection for it gave it the stamp of approval, and thereafter it commanded steady popularity until the end of the Tudor period. Until 1575, Professor Crane reports, the vogue was represented, first by metrical versions of the native and Carolingian themes of the Middle Ages, and then by prose translations from French versions of the medieval and of the early Renaissance origin. After 1575, the metrical compositions progressively yielded to prose, and translations of the Spanish romances were added. About the same time the influence of Ariosto and Tasso provided literary sanction to the genre. Lastly, drama, by drawing upon some of the themes and characters, also contributed to the preservation and popularization of the vogue.

Of the several romances of native origin illustrative of continuity we may consider two, *Guy of Warwick* and *Bevis of Hampton*. The first, appearing about 1300, tells of the adventures that are undertaken by the son of Warwick's steward to prove himself worthy of the hand of Felice, the Earl's daughter. When the prize is finally gained, Guy is smitten with remorse when he realizes that it was for a selfish purpose, love, that he had striven, and so makes amends by adventuring in behalf of God and faith.[18] These elements of knightly deeds, love, and faith assured its popularity. Expanded versions — four of them — one by Lydgate, began to circulate; and when the printing press came into being, several editions appeared within the century. Baugh further reports that the theme was incorporated into Elizabethan ballads and plays and found its way into chap books "that lasted on into the eighteenth century."[19] The second, also of medieval origin, is the story of a knight who is deprived of his rightful heritage but succeeds in recovering it. According to the plot, the knight is sold in his boyhood by his criminal mother and drifts with fortune until he finds himself finally in the service of a Saracen king and in love with his daughter. After performing numerous deeds in defense of Christianity and of his love, he returns to his native land and recovers his usurped rights. Rich in adventurous exploits which are described with vigor and humor, this romance remained quite popular in the sixteenth century.

Romances of the Arthurian *matière* enjoyed similar popularity. Outstanding among these, especially for storiology as well as for the usual chivalric properties, was *Sir Gawain and the Green Knight*.[20] More influential, of course, was *Morte Arthur*. About 1360, appeared a carefully wrought alliterative version of this, concerned primarily with Arthur's war with the Romans. By the end of the century there was another version, this one dealing with Lancelot's adventures. Then came Sir Thomas Malory's famous prose version, *The Book of King Arthur and His Noble Knights of the Round Table*.[21] Taken in part from English sources and from a recent French version, the work relates most of the anecdotes which tradition built around the legendary king of Britain. It is replete with knightly deeds and is thoroughly aristocratic in sympathy, hence the widespread belief that it was written for the purpose of bringing "back a decadent England to the virtues of 'man-hode, curtesye and gentylnesse.' "[22] But in view of the fact that Sir Malory himself was no model knight but one given to the invading of properties, cattle-rustling, and raping — the same woman on two different occasions — that is, to swash-buckling in general, his interest, despite his professions, was probably more in the telling of the story than in the preaching of social regeneration.[23] Certain it is that he told his story in effective prose, which is direct and often realistic.[24] His version fixed the Arthur tradition; and after it was printed by Caxton and reprinted by Wynken de Worde it became a classic.

Versions of medieval romances in French found their way to England early in the Renaissance period.[25] About the middle of the fifteenth century they began to be translated into English prose. Malory, it will be remembered, drew some of his accounts from a French "book." But it was Caxton who built up this source. Between 1475 and 1491 he published translations of seven French romances. Thereafter, many others followed,[26] and the vogue continued until the end of the Renaissance.

When this vogue was at its height, translations of Spanish romances began to appear. In general, the first versions came as retranslations from French. Among these were parts of the popular *Amadis de Gaula, Palmerin d'Olivia, Palladine of England*, and others, and the most productive translator was Anthony Munday. Although publication of these Spanish romances ceased about 1600, they had contributed significantly to the expansion of the romantic vogue.

One of the finest expressions of this vogue late in the sixteenth century was Sir Philip Sydney's *Arcadia*.[27] By title it is connected with Sannazaro's famous romance, as it is in the use of arcadian settings and of some elevated and sentimental language. And for these reasons it is popularly classified as a pastoral romance. But its story element is more pronounced (the love adventures of two princes, shipwrecked and disguised, in the land of Arcadia where they fall in love with the ruler's daughters); its action more vigorous, at times even heroic; its characters psychologically more realistic; and its purpose more didactic; so that it approximates an epic in prose. Apparently it was this combination of the pastoral with the epic that endeared it to the public. It could please those given to sentimentalism and those wanting sensationalism, those who craved sheer entertainment and those who desired some instruction with their pleasures.

About the same time as the Spanish romances began to appear came the influence of Ariosto and Tasso. This had the effect of elevating the dignity of the genre and of inviting a return to the metrical form. The result was Spenser's *Faerie Queene*. It is said that at first Spenser planned to "overgo" Ariosto, that is, to compose an extravagant metrical romance in which Leicester, represented as Arthur, "should achieve Gloriana (Elizabeth) by his matchless exploits, and then, ruling as King Arthur, should with her lead Fairyland (England) to triumph over the Paynim King (Philip II of Spain)."[28] This would have been in the tradition of an Arthurian romance. But Tasso's *Jerusalem Delivered* inspired him to ennoble the theme. Arthur became the epitome of virtue and magnificence, and the purpose became "to fashion a gentleman or noble person in virtuous and gentle discipline."[29] The transformation however was not thorough, and so we have an Arthurian romance drawn from Chaucer and Malory and Ariosto and an epic of romance influenced by Ariosto and Tasso.[30] The poem is a telling illustration of the persistence of the old tradition amid the transforming influences of the new. And when it is recalled that Spenser used the vigorous diction of the late medieval period and at the same time scattered throughout the body of the poem exquisite lyrics in keeping with the Elizabethan lyric vogue, the illustration becomes even stronger.

In closing this survey of the vogue of romance in Renaissance England it is fitting to point out that Milton, the great humanist, Hebraist, and Puritan, for a long time toyed with the idea of writing his masterpiece in the form of an epic of romance revolving about the figure of Arthur. This fact testifies to the power of attraction that the medieval tradition still possessed. On the other hand, the fact that he abandoned the notion and decided on the Homeric epic form and chose to write *Paradise Lost* shows that the tradition was already a fading tradition. But this was only in the age of the Stuarts.

1. Cited from J. W. H. Atkins, *English Literary Criticism: The Renascence* (2d ed.; London: Methuen & Co., Ltd., 1951), 60.

2. *Ibid.*, 61.

3. Ronald S. Crane, *The Vogue of Medieval Chivalric Romance During the English Renaissance* [an abstract of a Ph.D. Thesis, U. of Penn.] (Menasha, Wisconsin: George Banta Publishing Co., 1919), 12–13.

4. *Ibid.*, 18–22. For French criticism, extending into the sixteenth century, see Edelman, *op. cit.*, 173–7.

5. R. S. Crane, *op. cit.*, 4.

6. Cited from O. H. Green, *Spain and the Western Tradition*, I, 23.

7. So the style of the French *romans de chevalerie* is characterized by their noted master, Leon Gautier (cited from Edelman, *op. cit.*, 149). Similar criticism applies to the English compositions.

8. Cf. George Clark Sellery, *The Renaissance: Its Nature and Origins* (Madison, Wisconsin: University of Wisconsin Press, 1950), 112–19, for a succinct treatment of these.

9. For a sympathetic description of Ariosto's art see Wilkins, *A History of Italian Literature*, 185–92.

10. Cf. for example, the death scene of Clarinda, xii, 66–69 (trans. J. H. Wiffen [2d ed.; London: Bell and Daldy, 1872], 286–7).

11. On the relation of the *romancero* to chivalric literature see Mérimée, *op. cit.*, 171–80.

12. For a brief but informative statement on these cf. *ibid.*, 135–40, 195–201.

13. On all this see Edelman, *op. cit.*, 152–4, 158–61, and Raymond Lebique, "Contacts Français avec la littérature espagnole pendant la première moitié du XVIᵉ siècle," *Charles-Quint et son temps. Colloques internationaux du centre national de la recherche scientifique* (Paris: Editions du centre national de la recherche scientifique, 1959), 143–55.

14. George Madison Priest, *A Brief History of German Literature* (New York: Charles Scribner's Sons, 1910), 60.

15. For these and other examples see Walshe, *op. cit.*, 282.

16. For other translations see Karl Petry, *Handbuch zur Deutschen Literaturgeschichte* (Koln: Balduin Pick Verlag, 1941), I, 555–9.

17. For a later knight-errant see *The Diary of Jorg von Ehingen*, trans. and ed. Malcolm Letts (London: Oxford University Press, 1929).

18. For a fuller summary see Baugh, *op. cit.*, 178.

19. *Ibid.*

20. Summarized in Baugh, *op. cit.*, 236–7.

21. For a recent treatment of this work and its author see Chambers, *op. cit.*, 185–205, and Arthur B. Ferguson, *The Indian Summer of English Chivalry. Studies in the Decline and Transformation of Chivalric Idealism* (Durham, North Carolina: Duke University Press, 1960), 42–58.

22. Chambers, *op. cit.*, 196.

23. *Ibid.*, 196–8, 199–205.

24. *Ibid.*, 198–9.

25. For an example see R. S. Crane, *op. cit.*, 2.

26. A list of these is to be found in Crane's bibliography (*op. cit.*, 30–48).

27. For a penetrating analysis of the work see Clive Staples Lewis, *English Literature in the Sixteenth Century*, in the series *The Oxford History of English Literature* (Oxford: Clarendon Press, 1954), 331–42.

28. Baugh, *op. cit.*, 496.

29. *Ibid.*, 498. For a fuller treatment of the allegory and its purpose see C. S. Lewis, *op. cit.*, 380–8.

30. On its ties with the Italian models see Sells, *op. cit.*

VI *Literature during the Renaissance: The Novel*

Definition and Popularity

The term "novel" as applied to medieval and Renaissance literature does not denote quite the same thing as it does today. According to modern literary usage, a novel is a "fictitious narrative in prose" which attempts to "interpret human life."[1] In the Renaissance period the "novel" was less concerned with "interpretation" and more with narration and entertainment. Thus almost any kind of prose tale was looked upon as a novel. William Painter, for example, referred to the collection of tales which he "lifted" from such different sources as Herodotus, Livy, Boccaccio, and Margaret of Navarre as "novels."[2]

Besides the three usual properties common to the genre of the novel — prose, fictitiousness, concern with human life — the Renaissance novel had several characteristics peculiar to itself. In general, it was short and anecdotal, as it was intended for narration. Its plots were weak in development and so depended on excessive use of intrigue, which in turn tended to make the stories unrealistic and the characters artificial. Since the purpose was entertainment, some of the novels were amusing, some extravagant, and many of them highly and crudely erotic. On the whole, the story was paramount.

This genre was an expanding one during the Renaissance, and the reasons for its expansion were practically the same as those responsible for the growth of the prose romance. Crystallization of the bourgeois taste, progressive development of the vernacular, increase in literacy, and the appearance of the press operated in both cases. Two factors fostered the novel alone. One was the recovery of some of the Hellenistic and Roman novels, particularly the erotic compositions. Heliodorus' *Ethiopica,* Achilles Tatius' *Clotophon and Leucippe,* a picaresque bloodthirsty novel, Petronius' *Satyricon,* Apuleius' *Golden Ass,* and Longus' romantic story, *Daphnis and Chloe* — all appeared in the late Renaissance and were widely drawn upon for anecdotes and style.[3] The other factor was the social and economic dislocation of the late Renaissance which multiplied unemployment, increased vagabondage, and fostered disillusionment with the existing social order and mores. It was this condition which generated the Spanish picaresque novel, for example, and the English realistic novel as represented by Greene's *Cony-Catching* stories.

Novel in the Principal Western Countries

NOVEL IN ITALY   As in several other fields of Renaissance culture, Italy led the way in the novel. Following Boccaccio's *Decameron* and Franco Sacchetti's *Novelle*, numerous emulators compiled collections of tales. Among these only the foremost novelists deserve mention. The most influential was Matteo Bandello (*ca.* 1480–1561), a nobleman who became a Dominican friar and private secretary to the General of the Order who happened to be his uncle. A victim of the Spanish campaign in Lombardy against Francis I of France, he moved to the French court and was eventually rewarded with the See of Agen. While in France he prepared his *Novelle*, a compilation of over two hundred stories. Not a stylist of mark, and deficient in feeling, he yet proved to be a captivating storyteller whom all Europe followed. The stories, for the most part tales of trickery, are a picture "of society in dissolution."[4] Licentiousness and duplicity are their forte, even when their principals are clergy. He is not shocked at what he relates, but seems to laugh at the immoralities he so artfully depicts. They constitute evidence of the prevalence of cynicism in Italy. Even more dubious by moral standards were the novels of his two compatriots. Anton Francesco Grazzini (1503–1584), a Florentine writer of comedies, brought out a collection of stories under the title *Le Cene* (The Diners). Although told in a fresh style, these stories are repugnant, as they add carnal cruelty and the monstrous to the foul. Anton Francesco Doni, a vagabond monk making a living as a hack, published a collection of purported conversations held on the steps of the town cathedral (*I marmi* — The Marble Steps) in which he raked the world with capricious humor. Others that might be mentioned because they served as sources for non-Italian novelists were Fortini of Siena, a teller of smart but licentious stories, Antonio Cornazano who combined drollery with dirt, Agnolo Girenzicola, a cleric whose tales of clerical misconduct were less foul and more engaging in style, and Geraldi Cinthio, a Ferrarese nobleman, whose one hundred and ten stories in the *Hecatommithi* are characterized by force and vigor. The numerous others deserve no separate recognition except the observation that their very number testifies to the great popularity of the genre, which in turn implies that below the thin veneer of sophistication which Renaissance Italy presented to the world there was a great deal of coarseness and corruption.

NOVEL IN FRANCE France, the home of the *fabliau*, the forerunner of the Renaissance novel, did not have many outstanding novelists. The earliest of some note was Antoine de La Sale (1388–1461?). In the service of several French noble families, Antoine is better known for some compositions after the fashion of romances. Thus his *Réconfort de Madame de Fresne* has as its theme the saving of honor in the true chivalric custom; his *Petit Jean de Saintré*, his finest work, revolves about courtly love; and his *La Journée d'onneur et de prouesse* reveals its chivalric genre by its title. However, his familiarity with the literary fads of Italy led him to compile an influential book of stories. The compilation, named the *Cent nouvelles nouvelles*, he fashioned after Boccaccio, but many of the tales he borrowed from Poggio's notorious *Facetiae*, a collection of foul stories in Latin. As a result, his work is "extravagantly indecent."[5] What saves it is its wit and skillful storytelling.

The best known French novelist was a lady of royal blood, Marguerite d'Angoulême (1492–1549), sister of Francis I.[6] Her *Heptameron*, published posthumously, is too well known to require more than a brief comment. What might be said is that its tales generally exemplify the *jeux de l'amour et du hasard*, that some of them involved real personalities, that many of them lampooned the Cordeliers, that they are less offensive to good taste than those of the Italian novelists from whom she borrowed heavily, and that each story is closed by an epilogue which points out a moral lesson.

More independent and superior as a storyteller was Margaret's secretary, the sensitive Bonaventure Desperiers (*ca.* 1510–1544), who reportedly committed suicide to escape religious persecution. His one hundred and twenty-nine tales collected under the title *Les nouvelles recreations et joyous devis* were closer to the Gaulic *fabliau* than to the Italian *novelle* and reveal him as a superb storyteller. And the seventeen editions through which the work went by 1625 attest to his great popularity with the French readers.

Differing in tone were the novels of two commoners. The saddler Nicolas de Troyes, in his *Grand Parangon des nouvelles nouvelles,* although drawing on Boccaccio and Antoine de La Sale, presents his stories in the simple language of unlettered folk and gains much honest earthiness. Noel du Fail, a judge at Rennes, also deals with rural folk, but apparently with a nobler purpose than to laugh at his ruder compatriots. His *Propos rustiques et facetieux* (1547) and the *Contes nouveaux d' Eutrapel* may provoke a good deal of laughter at the naïveté of the country simpletons, but they are realistic pictures of rural society which command both sympathy and respect. Not infrequently behind his raillery there is biting criticism of the abuses of the time. The man finds no delight in relating dirty tales.

Another novelist of mark was the renowned expurgator and popularizer of Bandello, the historian François de Belleforest.[7] Referring the readers for the ludicrous and distasteful stories to Bandello himself, this taciturn French rhetorician selected those stories which lent themselves to eloquence and moralizing. He altered them to suit his purposes and added long ethical homilies, so that his Bandello was more than twice as long as the original.

With these borrowers and adapters of old tales should be included some of the writers who provided French versions of classical novels. Outstanding among these were Fenton, the translator of Achilles Tatius; Guillaume Michel, who rendered Apuleius; and Amyot, who did Longinus.

RABELAIS   Although a satirist rather than a novelist the famous François Rabelais (1494–1553) may well be treated with the novelists. A son of a country barrister, Rabelais was educated first in the traditional medieval manner, then in the humanistic fashion, and finally as a physician. In 1519 he joined the order of the Friars-Minor, but soon shifted to the Benedictines, and later still became a secular priest. But finding clerical life unpleasant, he turned to his medical profession and to writing. To his encyclopedic learning and worldly experience, Rabelais added boundless mental vitality and an extravagant sense of humor, and all these he compounded in his famous *Gargantua and Pantagruel*. The work is patterned after the manner of extravagant romances then popular and narrates the history of the legendary giant Gargantua (he sucked milk from 17,913 cows), of his son Pantagruel, and of his companion, the mockish Panurge. But its strength is less in the story than in its grotesque satire, in the robustness of its style, and in the appeal of its philosophy of a full and free life. Remaining an easy and at times a suspect Catholic, Rabelais satirized medieval institutions and ideals — especially scholastic education, idle monkery, seedy chivalry, silly private wars, futile church councils, and prognostication — and invited a life of a free mind, a strong body, and a full stomach; but he did so with such a lusty and grotesque humor and with such a vigorous compelling style that the satire was lost in the laughter.[8] The work therefore, despite its condemnation by the Sorbonne, became a "hit," selling more copies, he tells us, in two months than the Bible sold in nine years. Perhaps the best explanation of its popularity is to be found in the suggestion that it is "an expression of French common sense wedded to the elemental, earthborn strength and humor."[9]

NOVEL IN GERMANY The novel in Germany was slow in coming; and when it did come it failed to attain a respectable standard during the Renaissance, though it began to show literary promise and to gain in volume about the middle of the sixteenth century.

The novel as defined at the outset, namely, a short story in prose, appears to have evolved in Germany out of two sources. One was the "Schwankdichtung," that is, short witty anecdote composed in verse. Written for amusement, moral edification, or as a satire, these verse compositions naturally concentrated more on the tale than on poetics; and since they were widely received for their story element, it was natural that similar compositions be essayed in a medium closer to the people, that is, in their ordinary language.

Although not the earliest case of such transformation, we may refer to the popular composition *Till Eulenspiegel* as an illustration of the process. It is a collection of stories about a clever young man of peasant origin, Eulenspiegel, who may or may not have been a real figure of the fourteenth century but who was actually presumed to be real. Popular tradition represented him as a simpleton who was strong in body and who possessed an unfailing store of real cleverness and wit behind his apparent naïveté, a kind of a peasant Robin Hood who delighted in mischief, mostly at the expense of people who deemed themselves worldly-wise, townsfolk especially; and his doings made good subjects for storytelling. The first collection of tales about him was prepared in verse in Low German, and shortly thereafter appeared a prose version in the same dialect. Next came a poetic version in High German, and this in turn became the basis of a prose rendition. Published in 1515, this last version became a model for German short-story writing.[10]

The other source consisted of translations of medieval and Italian *novelle*. The *Gesta Romanorum*, a popular Latin collection of *exempla* for use in preaching, was translated in the fourteenth century, printed in 1489, and reprinted repeatedly. The *Decameron* was translated by some unidentified author about 1460, and it, too, became a popular model when printed in 1472. Similar other works were rendered into the native tongue,[11] and together with the translations cited and the prosified "schwankdichtung" they stimulated German short-story writing.

One of the first products of this progress was the *Schimpf und Ernst* (1522), a collection of stories by Johannes Pauli, a Franciscan monk. Undertaken "for the improvement of man," his stories are rich in wit and humor and are well told. Whether it was their intended moral edification or their entertainment appeal that attracted public favor, the fact is that the work became extremely popular, as its thirty editions must imply.

Another expression of this development was the genre started by Jorg Wickram of Colmar. Wickram was a versatile author who tried his hand at several different forms of literature. He was a meistersinger; he wrote biblical plays after the classical manner and Shrovetide plays reminiscent of mysteries, and he fashioned romances, both chivalric and those with peasants as characters. But it was as author of *Das Roll-wagenbüchlein* (1555) that he exerted the greatest literary influence. The composition is a collection of witty tales and anecdotes for weary stagecoach travelers, that is, it is literature of sheer entertainment. The publication caught the fancy of the public and became a model for several other works intended for man's relief from boredom. Among these we might single out as illustrations Michael Lindener's *Rastbüchlein* and Valentin Schumann's *Nachtbüchlein*.[12]

But while the genre made a significant start, it did not develop as fully as elsewhere. There were two main hindrances. One was the fact that the "schwankdichtung" still continued strong throughout the rest of the Renaissance. For sheer entertainment value the tales which Hans Sachs could tell in his homely doggerel were hard to equal, and prose storytelling necessarily suffered. The other reason was the diversion of prose into religious polemics, many of which were so satirical in character and so abusive in language that whatever literary merits they may have possessed were vitiated. Some of the less noxious ones, to be sure, became readable fiction, such as Johann Fischart's version of the first book of Rabelais' *Gargantua* (*Affenteurliche und Ungeheuerliche Geschichtschrift*), but such tolerable satirical treatments were relatively scarce while Protestant and Catholic spewed venom at each other. The polemical war was not conducive to respectable literature of a lighter vein.

Novel in Spain   Spain, on the other hand, saw the Renaissance novel highly developed. Like the rest of the lands it had a vogue of romances, and, in the *Amadis de Gaula*, it had a universal romantic novel. Contemporaneously with that vogue, two additional types made their appearance. One was the dramatized novel represented by Fernando de Rojas' *Comedia de Calisto y Melibea*, commonly referred to as the *Celestina*. Although written in dialogue form and divided into acts, it has the character of a novel and is generally so classified. It tells of the love of Calisto, a conventional type of Petrarchan lover, for Melibea, and of the role that the bawd Celestina and her helpmates Parmenio and Sempronio, two picaresque servants, had in bringing it to fruition. The theme corresponds to that of the Archpriest of Hita, but draws upon Ovid's *Pamphilus de Amore* and upon Plautus and Terence. Strong in characterization, particularly of Celestina, enticing by its eroticism and realism, and suggestive of the picaresque vogue, the work became exceedingly popular, as its sixty-three editions in the sixteenth century alone clearly confirm. The second was the picaresque, a genre so strong as to warrant more than just a passing mention.

The picaresque is sometimes defined as a romance of roguery. Like the romance of chivalry it had a hero, but instead of being a great knight the hero was a rogue, a person of low life. It dealt with adventure, but not with the adventure of knights; instead, it related the knavery of the peripatetic rogue who used his wit to cheat society into yielding him a livelihood. It treated of love, but in a carnal and vulgar way rather than in an elevated chivalric manner. Yet, while there is this remote similarity between the two genre, they were really poles apart. The picaresque did not deal with ideal society and its social ideals, but with actual society and its real customs and practices, too often far from honest and elegant. It did not put on "social airs," but was either hard and cynical or robustly humorous. Finally, it concentrated on characterization, however caricatured, rather than on storiology, its anecdotes simply being joined together by the consistency in the character of the principals. Finally, it pretended to be biographic or autobiographic in nature, whereas the chivalric romance is impersonal. All brave knights talk or act alike; all rogues talk or act as unique individuals. The picaresque, therefore, has some properties that make it a unique genre.

Among the best of these picaresque novels is *La Vida de Lazarillo de Tormes: y de sus fortunas y adversidades* by an anonymous writer.[13] As the title indicates, it is an account of the fortunes and adversities of Lazarillo. The story relates his experiences first as a servitor and companion of several masters, of a hardened blind beggar from whom he learned how to beg and cheat, of an avaricious priest, of a proud but starving hidalgo, of an indulgence peddler, and of a chaplain. It then depicts his fortunes as his own master, first as a water seller and then as a prosperous town crier, auctioneer of wine, and as a "complaisant husband of a canon's mistress." As to his wife's relations with the cleric, Lazarillo reports that his suspicions were roused by wagging tongues, and that he brought the unpleasant matter to the attention of the canon, but that the latter dismissed the charge with the advice that he, Lazarillo, was to "pay no heed to whatever people might say" but to concern himself only with what mattered most to him — his own advantage.[14] The story is a cutting satire on the society of the time, and particularly on the rampant vagabondage, on the proud but idle aristocracy, and on the immoral life of the clergy; but it is humorously and realistically presented with indelible characterization, and so commands interest not only as a mirror of the age but also as a literary composition.

The popularity of the work invited the composition of sequels and of independent imitations. Of the many that appeared, some deserve to be mentioned. Mateo Alemán produced the *Guzmán de Alfarache*, but he interlaced it with much moralizing. Francisco de Quevedo y Villegas wrote his *Historia de la vida del Buscón, llamado Don Pablos, ejemplo de vagamundos y espejo de tacaños* with vitriol. Northup describes the work as "one of the most heartlessly cruel books ever written."[15] Augustin de Rojas, himself a picaro, wrote the *El viaje entretenido*. To be included also are the two compositions by Cervantes himself. In his *El coloquio de los perros* he has a dog relate his adventures in the service of various masters, and in the *Rinconete y Cortadillo* he provides "the most graphic description of criminal life in Seville ever written."[16]

Even this much-abbreviated list suggests that the picaresque novel became a vogue. Before it declined in the late seventeenth century, many of its finest versions were translated into other European tongues and aided in the development of the realistic novel.

CERVANTES Combining the picaresque with the romances, Spain produced one work of universal acclaim, Cervantes' *Don Quixote*.

Miguel de Cervantes[17] was a man who aspired to be an ideal knight but found himself leading a life not much different from that of a picaro. Son of a poor apothecary surgeon, he enlisted with the Spanish forces, fought at Lepanto, and lost an arm. On his way back he was captured by African pirates and ransomed. After failing as a poet and a dramatist, he secured a government job, seduced one girl, married another but got separated from her, "knocked around," and finally ended in jail on a charge of losing some government funds entrusted to him. Obviously this life was no ideal life, but one of hard knocks, of frustration and failure, one of disillusionment; and out of it came the famous *Don Quixote de la Mancha*.

The story is too well known to justify even a brief synopsis. But its message and its properties deserve some attention.

The message, couched though it be in humorous language, is essentially a pessimistic one — how a man "ruins himself and others by his romantic and generous illusions and by his overconfidence in the goodness of human nature."[18] However, the pessimism is mitigated by the sympathy for the idealist that Cervantes evokes in the reader's heart, and this combination of commendation and censure of the cult of chivalry makes the work warm reading.

Its attractive properties are several. The atmosphere of the comic pervades it: not just hilarious nonsense, but the comic which results from the juxtaposition of the simple but practical with the glamorous but unreal. Characterization, although inclining toward caricature, is consistent and indelible. It is impossible to forget Don Quixote or his foil, the incomparable Sancho Panza. The style is an inviting one, leading the reader to believe that he is not merely a remote observer of the episodes but an immediate participant in them. Its masterful dialogues heighten the comic and give a sense of immediacy at the same time. Then there is the wealth of an inventive mind to capture the reader's fancy. In all, the work is a masterpiece of prose fiction excelling all romances and novels of the time.

NOVEL IN ENGLAND In England the novel was overshadowed by the lyric and the drama, but it was a thriving genre as the popularity of the prose romance might suggest.

Of the four distinguishable types of novels in Renaissance England, the earliest type consisted of translations from Latin stories circulating in the Middle Ages. Two collections of such translations made their appearance. One was the *Gesta Romanorum*, a collection of *exempla* for sermons compiled in the latter part of the thirteenth century and widely used on the continent as well as in England and translated into English in the fifteenth century. Two versions appeared about 1440, and another one late in the century. In the following century a modernized version was prepared by Richard Robinson and became popular. Between 1577 and 1602 seven editions of the work were printed, and by 1703 fifteen more appeared. The other was the *Legenda aurea*, a collection of tales about the lives of saints. Composed in Latin by Jacobus de Voragine, it was translated into English in 1438 and circulated as a complement to the *Gesta Romanorum*.

In the sixteenth century appeared the Italianate novel. One of the earliest collections was John Rastell's *A C. Merry Tales*. The tales were drawn from Sacchetti's *Novelle*, from the *Decameron, Cent nouvelles nouvelles*, Poggio's *Facetiae*, and from the German compilation *Till Eulenspiegel*. Subsequently two other Italianate versions appeared, William Painter's *Palace of Pleasure* and Geoffrey Fenton's *Tragical Discourses*. Painter's collection is given to eroticism and was intended, so he affirms, to "recreate and refreshe weried mindes, defatigued either with painefull travaile or with continuall care."[19] Apparently there were numerous tired minds who accepted the proferred "refreshment," for the work, aided by its "good and plain" style, became quite popular. Fenton, personally disreputable, was England's Belleforest, stuffing "every rift with rhetorical, proverbial, and moral ore."[20]

Included in this category, but showing some independence, were George Pettie's *A Petite Palace of Pettie his Pleasures* and George Gascoigne's *Adventures of Master F. J.* Pettie's work deviates from the *novelle* by its preference for classical over Italian sources and by its subordination of the story to rhetoric. Indeed, in this latter feature it already adumbrates the euphuistic novel. Gascoigne's story still follows the Italianate pattern, but it also has some properties of a real novel. It is a love story of a man who is invited as a guest in the hope that he would court one of the host's daughters, but who falls in love with the host's daughter-in-law instead, who first yields to him and then rejects him for another man. The tale is not a pretty one, but the plot is well handled, the characterization is believable — that of the injured daughter is particularly fine — and the language is quite convincing. These and other properties have gained for it the recognition as the first true novel in English literature.[21]

The third type was the euphuistic novel. Its principal model was the *Euphues* (1578) by John Lyly, a literary wit and hanger-on to Elizabeth's minister Lord Burleigh. The story is set in Italy, but some critics are of the opinion that it is based on what happened between Lyly and the daughter of the mayor of Brackley, John Thornborough, during Lyly's college days.[22] Its distinguishing feature however is not its story but its style, known as euphuism. It is an elegantly rhetorical style resulting from a combination of two stylistic devices used in excess: a decorative sentence structure which employs an abundance of antithesis, alliteration, balance, rhyme, and assonance, and academic pretension depending on excessive use of pseudoscientific simile.[23] "Staggeringly moral," it appealed to the prudery and affectation of the age, the high society accepting it because it depicted them as they would have liked to be.[24] This popularity led Lyly to write a sequel entitled *Euphues and his England,* and after him the mode was continued by Robert Greene. Greene's *Mamillia: A Mirrour of Looking-glasse for the Ladies of Englande* is notoriously dependent on Lyly, not only in style but in plot which he merely inverted. Several more of like nature followed, quite impossible by today's literary taste but apparently in demand in his day, for they were eagerly sought after by printers.

After some time, Greene, whose life was at complete variance with the elegant social atmosphere of these euphuistic novels, turned to a new style more in keeping with the underworld of London. This was the realistic novel of low society. In 1591 he came out with *A Notable Discovery of Cousenage* which has been described as an "exposure of the deceits practiced on honest citizens by the cardsharpers, pickpockets, and blackmailers who frequented Elizabethan London."[25] Its lusty coarseness, combined with wit and realism, caught the fancy of the readers and the warm reception of the work led him to dash off a series of sequels known as the *Cony Catching* novels,[26] and an account of the mad pranks of a notorious cutthroat, his brother-in-law Ned Browne, under the title *Black Bookes Messenger.* Greene's apparent popularity prompted others to imitate him, the foremost among these being Thomas Nashe. A learned, witty, and versatile writer, Nashe was capable of writing in any style; and of the realistic type his best is *The Unfortunate Traveller, or the Life of Jack William,* an account of the experiences of an English scapegrace page while on his journey to Italy to taste its pleasures. With this work, which is a parody of the shams of the contemporary society and at the same time a witty fiction of adventure in real life, the realistic novel was fully established. And with Nashe, who died in 1600, we may end our sketchy survey of the novel in England during the Renaissance.

1. Ernest A. Baker, the celebrated historian of the English novel, adopts the definition "the interpretation of human life by means of fictitious narrative in prose" (*The History of the English Novel* [New York: Barnes and Noble, Inc., 1929], I, 15).
2. *Ibid.,* II, 21.

3. For a brief summary of these and others see *ibid.*, II, 39–43.

4. Symonds, *op. cit.*, II, 206.

5. Nitze and Dargan, *op. cit.*, 117.

6. There is a sympathetic study of her and her work in Arthur Tilley, *The Literature of the French Renaissance* (Cambridge: University Press, 1904), I, 96–121.

7. It is as the author of *Grandes annales et histoire générale de France* in which he defended the hereditary rights of the French monarchy that he is best known.

8. It is on the strength of this, but wrongly, of course, that Rabelais was for a long time taken for a buffoon (Arthur Tilley, *François Rabelais*, "French Men of Letters," ed. A. Jessup [Philadelphia: J. B. Lippincott Co., 1907], 301).

9. Nitze and Dargan, *op. cit.*, 154.

10. On this see J. G. Robertson, *A History of German Literature*, 129–30.

11. For some examples see Petry, *op. cit.*, I, 488–99, 501.

12. For other examples see J. G. Robertson, *op. cit.*, 196.

13. Recently translated by J. Gerald Markley and published as no. 37 of *The Library of Liberal Arts* (New York: The Liberal Arts Press, Inc., 1954).

14. *Ibid.*, 67.

15. Northup, *op. cit.*, 186.

16. *Ibid.*, 184.

17. For a most delightful biography see Sebastian Juan Arbó, *Cervantes — Adventurer, Idealist and Destiny's Fool*, trans. Ilsa Barea (London: Thames and Hudson, 1955). For an excellent short treatment cf. Brenan, *op. cit.*, 175–98.

18. *Ibid.*, 179.

19. C. S. Lewis, *op. cit.*, 310.

20. *Ibid.*, 311.

21. Cf. Leicester Bradner, "The First English Novel. A Study of George Gascoigne's Adventure of Master F. J.," *Publications of the Modern Language Association of America*, XLV (1930), 543–52.

22. Synopsis in E. Baker, *op. cit.*, II, 58–59.

23. See C. S. Lewis, *op. cit.*, 312–3.

24. Baugh, *op. cit.*, 417.

25. S. Diana Neill, *A Short History of the English Novel* (New York: Macmillan Co., 1952), 21.

26. For the titles of Greene's numerous works see the index under "Greene, Robert" in E. Baker, *op. cit.*, II, 290–2.

VII

Literature during the Renaissance: Drama

I N COMPARISON with the developments in the lyric, romance, and novel during the Renaissance, progress in drama was decidedly greater. In lyric poetry a Renaissance Poliziano has his counterpart in a medieval Walter von der Vogelweide; in romance a Renaissance Tasso is prefigured by Chrétien de Troyes; in prose novel a Renaissance Bandello, by an earlier Sacchetti. But who in medieval drama can be a match for Lope de Vega or Shakespeare? Obviously no one, and this fact alone is sufficient indication of the remarkable advance drama made during the Renaissance.

If the purpose of this survey of drama were merely to ascertain the extent of this progress, then it might be enough to compare some dramatic composition of the Middle Ages with a good Renaissance drama. Such a comparison would certainly bring out the magnitude of the change. But our purpose is broader: as students of history we need to concern ourselves with the history of the Renaissance drama as a whole, with the ordinary as well as with the extraordinary compositions, and with the developments in the drama of each country, as these might well differ from one land to another. Only such a study can be expected to yield a realistic view of what happened in drama during the two centuries of the Renaissance.

Drama in Italy

RELIGIOUS DRAMA The most popular drama in Italy during the Renaissance was the religious drama, the *sacra rappresentazione*. Like its counterpart in northern Europe, it consisted of a series of dramatizations of biblical stories and hagiographical legends.[1] In general, each drama was preceded by a prologue which announced the subject and terminated by an epilogue which reaffirmed the intended moral lessons. The lessons were obvious: men giving up earthly pleasures to become monks, the return of the prodigal son, ladies preserving their honor in the face of great temptations or threats, and many others like them. Characterization, what there was of it, was stock and generally followed medieval patterns, peasants being cast as gawky, doctors as pompous, merchants as greedy, and beggars as sharp and impudent. Structure was free, that is, dramatic unities were not observed, and there was no division into acts. Finally, it was written in rhymed verse, *ottava rima* generally, and possessed considerable artistic finish.

Like the mysteries and moralities in northern Europe, the *sacra rappresentazione* lasted throughout the entire Renaissance period, from the thirteenth century until about the middle of the sixteenth. While they persisted in the smaller country towns for several decades longer, in the great urban centers, because of the rising tide of humanism, they gradually yielded to secular drama.

LATIN SECULAR DRAMA[2] Responding to the rise of humanism, Latin drama made its appearance early in the fourteenth century and paralleled religious drama throughout most of the Renaissance period. The earliest composition was the *Ecerinis* (1318) by Albertino Mussato, a Senecan-type tragedy based on the story of the Paduan tyrant Ezzelino da Romano and intended as an indictment of tyranny. It was followed by a few mediocre imitations. Of the comedies, most of which were satirical in character but with pretentions to edification, several deserve to be noticed. The *Paulus* (*ca.* 1390) by P. P. Vergerius sought to teach students what social evils to shun. Apparently the first of its kind in Italy, it served as an exemplar for other plays depicting student life. Leon Battista Alberti's *Philodoxus* (*ca.* 1426) has some claim to being a copy of Roman classical comedy; and indeed it was so regarded by many of his contemporaries, although its structure is quite medieval. Ugolino Pisani's *Philogenia* possesses the merits of depicting contemporary life realistically, as does Leonardo Aretino Bruni's *Poliscene*. Both drew quite heavily on Plautus, but their plots and structure still conformed to the medieval patterns. The *Chrysis* (1444) by Enea Silvio Piccolomini, who subsequently became Pope Pius II, was more coherently tied together despite its eighteen scenes, apparently because it depended more on Terence than on Plautus. Replete with bawdry, it is a reflection on the worldly ways of Italian Renaissance clerics. The best comedy in Latin according to some modern critics was Tommaso de Mezzo's

Epirota. It has a couple of believable characters and some effective scenes.

From the fact that some of these comedies were written by such first-rate humanists as Vergerio, Alberti, and Bruni, one would surmise that these comedies would borrow heavily from the classical compositions of Plautus and Terence. Indeed, it could hardly have been otherwise. On the other hand, the fact that these plays were organized around episodes and so were free in structure, that they often drew upon medieval stories and employed allegorical characters, and that many of them incorporated a good deal of vulgarity reveals their dependence also on medieval farcical drama. Hence they could well be regarded as hybrid compositions, quite transitional in character.

SECULAR DRAMA IN THE VERNACULAR: THE FARCE Latin drama naturally had a very limited following: it was primarily for the schools and court circles. For the general public drama had to be written in the vernacular and it had to depict the familiar. And because there were two broad types of audiences, the uneducated masses and those with some social pretentions, this vernacular drama naturally came to be divided into two categories, the comic, which itself was divided into the farce and the learned comedy, and the tragic and pastoral.

The Italian farce, according to one definition, was "a short play in verse representing a squabble, a prank, a jest, or a sport."[3] It was an outgrowth of medieval village plays, for the most part of the *contrasto* (dispute between lovers or spouses) and of the *maggio* (May dance), and as such its characters were vulgar, given to crude idiom, silly antics, and much bawdry. For the same reason it remained quite medieval in structure, except toward the end of the sixteenth century when it put on the formal dress of classical comedy.

Steadily gaining in popularity, it was to be found everywhere, from Naples to Padua and Venice. And because of this profuseness, opinions naturally vary as to which of the compositions are the best. But, perhaps, the following selections are as good as any to illustrate the nature and the history of the farce during the Italian Renaissance.

Anton Francesco Grazzini's (of Florence) *Il frate* depicts how a lusty, dissimulating friar worms his way into the household of one Amerigo to act as father-confessor to the family and as a lover of the adulterous wife. The play is merely a stylistic transformation of the medieval anticlerical farce. Grazzini's *La giostra* (*The Trick*) is even a more obvious copy of a medieval composition. The peasant Arzigogolo sells a team of oxen belonging to one Monna Papera and is promptly sued for damages. He engages a lawyer to defend him and is instructed to act irresponsibly by whistling back to every question addressed to him. The sly peasant follows these instructions most successfully, for he not only wins the suit but escapes paying the lawyer's fee by acting equally irresponsibly. The play is a clear copy of the French play *Maître Pathelin*, which, while appearing about 1464, is generally regarded as typically "medieval." The plays of the northern playwrights were even closer to the medieval tradition, as they were but more recent renditions in native north-Italian dialects of French medieval farces. This is exemplified by Giovan Giorgio Alione's *Farce of Zohan Zavatino and the Beatrix his Wife and of the Priest Hidden under the Poultry Basket* which, by its very title, betrays its dependence on medieval anticlerical farces.

By common consent the best writer of Italian farces was the playwright-actor Angelo Beolco of Padua (b. 1502) who went under the nickname Ruzzante (The Merry Flouter), a peasant character which he created as a role for himself. A man of learning, Beolco naturally fell under the influence of Roman comedy. But he did not allow this influence to override his belief in the necessity to adhere to reality. His characters, therefore, are north Italians, either simple peasants or bumptious burghers who have not completely shaken off the barnyard smells about them. Even those he borrowed from Plautus, such as the bragging soldier for example, he converted into contemporary Italian figures.

Of the many farces which he wrote, three have some distinction. The *Comedy Without Title* burlesqued Petrarchan love poetry; while the *Parlamento de Ruzzante* and the *La moschetta* (*The Flirt*) caricatured the bragging soldier who despite all his bravado lacked the courage to fight, either in war or for his wife whom he lost to more manly veterans during his absence. In their composition and themes these three plays clearly reveal the new influence of humanism, but at the same time their adherence to reality and their respect for local color prevented them from yielding to the classical trend entirely. In fact, it was this feature which made Ruzzante's comedies superior to those of other playwrights who fell for the fad of neoclassicism.[4]

SECULAR DRAMA IN THE VERNACULAR: THE LEARNED DRAMA Learned drama was one which observed the rules of classical drama, and borrowed the plots and characters from Seneca, Terence, and Plautus. If it possessed any independence, it was in the attempted naturalization of the scenes and characters, and in the occasional addition of new characters and further complications. It appeared early in the sixteenth century and took three forms, the comedy, tragedy, and pastoral comedy.

The learned comedy has as its reputed father the gentleman romancer Ludovico Ariosto. His *La cassaria* (*The Casket*), *I supposti* (*The Counterfeits*), *La lena* (*The Bawd*), and *Il negromante* (*The Necromancer*) clearly reveal his dependence on the Romans, while *La lena* exemplifies the happy practice of trying to naturalize the scenes and characters as Italian. However, it was not so much Ariosto's works as the *Calandria* by Bernardo Dovizi da Bibbiena which served as a model for the contemporary playwrights, especially as to structure and dramaturgical principles. Pietro Aretino's *La cortigiana* (*The Courtesan*), *Il marescalco* (*The Horse Doctor*), and *Ipocrito* deserve notice as fairly successful adaptations of farces to learned comedy without the loss of naturalism. Like Ruzzante, Aretino sought to depict his characters as Italians, except that he preferred to treat of townsmen rather than of peasants. One importance of these plays lies in the fact that they exercised considerable influence on Ben Jonson's comedies. Lorenzino de' Medici's *Aridosia* may be cited as an illustration of the overwhelming attraction that learned comedy held for the high society of the day. *Flora* by the poet Luigi Alamanni is generally regarded as the nearest imitation of true classical comedy, though the composition lacks distinction. The learned comedy most widely acclaimed is undoubtedly the *Mandragola* by Machiavelli.

According to some critics the *Mandragola* is not only the best known learned comedy of the Italian Renaissance but also the best one written then. As to structure and style perhaps it deserves the recognition, as it conforms to the rules of neoclassical drama. But its subject is not a pretty one; in fact it may be deemed unbecoming to a man of Machiavelli's intellectual stature.

The play depicts how a young man lusting for the love of a beautiful married woman tricks her husband with the aid of her mother and of a greedy friar into enabling him to know her carnally.[5] While the play may have some merit in its clever plot, in its vigor, and in its brisk dialogue, in its subject it is a travesty on the intelligence of Machiavelli's public.[6] The characters are impossible: the husband is a complete dolt, the friar an iniquitous dissimulator, the mother an unmotherly bawd, the young man a slick sexual werewolf, and the pretty wife a not-so-sweet woman who, upon discovering the pernicious trick, learns to be accommodating simply to spite her husband. Only the servant has some redeeming traits, if it be only his skill in connivance and his utmost concern for his master's pleasure. There is hardly a single redeeming act, as if mankind were wholly depraved — surely an absurd notion! Because of this mistaken philosophy, Machiavelli's play hardly deserves the high rating accorded to it.[7]

Tragedy in the vernacular was less popular than comedy, and the only justification for including it in this survey of drama is to illustrate its dependence on Seneca. Hence only three or four need be mentioned.

The honor of being the "first tragedy in Italian" is generally assigned to Antonio Commelli's *Filostrato e Panfila*. Taking its theme from Boccaccio's tale of Giomonda, this tragedy gave play to the element of horror and set a pattern for the exploitation of the terrible. Giovanni Rucellani's *Rosmunda* stands out as an illustration of the dependence on Seneca, while Gian Giorgio Trissino's *Sofonisba*, based on Livy's dramatic story of the Carthaginian princess' attempt to escape Roman captivity, actually tried to go back of Seneca to the Greek originals and to the rules of Aristotle. Successful in this respect, it won high praise, some commentators rating it above the works of Sophocles. Finally, Geraldi Cinthio's *Orbecche* may be selected as an illustration of overwrought sensationalism.[8] Promising "tears, sighs, anguish, terrors, frightsome deathe," it exploited the melodramatic without limit. From these few examples it can be seen that Renaissance tragedy in Italy turned out to be an exercise in composition after the Greeks, an exhibition of morbidity and of rhetoric after Seneca, and a parade of sensationalism.

In the field of pastoral comedy, also heavily indebted to classical influence, only three examples need be noted. Poliziano's *Orfeo*, a short and simple work written in two days, stands out as an exemplar, in some of its scenes, of true pastoral elements and as a step in the direction of opera. Tasso's *Aminta* is widely acclaimed as "the most perfect of pastoral plays," and Giambattista Guarini's *Il pastor fido* as the next "most perfect."[9] The debt of all three to the classics appears in the Arcadian characters and settings, and, in the last two works, in the attempted adherence to the rules of unity. Their themes are necessarily romance, romance that will not be denied and yet one which is *courtois*, saccharine, and sentimental. Their language is elevated, rich in lyricism and imagery. Symptomatic of an enervated society that would have its fancies tickled with feathery phrases and its sense of propriety soothed by having libidinousness don some half-concealing dainties, the pastoral comedy gained wide acceptance at the time and became a harbinger of the opera soon to come.

COMMEDIA DELL'ARTE The last dramatic endeavor of Renaissance Italy was the *commedia dell'arte*.[10] Although it attained its greatest development in the seventeenth century, it started in the late Renaissance and so belongs in this survey.

The distinguishing characteristic of the *commedia* was its lack of a finished script. The play was not written out in full; only the plot was outlined, and the actors, who were professionals — *dell'arte* means "of the profession" — improvised the dialogue and the action. However, the plots, taken from classical and the learned comedies, had the familiar stock characters and so the players knew from experience and from some suggestions in the scenarios what was expected from them, so that if it was improvisation, it was within set types and within fixed scenes.

The types consisted of two elderly men, one depicted as a love-mad *Magnifico* and the other as a pretentious academic; a boasting soldier, often represented as a despised Spaniard (the Spanish occupation forces were hated); four lovers with their loves misplaced; several *zanni*, or clownish characters, each with his own particular comic trait; and one or two simple-minded maids. Since the main purpose of the play was amusement and its general nature was that of a comedy of intrigue, the scenarios called for frequent farcical situations. Thus, much horseplay was combined with exaggerated typecasting. Once the spirit of the scene and its place in the scenario were established, the actor went through his antics and his dialogue "on his own," the amount of laughter he could evince being his main guide.[11]

Since the *commedia* developed after 1550, it would be logical to attribute its rise to Renaissance forces and circumstances. Certainly it owed much to the revival of Roman comedy, to the appearance of learned comedy, and to the professionalization of acting — all Renaissance developments. But on the other hand, the general farcical nature of the plays and the caricaturing are reminiscent of medieval farces and so point to the medieval comic spirit as a likely second source of the *commedia*.

In all, the Italian drama, while extensive, was not great. But, it was not without influence, for it was the first to incorporate some classical rules and so became a model for neoclassical drama in the rest of Renaissance Europe.

Drama in France

RELIGIOUS DRAMA In France as in Italy the Renaissance period saw the flowering of religious drama. Miracle plays, especially *Les Miracles de Nôtre-Dame*,[12] strong in the fourteenth century, continued to hold their own throughout the fifteenth. Moralities, such as the *Bien Avisé, Mal Avisé, L'Homme juste et l'homme mondain*, and others, depicting the struggle between good and evil, steadily grew in amplitude and in popularity in the fifteenth century. The mystery plays increased in number and reached their fullest form in the Passion Play in the second half of this century. Although all three types advanced beyond their medieval standard, it was the last that underwent the greatest development, and it alone can claim more than a passing mention.

The mystery plays, it will be recalled, were plays which depicted various episodes in the Bible as lessons in morality and religion. It was natural to have a steadily increasing number of the major biblical events presented in one continuous sequence of scenes — Adam and Eve in Paradise, The Fall, The Expulsion, Cain and Abel, and so on, up to man's redemption through the Coming of Jesus, His Life and Death, and His Judgment. When most of these episodes were so incorporated, the mystery play had become the Passion Play.

Although evolving out of the medieval mysteries, the Passion Play in France was primarily a product of the Renaissance period. It appeared at the outset of the fifteenth century, by 1402, when a Parisian organization, the *Confrérie de la Passion*, secured royal privilege for the staging of Passion Plays. The first complete play was put together by one Eustache Marcadé in 1440. About twelve years later it was expanded, improved dramatically, and refined stylistically by a canon of Le Mans, Arnoul Gréban. His version gained considerable popularity; it was itself revised in 1486 by Jean Michel, and the new revision went through fifteen editions.[13] In 1548 the *Parlement* banned the staging of mystery plays in Paris, but the ban was ineffective in the provinces and so they continued in the public eye until the end of the sixteenth century, that is, until the end of the Renaissance.

MEDIEVAL SECULAR COMEDY The religious dramatic fare was supplemented by secular comedy. Like the former, the first secular comedy was of medieval origin and attained its fullest development after 1450. It originated in the funny interludes between the sequences of the mystery plays and in the buffooneries of traveling comic entertainers (*sots*), and it copied the *fabliau* in exploiting the comic vein to be found in contrasting "the exaggerated and unnatural with hard common sense."[14] Thus, risen out of comic soil and nurtured on comic spirit, comic drama readily gained a following. Special confraternities, such as the *Basoche* (a gild of clerks connected with the *Parlement*) and the *Enfants san Souci* (a society of carefree gallants in Paris), appeared to stage it, and the genre took form and grew in numbers and in excellence. In the fifteenth century the number of farces alone exceeded one hundred and fifty. The finest farce, that of *Maître Pierre Pathelin*, about a lawyer outwitted by his own simple client whom he had successfully coached for a trial,[15] appeared about 1464. And the most distinguished composer, Pierre Gringoire, Louis XII's entertainer and satirist, and prince of the *sots* of the *Enfants san Souci*, began his productive career shortly after 1500. His *Jeu du prince des sots*, a combination of *sottie*, *farce*, and *moralité* designed to win public opinion to Louis XII's Italian policy, and showing some capacity for characterization, appeared in 1512, and his *Monde et abuz* in 1513. If Francis I found his work "medieval" and preferred the Italianate tragedy, the house of Lorraine accepted him and his "medieval" genre. The "medieval" comedy, with all its coarseness and crudeness had a hold that could not be shaken easily. Not until very late in the Renaissance, actually in the second half of the sixteenth century, was it to find itself slowly yielding ground.

CLASSICAL DRAMA The new dramatic form that began to challenge the prevailing genres was classical. A number of translations of Greek and Latin masterpieces — Scaliger's Latin version of *Oedipus Rex*, Lazare de Baif's French version of *Electra* (1537) and of *Hecuba* (1544), Sibilet's *Iphiginie* (1549), Ronsard's *Plutus* — served to inaugurate the trend. Translations of Italian works, comedies especially, which were patterned after the classics — Ariosto's *Suppositi* by Jacques Bourgeois and his *Negromante* by Jean de la Taille — added to the trend. Compositions of drama in colleges adopting humanistic curricula — at the College of Bordeaux, Buchanan staged *Alcestis* and *Medea* — aided in spreading the movement; and together these translations and college presentations secured for classical drama a place in the annals of French drama.

In the field of tragedy two types developed. One type concerned itself with great personalities of Greek and Roman times, such as Agamemnon, Caesar, Cleopatra, Dido, and Darius, and may be regarded as classical drama in theme as well as in form. The other type dealt either with biblical themes or with contemporary events, that is, non-classical themes, but in the form of classical drama. For both types Aristotle served as instructor and Seneca as model. The rules of unity were admitted and sometimes respected, but the art of dramaturgy yielded to Senecan morbidity and declamation. In consequence, characterization was weak, depending more on rhetoric than on action, and plots were without compulsion. On the whole, these compositions seemed more like academic exercises than plays for the theater.

Among the several dramatists who tried their hands at this style of drama, three or four may be singled out as worthy of some notice. Etienne Jodelle, a member of the Pléiade and writer of *La Cléopâtre captive*, of *Didon se sacrifiant*, and of the comedy *L'Eugéne*, is looked upon as the initiator of this French classical tragedy and through it as the founder of modern theater in France. Louis Desmasures, composer of the trilogy *David combattant, fugitif, triomphant*, may be cited as an illustration of the adoption of the new form for the dramatization of religious themes. Jean de la Taille's *Saul le furieux* and *Gabéonites*

belong to the same category and have some dramatic merit. Representing a similar adoption, but for the dramatization of contemporary
events, were Chantelouve with his *Coligny* (1575), Gabriel Bounin
with his *Sultané* (1560) and Pierre Mathieu with his propaganda pieces,
Esther, Vasthi, Aman, Clytemnestre, denouncing the supposed weaknesses of the French royal family, and the *Guisiade* exalting the virtues
of the Guises. The foremost was Robert Garnier. Six of his plays —
Porcie, La Cornélie, Marc Antoine, L'Hippolyte, Troade, Antigone —
narrowly Senecan, show some energy and considerable literary merit.
His masterpiece, *Les Juives*,[16] which dramatizes Zedekiah's misfortunes
at the hands of Nebuchadnezzar, though still defective in dramaturgy,
employs the technique of dramatic suspense effectively; some of its
characters tend to become realities; and its style combines vigor with
considerable simplicity and grace.

In the field of comedy there was a similar attempt at classicization.
Plautus and Terence were followed as exemplars and the medieval
types were publicly decried. Jacques Grévin, for example, in his *Mau-
bertine ou la trésorière* and *Esbahis*, allegedly promised that "in his
theater . . . the audience will not 'see either farce or morality,' but true
comedy based on the Roman pattern."[17] Antoine de Baif's *Brave* is
merely an adaptation into French of Plautus' *Miles Gloriosus*. Yet
critics are of the opinion that this attempt to follow the classical pattern
did not eliminate the medieval comedy from continuing to serve as a
nucleus of the new comedy.[18]

As stated before, French comedy of the Renaissance owes much to
the translations of the Italian *commedia erudita*. Adaptations followed,
and those of Pierre de Larivey of Troyes are generally admitted as the
best. They are drawn from the original Italian — thus *Les esprits* (*The
Wits*) comes from Lorenzo de' Medici's *L'Aridosia*, and *Le Laquais*,
from Lodovico Dolce's *Il ragazzo*[19] — but are suited fittingly to the
French scene. Retouched enough to give the impression of being distinct works, they reveal considerable capacity for delineating character,
for exploiting theatrical potential, and for adapting style to needs, all
the way from provincial colloquialisms to a clear and vigorous prose.
Occasionally they may have stooped to caricature to elicit laughter,
but in general they did not allow the comic spirit to degenerate into

buffoonery. That these works possessed some merit is best attested by the fact that *Les esprits* was used by Molière in *L'avare* and by two later dramatists.[20]

Such then is the history of drama in France during the Renaissance. Much of the drama is clearly medieval in character and origin, and only toward the very end of the period did classical and Italianate types appear. Except for a minority of Frenchmen, an influential minority to be sure, the French populace as a whole still wanted the "medieval" fare.

Drama in Germany

CONTINUATION OF MEDIEVAL RELIGIOUS AND POPULAR DRAMA In Germany the prevailing type of drama until the Reformation was what has always been identified as medieval drama, both the religious and the secular. Religious drama was, of course, represented by the moralities and mysteries, and these continued to be staged without any significant changes as to purpose and themes, and gilds, town councils, and princely patrons continued to be deeply involved in the production of them.[21] There were some improvements in plots, staging, characterization, and literary style, as is well exemplified by *The Redentin Easter Play (ca. 1464).*[22] But any improvement was bound to enhance the popularity of this type of drama and so its life was prolonged throughout most of the Renaissance period, until approximately Luther's time, when some opposition made its appearance. The Passion Play was challenged on the ground that it invited whimpering over the death of Jesus, and the miracle plays dropped those themes which derived from the legends of the saints. On the other hand, the Lutheran emphasis on the Bible increased the use of scriptural themes. Hence the final result was not much different from the earlier compositions, if the elaborate "Oster-spiele" of Lucerne, which did not attain the fullest form until 1586, are any indication.[23]

No less pervasive and persistent was the secular drama, often referred to as "popular" drama and consisting for the most part of Shrove-tide plays.[24] These were short comedies on such ever-popular themes as the outsmarting of doltish husbands by shrewish and unfaithful wives, priestly peccadilloes and more serious perversions, conflict of wit between rustic simpletons and supposedly more worldly-wise burghers, misplaced confidence, mistaken identities, and so forth. In general farcical and laden with coarseness and even with barroom obscenities, they provided rowdy entertainment for the urban masses.

Deriving from the breath and habits of ordinary man, these plays were both numerous and persistent throughout most of the Renaissance. There are, for example, some one hundred and fifty of them from the fourteenth and fifteenth centuries that have been preserved. The Reformation movement with its denunciation of levity did cut into their audiences and chastened their content. However, neither the reduction nor the "sterilization" was sufficiently great to eliminate the fad, as the popular plays of Pamphilius Gegenbach — *Die Zehn Alter* (1515), *Die Gouchmatt* (1516) and *Der Nollhart* (1517) — and as many of Hans Sachs's two hundred plays are really quite close to the Shrovetide plays. Indeed even some classical plays — even those written by Lutherans — accommodated themselves to the popular dramas. We are told, for example, that Burkard Waldis' *De Parabell von vorlorn Szohn* written in Latin and with pretentions to being a humanistic piece of composition was "closer to Shrovetide comedy than to Terence and Seneca."[25]

CLASSICAL DRAMA Although this drama of medieval origins remained popular, beginning with the fifteenth century, drama based on classical models began to attract public attention also. Old Latin plays were translated and some were adapted to the German scene — Albrecht von Eyb's (1420–1495) adaptation of Plautus' *Menaechmi* and *Bacchides*; and new plays patterned after the classic mode and written in Latin began to appear. Of these, some were school plays moralizing on prodigal students and serving as exercises in proper composition in Latin. Macropedius' *Rebelles* and Stymmelius' *Studentes* were two of the best in the field. Others were polemics for or against the New Learning. Kerkmeister's *Codrus*, for example, was a violent criticism of obscurantist schoolmen and of their dog-Latin, while Wimpheling's *Stilpho* was a case study of the ill effects of the old pedagogy on a dull student as well as a satire of clerical greed. Philip Nicodemus Frischlin (1547–1590) of Würtemberg, Tübingen, and of wheresoever his unbridled satirizing necessitated his going, carried these notions further. In one play, *Priscianus vapulans*, he depicts the displeasures of Priscian, the famous Roman grammarian, at the "barbarism" of medieval Latin. While in another, *Julius Caesar redivivus,* intended as a compliment on Germany's political and humanistic achievements, he had the ghosts of Caesar and Cicero rise from their classical past and survey what he believed to be the power and glory of Renaissance Germany in contrast with the chaos in Italy. Still others belong to the "situation" type of plays, mostly comical. Reuchlin's *Henno,* a *"fabliau* of husband and wife and neighbors," part of which he based on *Maître Pathelin,* was one of the more popular ones; and closely following it in popularity were the *Andrisca* and *Bassarus,* two farces on peasant life by Macropedius, noted for his biblical dramas.

POLEMICAL RELIGIOUS DRAMA   This classical trend locked arms with the Lutheran movement and gave rise to a crop of polemical religious plays. Catholics and Lutherans exchanged vicious blows; Lutherans rebuked the shortcomings of the Protestants themselves or elaborated on some biblical lessons. Simon Lemnius spewed obscenities on Luther in the *Monachopornomachia.* On the other hand, Nicholas Manuel of Bern ridiculed the practice of saying Masses for the dead by depicting the priests as *Todtenfresser* (Eaters of the Dead), and the theory of Indulgence in the *Ablasskrämer* (*The Indulgence-Monger*). Thomas Naogeorgus (Kirchmayer), given to *saeva indignatio,* in his *Pammachius* cast the pope as Antichrist laboring to subvert true faith; and in his *Mercator* he dramatized, crudely and realistically, the contrast between good works and justification by grace as means of gaining heaven. But he also wrote plays about ministers who were remiss in their duties and about those who deserted the Protestant cause. Paul Rebhun's *Susanna* (1535), written artistically, with verse forms suited to the situations, and Sixt Birck's *Ezechias* and *Joseph* (1532–1534) are illustrative of the better type of biblical plays.[26]

Combining these various trends and representing the prevailing character of German drama during the Renaissance were the works of that folksy *littérateur* Hans Sachs (1494–1576).

SACHS'S POPULAR "MEDIEVAL" DRAMA[27]   Although Sachs began his dramatic output with classical themes (*Lucretia* and *Virginia*) and from time to time returned to antiquity's storehouse for his stories, he was no adherent of the classic mode. In fact, he seems to have been unfamiliar with the rules of classical drama and so in drama as in poetry his forte was in "medieval" styles. The farce was his best. In this medium he was able to delineate individual character as well as types and to exploit the comic situations which he so readily detected in human traits and weaknesses; and even if many of these plays were propaganda in behalf of Lutheranism, we can still enjoy them as pleasant examinations of mankind. Such, for example, is his *Der farendt Schüler ins Paradeis*, probably his best known composition. A simple wife is persuaded by a sharp student to part with some clothes and money, professedly to be taken to her deceased husband in Paradise. She is berated for this by her second mate who believes himself to be, and, indeed, to all appearances is, superior to her. The indignant husband takes off after the sharper, but instead of recovering the clothes and money he is tricked into losing his horse to him. Returning on foot, he pretends to his wife that he added the horse to the articles she had entrusted to the obliging student but pleads with her to keep the incident secret, only to find out that it was already known to the whole village. No deep study of man's nature, the play nevertheless pokes fun at some human traits and ridicules, somewhat less tenderly, the countryfolk's naïveté in matters religious. Close as it is to the tradition of the *fabliau,* it is "medieval" rather than "Renaissance." On the other hand its kindly humor renders it acceptable to all ages. The same can be said of his other popular compositions, *Der Rossdieb zu Funsing mit den tollen Bauern, Das heisse Eisen,* or the two versions of God's visitation of Eve's household.[28]

Thus German drama during the Renaissance, while admitting some classical influences and responding to the polemical needs of the Catholic-Lutheran conflict, continued to adhere to tradition quite strongly.

Drama in Spain

EVOLUTION Undistinguished in the Middle Ages, Spanish drama during the Renaissance passed through several stages and attained both excellence and popularity. First appeared bucolic drama, fashioned after Vergil's *Eclogues*, classical in aspirations and written for the courts. Then came the improvisation of the popular theater — the erection of a temporary stage, and the composition of *comedias*, somewhat after the manner of the Italian *commedia dell'arte*. This step proving popular, companies of players came into being, and the demand for compositions with popular appeal increased. This was Lope de Vega's chance, and with him the great Spanish "Renaissance" drama came into being.

Before taking up Lope de Vega we might expand a little on each of the foregoing stages. The first stage was inaugurated by Juan del Encina (1469?–1529?), a student of the humanist Nebrija (translator of Vergil's *Eclogues*) and a priest whose rapid promotions finally took him to the papal courts of Alexander VI and Leo X. By training he was inclined toward the classics, but his priestly calling seems to have preserved his interest in the old liturgical drama. He combined the two by freshening the latter with the Renaissance pastoral both in language and in spirit, and produced the *Égloga de tres pastores*. Encina's contemporary, Gil Vincente (1470–1539?), a lesser scholar but a more discerning student of life, produced superior work. His farces are brilliant, particularly the *Ignez Pereira* which tells of a peasant girl's marriage first to a ne'er-do-well knight and then to a solid peasant, but in their depiction of the realities of life these plays are more reminiscent of the medieval farces than they are of Terence or Plautus. The medieval influences are further exemplified by his religious dramas built on mystery plays — *auto dos quatro tempos, auto de los reyes magos* and the three Barcas, *auto da Barca do Inferno, do Purgatorio,* and *de la Gloria* — and in the two tragicomedies — *Amadís de Gaula* and *Don Duardos* — which follow the medieval traditions of romance.

The process of popularization was begun by Lope de Rueda (1510?–1565). As the first "barnstormer" he began to democratize drama. Influenced by the Italian comedy of masks, but holding close to the native environment, he composed farces — *pasos* (incidents) — of considerable appeal. This trend was furthered by Juan de la Cueva (1550?–1620?). Also preferring themes which had their roots in native tradition, he addressed his works not to any social class — such was the bucolic drama, for example, of Gil Vincente — but to the nation at large. He did, however, move in the direction of sensationalism; but that may have been in response to the demands of the popular taste. At the same time he began to pay attention to plot, to organization in acts, and to variation in meter. His best work is probably his *El infamador*.

Lope de Vega Building on the lessons of his predecessors and carrying the mode to its highest level was the prolific Felix Lope de Vega Carpio (1562–1635). With his exciting life, not far removed from that of a picaro, we need not be concerned, except to recognize that he had a zest for love and life, that improprieties did not sit heavy on his conscience, and that both of these attitudes conditioned his art. But perhaps the most commanding influence on his work was his adherence to the demands and the taste of his public. Thus in his *The New Art of Writing Plays in This Age* he wrote

> When I have to write a comedy I lock in the precepts with six keys, I banish Terence and Plautus from my study, that they may not cry out at me; for truth even in dumb books is wont to call aloud; and I write in accordance with that art which they devised who aspired to the applause of the crowd.[29]

And the demands of the crowd were exacting indeed. In his words "the wrath of a seated Spaniard is immoderate, when in two hours there is not presented to him everything from Genesis to the Last Judgment."[30] Lope de Vega did not intend to tempt this "wrath."

Two other facts influenced his work. One was his idea of poetry. He believed that "poetry must cost great trouble to the poet, but little to the reader," that is, the composition must be smooth and easy, fine but not overdone. The other was the demand of the theater business. The day of the "Broadway long-runs" had not yet come. Plays ran a day or two, so that a multiplicity of plays was absolutely necessary. Hence his productivity. We still have four hundred and seventy of his plays, and his whole output exceeded 1,500 plays! Obviously his imagination must have been fertile and his pen facile.

From these several conditions we can almost guess what the chief characteristics of his drama would be. Quick movement, unexpected turns, and liveliness would be their tempo; variety and imaginativeness, their wealth; lyricism and lightness, their charm; humaneness and avoidance of tragic heaviness (*El castigo sin venganza* (*Punishment without Vengeance*) being an exception), their warmth. Characterization is not of types but of individuals in action, and his individuals are Spaniards of all classes who move in Spanish settings and in a Spanish atmosphere. And the principal theme is the universal one of love, not deep, elemental passion, but earthy and intriguing.

To select his choicest work is, of course, next to impossible. Estimates necessarily vary with each critic. But we may allow ourselves three or four illustrative choices. His *Castelvines y Monteses* deals with the story of Romeo and Juliet, but unlike the heavy tragedy of Shakespeare, it is "a strange mixture of lyrical ecstasy and clownish merriment."[31] *El mejor alcalde el Rey* (*The King, the Greatest Alcalde*) is a panegyric on royal justice, the king rescuing a peasant maiden from a defiant nobleman who was forcing himself on her. *Fuente Ovejuna* (*The Sheep Well*) is a variation on this theme: the savior is not the monarch but all the villagers, who kill the abductor and then, when an inquest is held to discover the murderers, endure the rack but refuse to betray their colleagues. *El perro del hortelano* (*The Gardener's Dog*) shows Lope's use of the unexpected. A countess falls in love with her secretary who is in love with one of her maids. The secretary succumbs to the allurement of his mistress, but to marry her he has to pose — and she is willing to accept the pose in order to have him — as a nobleman. *El acero de Madrid* tells how a lovesick maiden tricks a sticky chaperon into letting her go where she could meet her lover. *La Dorotea* depicts the inward struggle of a woman who is both a wife and mistress and faithless to both her husband and lover. It may have been taken from Lope's own experience with his wife.

UNPOPULARITY OF HEAVY DRAMA; AND SUMMARY   The last playwright who should be included in a survey of Spain's drama of the Renaissance is the Mercenarian friar Gabriel Téllez (1584–1648) whose nom de plume is Tirso de Molina. Although a supporter of Lope de Vega's free romantic *comedia*,[32] he is decidedly opposite to him in spirit. Instead of the raciness and commonplace earthiness of the latter, he has the intensity and the epical quality of Marlowe. In the *El burlador de Sevilla* the principal character, Don Juan, is possessed of an overpowering inner force that brooks no opposition to his feats of seduction, and with this deep characterization go a dynamic plot[33] and incisive language. But the Spaniards were not of English temperament. They preferred to be entertained rather than stunned, to laugh with Vega than to suffer with Téllez, and so his plays did not win a following.

Spanish drama in the Renaissance then admitted the influence of classical drama at the outset. It retained the classical structural framework of acts and the classical focus on plot and dramaturgy. However, in responding to the popular taste it subordinated the latter two elements to devices for eliciting laughter. Also it drew heavily on the contemporary scene, but in doing so, it necessarily absorbed much that was medieval, for the ordinary Spanish scene remained fundamentally medieval.

Drama in England

RELIGIOUS DRAMA In Renaissance England drama had a history similar to that of France. Medieval plays continued their development; classical types emerged and grew; and finally came Shakespeare's ascendant star.

The mystery plays, it will be recalled, originated in the Middle Ages. Yet while medieval in origin, they remained popular until the close of the sixteenth century. The Chester Cycle was still being enacted as late as 1575; the Coventry plays did not cease until 1580; and the Wakefield Cycle continued until banned by the Ecclesiastical Commission of Elizabeth. The moralities kept improving throughout the fifteenth century. The *Pride of Life*, a summons to death, appeared about 1400; *Wisdom*, depicting the return to Christ of a mind that was lost to the devil, appeared some sixty years later; *Mankind*, which depicts the chiding of man for forgetting the goodness of God, was written about 1471; and *Everyman*, the best of all moralities and probably based on the Dutch play *Elcherlijk*, which was printed about 1495, was prepared some five years later.[34]

How long these religious plays would have continued if Elizabeth's government had not banned them cannot be answered. Some were beginning to fade out by themselves without state interdiction, especially the morality plays. But the mystery plays remained popular and were reluctantly relinquished only under the steady pressure of the Ecclesiastical Commission who deemed them papistical.[35]

INTERLUDES Emerging from the religious plays and pointing to the classical drama were the interludes. These abandoned the universal for the topical, and turned courtly or realistic. Also, where most of the former were anonymous, the interludes bear the names of their authors. Among the several noted writers of this type of plays three may be selected as more or less typical. Henry Medwall, chaplain to Cardinal Morton, prepared a courtly interlude called *Fulgens and Lucrece*. This dealt with classical personalities, but wove in some good low comedy. He also wrote *Nature*. The theme of this was man's toying with the Seven Deadly Sins. The mixture then is quite noticeable. The second example is John Heywood, husband of More's niece, Joan. A good-natured Catholic, he was connected with the courts of Henry VIII, Edward VI, and Mary, and prepared plays for their entertainment. The type of play that he produced is nicely exemplified in the *Four P's*. He has the Palmer, Pardoner, Pothecary, and Pedlar vying with each other to determine which was the most clever prevaricator, the Palmer winning. Sometimes he has only three principals, but the plan — we can hardly call it a plot — remains the same. In *Gentleness and Nobility*, a debate between a merchant and a knight as to who is the better gentleman is turned into a success for a plowman who enters into the list as a third adversary.[36] It is clear that in plays like these there is little room for characterization of individuals, and considerable opportunity for rowdiness (cf. his *Pardoner and Friar*). In this sense, then, they are comparable to the medieval farces. On the other hand, the superior handling of the principals, the raciness of the language, and the casualness of the mundane atmosphere indicate departure from the farces. The third example is the poet John Skelton, and he is chosen mainly to illustrate that the interlude often took the form of satire or outright propaganda. In his *Magnificence* there is an obvious indictment of Wolsey, who is accused of giving counsel that is likely to bring harm to the king and country.[37] Put to use in political or religious propaganda of the time, the interlude might be expected to partake of its age. That it did, but not wholly. The *Magnificence*, for example, is still structured after the pattern of a morality. The titles of some other political interludes — *Wealth and Health, Impatient Poverty* — are in themselves indications that the ghost of morality is still present in the interlude.

As the interlude, turned into a propaganda vehicle, began to decline during the reign of Elizabeth, the classical drama emerged. The movement started with the composition of school plays patterned after the models of antiquity. Subsequently came the adaptation of classical comedy to the English scene, and the new drama was born. Among the better early examples of this comedy were Nicolas Udall's *Ralph Roister Doister* (1553–1554), a picture of London bourgeois society, and *Gammer Gurton's Needle* (1553), a humorous treatment of rustic society, by the enigmatic "Mr. S."[38] Subsequently appeared a number of more refined plays. *Dammon and Pythias* and *Palamon and Arcite*, written by Richard Edwards for the Chapel Children, a court choir of twelve boys who at times doubled as actors in court plays, combined decorum of character and propriety of language with successful plots. John Lyly's *Campaspe* as well as his other six plays, all played before Elizabeth, carried the elegance of language to the same high degree as his popular novel *Euphues*. Most of them were taken from classical mythology and followed the classical form, though infrequently they departed somewhat from the unities prescribed by the classical rules.

CLASSICAL DRAMA This trend in comedy was soon joined by the rise of classical tragedy. Translations of all nine of Seneca's tragedies appeared and began to be used as models for compositions in English. The first work of this type was *Tragedy of Gorbuduc* (1562) or *Tragedy of Ferrex and Porrex* as it was called in its second edition. Written by two members of Parliament, Thomas Norton and Thomas Sackville, it was intended to point out to the Queen the dangers that are likely to befall the realm if the problem of succession is left unsettled. The theme is derived from Britain's legendary past, but the structure and the mechanics are noticeably Senecan, as are the elevated rhetorical language and the high purpose. It deviates from the pure classical tragedy by failing to observe the rule of unities and by making the tragedy depend not on fortune or some vindictive gods but on the reasoned actions of the hero himself. Similar compositions, some more strongly Senecan, followed shortly. *Jocasta* by George Gascoigne and a collaborator was produced by Gray's Inn and *Gismond of Salerno in Love* by the Inner Temple. These were all topped by the works of Christopher Marlowe (1564–1593).

Marlowe was a bold spirit, and the tragedy he wrote was high and powerful. A Cambridge graduate, he employed scholarship to enhance the realism and the dignity of his productions. A gentleman who carried himself high among the "cafe society" of the day, even though he died in a tavern brawl, he wanted no part of the ordinary. His heroes strove for mighty ends — Tamburlaine for the conquest of whole peoples, Faust to gain overpowering knowledge, the Jew of Malta to secure inordinate wealth — and his language, fit for these heroes and spoken through the medium of the blank verse, has been made memorable by Ben Jonson who called it "Marlowe's mighty line."

This "mighty line" lends itself to much high oratory, a feature which characterizes the Senecan type of tragedy; and the characterization of heroes as individuals rather than as types adds further evidence that Marlowe was writing after the classic mode. Yet, as Nicoll remarks, the connections with the morality are also present, in form, in "abstract personifications and in the display of the Seven Deadly Sins."[39] On the other hand, and still following Nicoll, Marlowe is ahead of the classical tragedy when, instead of presenting a character already "set" at the outset of the play, he develops the characters of the principals as the play proceeds. Thus Faustus moves "from confident assurance and untroubled ambition to a realization of his error and to an abject dismay of the forces of hell surrounding him."[40] If we note that by treating his principals as individuals whose characters develop *pari passu* with the play he was able to attribute their fall to their own motives and actions rather than to Fate alone in the manner of earlier tragedy,[41] we can see how basic Marlowe's contributions were to Shakespearean drama.

SHAKESPEARE   Three additional influences helped to fashion the drama of Shakespeare. One was the property of the exciting and the horrible. This was principally the contribution of Thomas Kyd (1558–1594). In *The Spanish Tragedy*, which makes Seneca seem tame, sensitive dignity gives place to shocking sensationalism, and the flash of fury and the stench of gore are everywhere. The English audience accepted it with excitement and called for more; some, no doubt, because mere shock gave them thrills; others, perhaps, because the suffering which man, in knowingly overreaching himself, justly brings upon himself stimulated their tragic qualm. The second influence came from the romantic comedies on fictionized English historical themes. Greene, who was no lover of Lyly's eloquence and Marlowe's grandiloquence, set the pattern for these with his *Friar Bacon* and *Friar Bungay* and *James V*. Thomas Lodge joined him in producing *A Looking-Glass for London and England*. London, afire with nationalism, received them with applause, and others like them were produced by his followers — *Fair Em, The Famous Victories of Henry V, Sir John Oldcastle,* and several more.⁴² The third influence was the cultural tradition of the immediate past, that is, of the Middle Ages. The society for which Shakespeare wrote had not yet rejected its heritage. It still admired the *courtois*; it loved romantic tales and true love ending in happiness; it was sensitive to moral teachings and sophisticated in the religious allegorism employed to communicate them.⁴³ To all these influences Shakespeare proved to be receptive, and since they really were indications of what the public desired in its dramatic fare, his acceptance of these influences naturally won him public favor.

If Aristotle was "the master of them who know," Shakespeare (1564–1616) was "the master of them who wrote dramas." He borrowed heavily from his contemporaries: the blank verse and high purpose from Marlowe, the mechanics of heightening drama and the accompanying deep passions and crude realism from Kyd, the dramatic potentialities of historical plays both from Marlowe and from Greene and his school, and the pleasant world of fancy from the sweet-tongued court poets of the day. He ransacked the great storehouses of Amyot's *Plutarch* and Holinshed's and Hall's *Chronicles* for dramatic themes and for characters. He stole whole lines from his competitors or by revision made older plays his own. But all this borrowing would not have fashioned fully the mastery of drama that was his. On top of these, and helping him to make the most of them, was his experience with the theater as actor and promoter. This enabled him to discern the best dramatic properties of each and so to exploit their potential to his advantage. Lastly, it must be recognized that he had the great gift of discerning the universal in the immediate and of portraying it without making the individual a mere type.

It is customary to see three periods in the history of Shakespeare's compositions. The first is regarded as the period of the fanciful plays of a young man. Such works as the *Midsummer Night's Dream* may seem to justify such a classification, but if it is noted that the Kydian-like

Richard III appeared during this same period also, it might be more accurate to characterize this first period as that of a novice seeking to acquire experience in the art of playwriting by trying out several different types of drama in accordance with the tastes of the public. And so, with one eye on what his competitors were doing and with the other on his public, he essayed a light satire (*Loves Labour Lost*), some farces (*The Taming of the Shrew, The Comedy of Errors, The Merry Wives of Windsor*), a number of historical plays (*Richard III, Henry VI,* in three parts, *King John, Richard II*), and some tragedies of the vendetta type (*Titus Andronicus, Romeo and Juliet*). Once the period of apprenticeship was over, Shakespeare entered the middle period, the great period, of his career. Essentially it is the period of the great tragedies — *Hamlet, Othello, King Lear,* and *Macbeth* — but it also includes the Roman plays (*Julius Caesar, Antony and Cleopatra,* and *Coriolanus*) and some heavy satirical comedies (*Measure for Measure, All's Well That Ends Well*). In this middle period, without abandoning his function as a professional entertainer, Shakespeare becomes a student of the inner man and of society. Thus, for example, in *Macbeth* we see how two characters in great love lead each other under the drive of ambition to utter destruction. Antony and Cleopatra also are the victims of their own character, whereas Troilus and Cressida in the play of the same name are the victims of environment, and Romeo and Juliet in a play of the first period are merely the unfortunate victims of chance.[44] Thus also in *Measure for Measure* Shakespeare advocates the need of sincerity and common sense in public life. The third period is that of experience and maturity mellowing into tolerance and romance. At times the great man seems to smile at and with the world, though not without disapproval of wrong. At other times he chuckles as if he were enjoying his own artistic skill. The period is characterized by *The Winter's Tale, The Tempest,* and *Cymbeline.* The period ended with him assisting Fletcher in the historical plays, one of which, *Henry VIII,* when first staged in Shakespeare's famous theater, the *Globe,* led to its destruction — one of the cannons used in connection with the play misfired and set the structure aflame. Shakespeare's creative days were over.

Such in brief is the history of Shakespeare's dramatic compositions. Now, what of the merits that rate these works so highly in the scales of world literature? These obviously cannot be listed categorically, for each critic has his own respective standards of literary values. Still we might suggest some of them.

One of these merits, and probably the greatest, may be found in the elevation of the particular into the significant and eternal without its transformation into the typical. Thus the love of Antony for Cleopatra cannot be dissociated from the two; it is the love between two particular people. Yet, at the same time, it transcends the immediate and becomes timeless, and this Shakespeare achieves without treating it as a mere case study of inordinate passion. The same is true with Falstaff. Very much an individual, a bragging, big-bellied, good-humored, self-interested comic, he is always a Falstaff, and never a specimen. Perhaps Shakespeare was able to impart this property to his plays as a consequence of his understanding of human nature and his ability to portray it with proper realism. His characters are not abstractions which have to remain one-sided. They are real people who have their good moments and qualities as well as their bad ones, however preponderant the latter might be. Such people can evoke sympathetic understanding, an indispensable reaction if the play is to bring satisfaction to the audience.

Another strong feature of these dramas is the superb mastery of the language. The blank verse is expertly exploited to bring out the desired dramatic effects. The lyric sings or weeps as the circumstances require. There is also the fitting use of prose and of the colloquial.

Their third quality is their breadth of spirit. The idea that life is great and meaningful and enjoyable appears constantly; and the fact that the message is conveyed more by implication or suggestion than by open declaration heightens its appeal. Whether it is the result of chance, as in *Romeo and Juliet,* or of personal weakness, as in Hamlet's indecision, the challenge to life's fulfillment merely magnifies the richness of life. Nor is its realization to be compassed without regard to responsibility, Falstaff to the contrary notwithstanding. On the contrary, the fullness of life was to be attained in concord with at least three limiting principles: that of morality, that of fixity of the social order, and that of man's insignificance in relation to the cosmos. The result is a freedom bound by responsibility and by reason. Indeed, to some critics it is this "reasonableness" that makes Shakespeare so acceptable and so lasting.

:atures are to be found, such as rich imaginativeness, elevated tone, and warm patriotism. But whatever the properties that make his works appealing, the enigmatic fact remains that the popularity of the plays seems to be growing with time.

Now, how to classify these plays? They are classical in structure, and some observe the prescribed unities. There is the Senecan rhetorical rant, and the Senecan vendetta theme. There is the Plautan comic spirit. There is the imitation of the school plays. Thus the role of the classical mode is commanding. But there is also the warm reflection of the contemporary spirit: the cult of the aristocratic is ever-present, the ardor for the Tudor monarchy and the dependence of England's destiny on them, and the gaze at the horizons of the future. These reveal that the plays are in a sense a national by-product of England's Renaissance. Yet, if the structure is classical and the animating spirit contemporary, there are certain features which tie the plays with the past. In spite of the fact that it was "for gain, not glory, that Shakespeare winged his roving flight," and that his aim was "to please," his plays are intended as lessons against evil.[45] Without being morality plays they retained the function of these plays, and in so doing perpetuated the medieval *raison d'être* of drama. Again, some of the history plays, although an expression of Tudor patriotism, preserved, in their representation of the fall of high princes, the medieval concept of tragedy.[46] Thirdly, his notion of a comedy "as a story starting in trouble, ending in joy, and centered in love" and conforming in philosophic essentials to the "Christian understanding of reality" is medieval and not in keeping with the Renaissance comedy which followed the classical pattern.[47] Then, even if this does not affect the composition of the plays, we cannot overlook the fact that the religious philosophy and the metaphysics expressed in all his plays are generally in keeping with the medieval tradition.[48] And so without fully breaking with the medieval,[49] Shakespeare's plays reflect the pervading influences of the cult of classics and of the contemporary national air.

General Appraisal of Developments in Drama

This survey of drama country by country can be supplemented by some generalizations about the development of drama as a whole. Some of these observations are readily ascertainable from the survey. Others, adumbrated here and there, will need to be made more concrete at this point.

One readily noticeable feature common to the history of Renaissance drama in all lands was the continuation of the so-called "medieval" drama, both the religious and the popular type. Indeed, as the survey reveals, the "medieval" mystery, miracle, and morality plays and the people's comedy not only continued but actually attained their ripest stage during the Renaissance, as in the case of the Passion Play of Lucerne and of the Shrovetide plays of Hans Sachs.

Another fact that was common was the emergence of a "national" type of drama, that is, drama which was peculiar to the country of its origin, such as the *commedia dell'arte* in Italy, the anti-Catholic plays in Lutheran Germany and in other Protestant lands, the historical and nationalistic compositions of Shakespearean England, or the "theatrical" drama of Spain. To the extent that drama was becoming more responsive to the national atmosphere, it was naturally less responsive to the universalism that dictated the character of medieval drama; that is, Renaissance drama, at least toward the end of the Renaissance period, was becoming independent of medieval traditions.

The great development was, of course, the emergence of the classical type of drama. As a result of the ardent pursuit of classical letters, comedies were patterned after Terence and Plautus and tragedies after Seneca; and indeed the first stage in this imitation actually consisted of drama in the language of antiquity, Latin. Then the imitation was extended to include secular drama in the vernacular, and finally even biblical drama. Encouraging this imitation was the Aristotelian dictum concerning the rules of dramatic composition. His injunctions about the necessity of observing the dramatic unities were taken seriously and led some dramatists to adopt classical drama as models for imitation.

But the fact that Renaissance drama was influenced by the drama of antiquity and by certain humanistic influences does not mean that it escaped all influences of "medieval" drama and of medieval social and religious philosophies. Although this influence of the "medieval" on the "classical" drama of the Renaissance has been suggested here and there in the survey, it has not been emphasized as much as its importance requires.

One of the more obvious contributions of "medieval" drama to Renaissance drama was the provision of a "considerable repertory of well-defined characters." "The proud tyrant" of the Renaissance drama was patterned after the Herods and the Pilates of the medieval drama; "the braggart soldier," after "the soldiers of Herod and of the high priests"; "the comic yokel," after "the shepherds at the Nativity"; and "the witty servant, the shrewish wife, and many others," after their respective counterparts.[50]

Another impact was in the field of Renaissance comedy. It is true that Terence and Plautus served as models for dramatic techniques and provided some ideas for plots and characters, but it was also from the medieval farces that many elements of low comedy were borrowed.

Greater than the influence of medieval farces was that of certain medieval social mores and medieval literature. It is true that structurally and stylistically the prime model for Renaissance romantic comedy was the classical comedy; but in the all-important matter of ideals the influence came from the immediate past and not from antiquity. Classical comedy treated man as if he were hopelessly steeped in vices, follies, and ignorance, and it burlesqued or satirized these seemingly without limit. Renaissance comedy, on the other hand, if it was not base eroticism (*Chrysis* of Aeneas Sylvius) or venomous cynicism (Machiavelli's *Mandragola*), generally stressed the elements of romance, admitted the possibility of human merit, and ended on a note of optimism. Its ladies are attractive and witty, courtly females, not just rowdy courtesans; its loves are sincere though *courtois*, not carnal; and its endings are happy.[51] While some of these differences in the matter of love may be partially attributed to the influences of classical idyllic literature, it is unquestionable that the more proximate influences were medieval. The attitude to women was influenced by the adoration extended to them in the chivalric romances, and the happy endings were due to the Christian notion of man's ultimate bliss.

Another of these influences affected the school drama and the interludes. The school drama, intended to be staged by students for the edification of their companions, naturally included elements from the morality plays. Not only was the theme moral in purport, but frequently the apparatus of the moralities, abstractions of Virtues and Vices and devils, were taken bodily from the moralities. The same appears to be true in connection with the interludes — in fact, in England they were sometimes actually called moralities.

Finally the influence even extended to tragedy. Seneca, it was pointed out, served as the classical model for the structuring of the dramas, for the dramatic techniques, and for the elevated language. He also helped to fashion the notion of tragedy as a play which traces the operations of great ambitions and the subsequent fall, both of which entail repugnant crimes, horror, and bloodshed. Renaissance tragedy accepted these elements but introduced one vital change. In Seneca the rise and fall are the result of Fate, something greater than man; man can scarcely do anything but follow Destiny's course. In Renaissance tragedy, in its early stages, there is a similar determining force, but rather than Fate, it is the allurement of the earthly. Man surrenders to mundane interests and then pays the due price. It is the theory behind Boccaccio's *De casibus virorum illustrium* (*On the Fall of Illustrious Men*) in which Boccaccio, smitten by remorse at his dallying with love literature of questionable morality, wrote up the histories of some hundred great historical and legendary figures who had sold their souls to earthly interests and paid the price of a disastrous fall. Here man is as helpless as in Seneca's plays, but instead of Fate it is the Sin of yielding to the earthly which causes the fall. Subsequently, under the influence of later medieval philosophy and religion that the earth in itself is not evil, that its enjoyment by man was intended by God, and that man is accountable for his own sins, the theories of Seneca and Boccaccio and their continuators yielded to the notion that, while there are great forces outside man with which he has to cope, in the last analysis it is man's own actions which shape his destiny. Tragedy then becomes the story of a man capable of nobility, struggling against his own weaknesses, heroically succumbing to them, and then justly reaping the price of failure. Thus, not Fate and not tempting earthliness, but man himself prepares his own tragedy; and this idea, the heart of all great Renaissance tragedy, came not from revived classicism but from medieval religious philosophy.[52]

Summary

With this conclusion we have come to the end of the survey. Clearly the survey shows that in the course of the Renaissance period drama changed from "medieval" to "Renaissance" drama. But the survey also shows that "Renaissance" drama did not appear until the last few decades of the period, whereas drama which is generally regarded as "medieval" (such as, the mystery plays, moralities, and farces), and drama which combined medieval and Renaissance characteristics (such as, the interludes and the Latin drama written in schools) prevailed throughout most of the Renaissance period. Hence we should be careful not to confuse "Renaissance" drama, that is drama patterned after classical models, with all the drama written during the Renaissance period. If we keep this distinction in mind, our appraisal of the history of drama during the centuries of the Renaissance will be more realistic.

1. For an example of the extravagant staging, see Symonds' description of one of these dramas in *op. cit.*, II, 55–56.

2. For a recent survey of classical Latin drama in Italy during the Renaissance see Liecester Bradner's "The Latin Drama of the Renaissance (1340–1640)," *Studies in the Renaissance*, IV (1957), 31–35. This survey will be utilized for reports on Latin drama in other lands.

3. Marvin T. Herrick, *Italian Comedy in the Renaissance* (Urbana, Illinois: University of Illinois Press, 1960), 26. Much of what follows on Italian comedy is based on this work.

4. For a more thorough analysis of these see *ibid.*, 43–55.

5. For a brief synopsis of the plot see *ibid.*, 80–85.

6. Symonds (*op. cit.*, II, 263) appraises it as a "study of stupidity and baseness acted on by roguery."

7. But cf. Liecester Bradner ("The Rise of Secular Drama in the Renaissance," *Studies in the Renaissance,* III [1956], 11) who argues that Machiavelli represented evil extravagantly because he wished to make it appear abhorrent.

8. On these tragedians see Wilkins, *A History of Italian Literature*, 238–40, 252.

9. *Ibid.*, 154–5, 271–2, 290.

10. The subject is treated at length in Winifred Smith, *The* commedia dell'arte. *A Study in Italian Popular Comedy*, "Columbia University

Studies in English and Comparative Literature" (New York: Columbia University Press, 1912). For a short treatment see Wilkins, *A History of Italian Literature*, 264–7.

11. W. Smith, *op. cit.*, 27–28.

12. For a synopsis of three of these see Allardyce Nicoll, *World Drama from Aeschylus to Anoulh* (New York: Harcourt, Brace and Company, 1950), 161–62.

13. For meaningful summaries and appraisals of some of these Passions see Cohen, *Le théatre en France au moyen âge*, 39–59.

14. Nitze and Dargan, *op. cit.*, 109.

15. For a brief summary see *ibid.*, 112–3 and cf. Cohen, *Le théatre en France au moyen âge*, 125–40.

16. For a synopsis see Arsène Darmesteter and Adople Hatzfeld, *Le seizième siècle en France* (3d ed.; Paris: Librairie Ch. Delagrave, 1886), 170–2.

17. Cited from Nicoll, *op. cit.*, 202.

18. *Ibid.*, and Darmesteter and Hatzfeld, *op. cit.*, 176.

19. For his other plays see Nicoll, *op. cit.*, 202.

20. *Ibid.*, 202.

21. Cf. Derek van Abbé, *Drama in Renaissance Germany and Switzerland* (Victoria: Melbourne University Press, 1961), introduction, xi–xiii, also p. 2, and note the references to the religious plays in the appendix (123–5) which lists the plays performed between 1500 and 1540.

22. Recently translated by A. E. Zuker and published as no. XXXII of the *Records of Civilization Sources and Studies* (New York: Columbia University Press, 1941).

23. For additional references see Van Abbé, *op. cit.*, 22–23.

24. *Ibid.*, 5–6.

25. *Ibid.*, 28–29, 31–33.

26. For an informative analysis of Rebhun's and Birck's plays see *ibid.*, 58–74, 78–91.

27. Cf. Robertson, *op. cit.*, 164–5, and Maximilian J. Rudwin, *The Origin of the German Carnival Drama* (New York: G. E. Stechert & Co., 1920), 55–59.

28. For summaries of some of these plays see Nicoll, *op. cit.*, 168–70.

29. Cited from Barrett H. Clark, *European Theories of the Drama* (revised ed.; New York: D. Appleton-Century Co., 1936), 89–90.

30. Cited from *ibid.*, 91.

31. Nicoll, *op. cit.*, 213.

32. Cf. the fictitious dialogue of his in *Cigarrales (Orchards) de Toledo* in B. H. Clark, *op. cit.*, 94–95.

33. For a summary of the plot see Brenan, *op. cit.*, 214–5.

34. For a fuller treatment of these see E. K. Chambers, *op. cit.*, 53–64. For a lengthy study turn to Hardin Craig, *English Religious Drama of the Middle Ages* (Oxford: Clarendon Press, 1955), 151–354.

35. On the disappearance and suppression of religious drama see Craig, *op. cit.*, 354–89.

36. Concise summaries in Baugh, *op. cit.*, 361–2.

37. *Ibid.*, 362.

38. For studies on the identity of "Mr. S." see *ibid.*, 449, n. 2.

39. Nicoll, *op. cit.*, 271.

40. *Ibid.*

41. Cf. Willard Farnham, *The Medieval Heritage of Elizabethan Tragedy* (Berkeley: University of California Press, 1936), 401–13.

42. For others see Baugh, *op. cit.*, 458.

43. For this last influence on Shakespeare see Nevill Coghill, "The Basis of Shakespearean Comedy. A Study in Medieval Affinities," *Essays and Studies Collected for the English Association*, 3d series, 1950, 1–28.

44. Baugh, *op. cit.*, 538.

45. This is the principal thesis of Coghill's article cited above, n. 43. Cf. particularly 17–28.

46. See Atkins, *English Literary Criticism: The Medieval Phase*, 156–61.

47. Coghill, *op. cit.*, 9–14.

48. On this point the reader is urged to consult E. M. W. Tillyard, *The Elizabethan World Picture* (New York: The Macmillan Co., 1944).

49. The subject of the medieval in Shakespeare has been treated by Farnham, *op. cit.*, *passim*.

50. Leicester Bradner, "The Rise of Secular Drama in the Renaissance," *Studies in the Renaissance*, III (1956), 8.

51. On this difference see Coghill, *op. cit.*, 1–28.

52. This whole thesis is carefully worked out by Farnham in *op. cit.* The entire book is devoted to this theme.

CHAPTER **VIII**   *Architecture*

I F WE WERE interested only in the stylistic changes in architecture
during the Renaissance period, then a comparison of one or two
buildings erected in the Renaissance style, as for example, the cathedral
of St. Peter's in Rome and the Louvre, with a couple of medieval Gothic
structures such as the cathedral of Notre Dame in Amiens, would be
enough. But if we are interested in finding out how widespread was
this change in style, as indeed we should, then we really need to be
familiar with the history of architecture during the period. We should
know what style prevailed at the outset of the period, how long its
prevalence lasted, and to what extent it was displaced by the new style.
Only such a comprehensive survey can lead to a sound historical view
of what actually happened in architecture during the Renaissance.

Romanesque and Gothic Styles of Architecture before the Renaissance

One old style of architecture was the Romanesque. To be sure it was
not a living style during the Renaissance; it had reached its fullest development by the end of the twelfth century and was supplanted in the
next century by the Gothic. But even so, its influence was inescapable.
Its monuments were everywhere present, from the cathedral of Durham
to that of Pisa and from that of Santiago de Compostela to that of
Magdeburg (the *Liebfrauenkirche*), and continued to declare their
identity. A sixteenth-century architect of Pisa, Siena, or Angoulême
lived in the shadows of the Romanesque more than in those of the
Renaissance. It seems unlikely, therefore, that he would have escaped
its influence. The Roman arch and vault, the monumentality, the
effective employment of mass, the vigor of the elemental were all there
to leave their mark on him even if he may have been oblivious to that
influence. If the influence cannot be easily documented, the possibility
of this influence cannot be ruled out.

The other old style was the Gothic. But, although old, it was still very much alive and will, therefore, require more than a passing mention.

To begin with, first, what is Gothic? The right reply is of course, which Gothic? Early, High, or Late Gothic, if we let chronology be the determining factor? or the Gothic of Isle de France? the Gothic of North Italy? the English Perpendicular Gothic? the Rhenish Gothic? and so on, if we let geography dictate our choice? The point implicit in these questions and one to be kept in mind is that the Gothic underwent a steady development and that its changes were not simultaneous nor similar everywhere. Provincial artistic tradition, zealous town rivalries with each community trying to build a grander cathedral, individualism of the masterbuilders invading the structures, constant experimentation with tried techniques, and the prolonged building periods extending anywhere from two generations to more than two centuries — all contributed to variation in the style. And the range of variation is truly great. From the early Gothic of Noyon cathedral (begun *ca.* 1150) and the pristine Gothic of the cathedral of Chartes (started in 1194) to the lavish Gothic of the cathedral of Milan (1387 ff.) there is a wide difference. The single-towered Gothic of the cathedral of Ulm is quite dissimilar from the Moorish-Spanish Gothic of the cathedral of Seville. This then is the first notion about the Gothic that should be recognized, namely, its progressiveness and diversity.

But the recognition of this variation and stylistic development should not of course obscure the opposite fact that these variant Gothic styles, once the basic elements of the structural system — the diagonal rib, the pointed arch, the tall shafts, the long windows, the thin wall, and the reinforcing buttresses — were brought together, possessed some structural and aesthetic properties in common. The ground plans, however differing in detail, were usually in the form of the Latin cross. Generally also, Gothic structures were divided into three parallel sections, longitudinally up to the transept, with the central section, the nave, wider than the two side aisles and separated from them by a row of piers along each of its sides. This longitudinal division was matched by a corresponding triple vertical division of the façade with two tall towers flanking the lower middle section. This latter division, however, was not as universal, there being some fronts with more divisions and some that emphasized the middle section. Another common element and the one truly identifying element was the pointed arch which was adopted to impart greater height to the building both aesthetically and structurally. By carrying the eye upward without turning it down as the round Roman arch does, it adds to the impression of elevation. Structurally it enabled the builder to convey a greater part of the roof's thrust along the vault's vertical, and so more stable, component and so to raise the roof on higher pillars. Then, to reinforce the pillars which were heightened almost to the critical point, the Gothic structures generally employed the flying buttresses to transfer some of the lateral thrust of the roof to another series of upright buttresses which paralleled the interior piers. The resulting structure therefore amounted to two parallel series of piers reinforcing each other and supporting a steep gabled roof like stilts. Because most of the weight of the superstructure rested on these uprights, heavy walls were not necessary. So masonry was reduced to the minimum and replaced by windows, tall and gothic-arched like the interior vaults; and since windows do not enclose, the resultant structure became an art of lines and space and not an art of mass. Other properties were those of height and linearity, of elegance and grace, and of myriad ornamental detail.[1]

Out of these various properties the Gothic gets its character, a compound of rationality and emotion.

Its rationality manifests itself in the way each of its structural elements declares its function, in the same sense as each step in a scholastic argument makes palpable the reasoning that leads to the inevitable conclusion. It also comes out in the patent relatedness of its members and, more importantly, in the logical arrangement of these parts in an intelligible synthesis. Finally, it reveals itself in the reconciliation of its opposites, as in the case of verticality versus horizontality, the *sic* and *non* so to speak of the structure, into an acceptable harmony.[2]

The second property, that of emotional language, is more easily felt than explained. Some of it consists of the feeling of spiritual security that comes from the structure's rationality and interior harmony. Much of it is a sense of exaltation which is stimulated by the predominance of the verticals. Wherever one turns his eyes, the emphasis on the verticals stimulates a sense of exaltation, and each linear element fairly accentuates the sense. There is no "let down"; instead there is excitement, a constant and directed stimulation which grows upon one. On the outside, too, the ascending lines of the main towers and of the several finials carry the eye into the sky and create the impression that the structure soars. Some of it is a sense of awe with which the vastness of the interior overwhelms one. This derives not only from the magnitude of the building, but also from its vast expanse of windows, both of which seem to unite the interior and those it encompasses with the sky above. In sum, the emotional language of the Gothic is one of animation, elevation, and exaltation.

A third element might be added, namely, the symbolism of the style. Indeed, it is implied in the union and the encompassment referred to in the preceding paragraph, namely, "the disappearance of the boundary between Man and God," for Christ, the son of God, suffered and died as man out of love of man.[3] But however noble the meaning, it is clear that the symbolism can only be obvious to the Christians. In other words, the meaning is not inherent in the style but has to be learned by the viewer. Still, since all art is seen introspectively as well as objectively, perhaps this third element might be included among the elements which impart to the Gothic its particular character.

Such is the nature of the Gothic architecture. Remains now the task of examining the history of this style during the Renaissance.

Gothic during the Renaissance

In the land of its origin, namely France, the Gothic continued to be employed both in the construction of new churches, once the ravages of the Hundred Years' War ceased, and in the completion or repair of older structures. The use of the Gothic in the latter process is of course understandable. It is exemplified in the towers of the cathedral of Amiens, completed about 1366–1402, and in its *fleche* which was not raised until 1529; in the northern tower (completed about 1510) of the cathedral of Chartres; and in the righthand tower and the central doorway, gable, and rose window, of the western façade of the cathedral of Rouen (1485–1514?). Some examples of substantially or completely new churches erected in the Gothic are *Notre-Dame de l'Épine* near Châlons-sur-Marne (1410 ff.), *San Maclou* (1437–early sixteenth century) at

Rouen, *St. Jacques* at Dieppe, *St. Gervais,* and, to some extent, *St. Eustache* at Paris.

A comparison of these structures (Plate 1) with thirteenth-century Gothic will readily reveal some differences. Lavishness of ornamentation, even unto excess, is the first noticeable characteristic; and much of that lace-like screen appears unintegrated with the structural forms. False gables and numerous finials, both crocheted, add to this excess of ornamentation. In the interiors the same abundance of decorative tracery is present, and the flamelike designs in the windows are noticeably characteristic. Indeed, it is from these shapes that the whole style derives its name, the flamboyant Gothic. On the other hand, the interiors reveal an economy of structural forms, almost to the point of inadequacy. The whole, therefore, while exhibiting superlative mastery of stone cutting, leaves the impression of being deficient in structural firmness. It is like the poetry of *rhétoriqueurs,* intricate, aureate, and fashioned but lacking in substance and greatness. This disparity has tempted some critics to regard the style as decadent, but that is perhaps because they have their eye on the monumental style of the Renaissance.

In England the Gothic church architecture continued uninterrupted into the Tudor period. Exemplifying this continuation are such famous monuments as the cathedral of Winchester, which was built in the latter half of the fourteenth century, King's College Chapel erected between 1472 and 1530, and the fine chapel of Henry VII constructed between 1502–1520. These examples do not cover the entire Renaissance period, but that does not mean that the Gothic gave way to some other style. There was no other style, in fact very little church building in any style, from the time of Henry VIII's break with Rome through the rest of the Tudor period.

Just as the late Gothic in France admitted variations, so did the late Gothic in England. In fact two important variations evolved, the Curvilinear Decorated as represented in the cathedrals of Winchester and Gloucester, and the Perpendicular of Henry VII's chapel. The first is named after the tracery on the windows, there being little to distinguish the building structurally from the High Gothic. The Perpendicular owes its name also to the design on the windows, from the intersection of the vertical mullions by horizontal transom bars. But in the mature form of the Perpendicular the horizontal lines of the transoms are continued as prominent string courses in the masonry. The result is a pleasing effect of verticals cut by horizontals as evidenced by Henry VII's chapel (Plate 2). Another characteristic change, this time in the interior, was the fan vaulting. Instead of the usual Gothic vaulting which produced a segmentation of the ceiling, the builders allowed fine ribs to spread out from the piers in an ever-widening fan, as in the cloister of the cathedral of Gloucester, until the fan took the form of a nearly-full circle, as in King's College Chapel and in Henry VII's chapel at Westminster (Plate 3). The resulting ceiling is not only a marvel of suspension but a fortuitous means of magnifying the impression of the structure's spaciousness.[4] In sum, the Gothic in England remained a living and an elegant style throughout the Renaissance period.

In Germany the Gothic continued until the middle of the sixteenth century. This is nicely exemplified by the cathedral of Ulm which was under construction during the fourteenth, fifteenth, and sixteenth centuries. Indeed the spire was not completed until the nineteenth century. The fact that the sixteenth-century portions of the structure do not clash with those constructed earlier would support the proposition that there was no radical change in the Gothic style.

The properties of this style are a strong emphasis on the perpendicular, with numerous piercing finials to accentuate this, and lavishness of decorative stonework. It is, of course, of the single-tower design.

This emphasis on the verticals is repeated in the interior of the chapel of St. Vitus at Prague and in the nave and tower of the equally famous *St. Stephen's* at Vienna.

While the perpendicular style persisted, German Gothic during the Renaissance period adopted several distinguishing modifications. One of these changes appeared in the vaulting of the interiors. In an increasing number of churches, straight-line ribs yielded to graceful curvilinear ribs, the stone of the rib itself being so carved as to give the impression of a gentle twist; and the combination of the twist and the "S" curve produced a gentle flowing effect. Designed by Benedict Ried von Piesting, this departure is best expressed in the church of St. Barbara at Kuttenberg (1512–1548, Plate 4) and in that of St. Anne at Annaberg (begun in 1499).⁵ Another notable modification was the employment of brick instead of masonry. The substitution naturally precluded the possibility of the kind of decorative design to which masonry lends itself, and so the brick churches are clean-surfaced. In addition, the wall surfaces are necessarily greater and make the structures look more like architecture of mass than of line and space. The classic example of this brick Gothic style is the *Frauenkirche* at Munich (Plates 5 and 6), built between 1468 and 1488, but the home of this style was the Baltic area from Lubeck eastward. A third departure was the "hall" church. This type of church had its aisles made as high as its nave, and two consequences necessarily followed. The triforium and clerestory were eliminated, opening the church, as it were, from wall to wall and enhancing its spaciousness. Secondly, with the elevation of the aisles equal to that of the nave, it was possible to cover the church with one large single roof. Of necessity the roof was tall and steep and became a striking feature of the structure. Although introduced as early as the eleventh century (chapel of St. Bartholomew at Paderborn),⁶ the style continued in use during the Renaissance, the *Wiesenkirche* at Soest (begun in 1331) being an early example and the St. Vitus at Prague being an outstanding later example.

In this survey of the Gothic in Germany during the Renaissance, only a few structures have been cited, not because such structures were few, but because there is no need to multiply illustrative examples. Many others could be cited, all pointing to the prevalence of this style.

In the Low Countries, flanked by the Gothic of France and Germany, the Gothic continued long into the Renaissance. Among the several famous examples of late Gothic are the church of St. Bavo at Haarlem and particularly the church of St. Jan at s'Hertogenbosch which was begun in 1419 and completed in 1498.

At the other extremity of western Europe, in Spain, the Gothic acquired some properties from Moorish architecture. An excellent example of this mixed style is the cathedral of Seville, which was more than a century in building (1403–1519). In the interior the Gothic is proclaimed by the pointed arch, yet the Moorish influence is present in the unsatisfactory differentiation between the essential components of the church — nave, aisles, transept — and in the excessive use of pillars imparting to the church the character of a many-pillared hall. On the exterior the noticeable Moorish features are the wide wall areas, small windows, decorative-like buttresses, and profuseness of ornamentation around the doors. Another example of this mixed style is the Royal Chapel which Enrique de Egas built in Granada (1506).

Although Gothic architecture never was the prevailing style in Italy, some Gothic structures were erected, particularly in Lombardy which always maintained close contact with trans-Alpine Europe. The foremost of these is the cathedral of Milan, sometimes characterized as "the most sumptuous church in the world."

Designed by an unidentified Gothic master in 1386, and in process of building for more than a century under the direction of German and French architects, the church naturally acquired late Gothic characteristics. The exterior is prolific with verticals and with statuary. Finials are numerous but irregular in height to the point of giving the structure a meaningless skyline. The interior has lace-like vaulting and is rich in dazzling decoration. But at the same time, because of the mandatory recommendations of a number of Italian consultants, the building has features which distinguish it from true northern Gothic. One is its lesser height; another, the sexpartite vertical division of its façade; and still another, the weakness of its buttresses both structurally and aesthetically. The remarkable fact is that so much Gothic went into an Italian edifice during the first century of the Renaissance.[7]

Farther south, the continuation of the Gothic into the period of the Renaissance is to be found in the cathedral of Florence, the *Santa Maria del Fiore*. True, it was begun in 1294, but its construction continued long into the Renaissance without any major structural adjustments that might indicate resistance to the medieval style.

The original plan of Arnolfo di Campio yielded in 1357 to an enlarged one of Francesco Talente and the construction proceeded on into the second quarter of the fifteenth century when Brunelleschi added the celebrated dome (1420–1434). Admittedly the dome is a declaration of Renaissance architectural style, as is the octagonal crossing which replaced the usual rectangle produced by the intersection of the transept and the nave, but the rest of the structure conforms in principles to the Italian Gothic, with its wide-open spacing between the columns, its unmolded arches, its bracketed cornices, and with its lack, in the interior, of an adequate sense of scale.

The continuation of the Gothic in the Renaissance period was not limited to religious structures. Secular buildings also, both civic and private, continued to be erected in the Gothic style throughout most of the era. Among the civic structures the outstanding examples are the Cloth Hall at Ypres; the town halls of Bruges, Brussels, and Louvain; the Exchange in Frieburg-im-Breisgau; and the Palais de Justice in Rouen.[8] As to private buildings, one need only recall the paintings of those picturesque German, Dutch, and French towns with the multiple-storied houses hugging the crooked streets, or the country houses of the French and English gentry to reassure oneself of the persistence of the Gothic style.

Renaissance Style: Properties

Strong as the Gothic remained during the Renaissance, it, of course, did not go unchallenged. The Renaissance gave birth to a new style, an imitation of the classical fashion. Humanism evoked as much admiration for classical art as for classical letters. Architects sought out Roman ruins, measured them, and analyzed them with the help of the treatise of Vitruvius, the *De Architectura*. Then they prepared books elucidating the principles of classical architecture and illustrating them with designs for palaces and churches — Leon Battista Alberti's *De re aedificatoria* (1485), Giacomo Vignola's *Regole delle cinqui ordini* (1562), Andrea Palladio's *Quattro libri dell' architettura* (1573), and Sebastiano Serlio's *Quinto libri d'architectura* (after 1537).[9] And before long their enthusiasm led them to try their hands at the classical style itself.

The new style was notably different from the Gothic. Philosophically it consisted of the modeling of mass as against the Gothic management of space, and so solid walls took the place of skeletal framework. Moreover, it stood for equipoise and authority as against Gothic restlessness and movement, and so planes, centrality, strict geometric figures (circles and squares), and equally strict metrical relationships — both based on the anthropometric principle that proportions of the human body should be the basic unit in the structure[10] — replaced lines, axes, and disproportionate ratios. Structurally the pointed arch yielded to the round arch; the segmented ceiling, to the more ponderous barrel vault; and the soaring towers, to the encompassing dome. Aesthetically the agitated surfaces of the Gothic were replaced by disciplined grace brought about by the use of the quiet Greek orders and by a play on regularity, horizontality, symmetry, and harmony. In addition, the classic decorative motifs of acanthus leaves, scrolls, and egg and dart moldings replaced the Gothic tracery. The end product, therefore, was noticeably monumental.[11]

In addition to these general properties of classical architecture as distinguished from those of the Gothic style, one very notable difference appeared in the form of the church. The traditional cross was replaced by a centralized (rounded) structure, and the reason, as Wittkower explains it on the basis of the Renaissance theorists on architecture, was the Neoplatonic-Pythagorean concept, then current, that perfection translated into geometry takes the form of a circle, the very form which was thought to represent God himself.[12]

Renaissance and Gothic Styles Combined

The first stage in the appearance of the new style was the use of some of its decorative elements as an overlay on the Gothic, with only an occasional invasion of the fundamentals. As might be expected, this stage appeared in Italy first and went further than elsewhere in Europe.

Three examples of such an adaptation are to be found in the church of St. Francis at Rimini, in the Pazzi Chapel at Florence, and in the Palazzi Corner-Spinelli at Venice. In the first a Gothic church is provided with a classical dress, the old sides having been covered with new arcades (Plate 7). In the second, Alberti combined the Roman arch with a Roman wall to provide a classic façade for an old Gothic church; and in the third Conducci dressed the front of a traditional medieval palace with a veneer of classical forms. In themselves the arcade of the Rimini church and the façades of the Pazzi Chapel and of

PLATE 1 — *San Maclou,* Rouen. By permission of N. D. Giraudon.

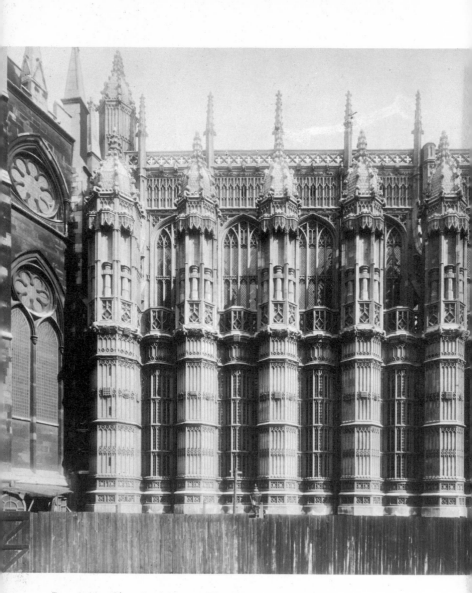

PLATE 2 — Chapel of Henry VII, Westminster Abbey. By permission of Marburg-Art Reference Bureau.

PLATE 3 — Chapel of Henry VII, Westminster Abbey. Fan vaulting. By permission of Marburg-Art Reference Bureau.

PLATE 4 — St. Barbara at Kuttenberg. S-curve vaulting. By permission of Bildarchiv Foto Marburg.

PLATE 5 — *Frauenkirche* at Munich. Brick-wall church. By permission of Bruckmann-Art Reference Bureau.

PLATE 6 — *Frauenkirche* at Munich. Brick-wall church. By
permission of Bruckmann-Art Reference Bureau.

Plate 7 — Church of St. Francis at Rimini. By permission
of Alinari-Art Reference Bureau.

PLATE 8 — *Château de Blois,* Wing of Louis XII. Exterior façade. By permission of N. D. Giraudon.

PLATE 9 — *Château de Blois*. Interior view. By permission of
N. D. Giraudon.

PLATE 10 — *St. Peter's* at Rome. Interior. By permission of
Alinari-Art Reference Bureau.

Plate 11 — Rucellai Palace at Florence. By permission of Alinari-Art Reference Bureau.

Palazzi Corner-Spinelli are excellent classical monuments; but for an age which pleaded so much for architectural purity and harmony to have yielded to this adulteration is quite incredible; incredible, that is, unless it is assumed that in practice the Renaissance architects were less opposed to the traditional than their theorizing might imply. They could even undertake the integration of the Gothic with Roman with unhappy results, as Alberti's façade for the *Santa Maria Novella* in Florence clearly illustrates.[13]

Another example of this adaptation in Italy, but one which invaded the structure basically, was Brunelleschi's dome on the cathedral of Florence. On a structure with a strong longitudinal axis he superimposed an element that properly belongs to a centralized church. The result is a glaring contradiction and, indeed, in the interior, the dome is aesthetically ineffective. The appeal of the Renaissance style was apparently strong enough to overcome any apprehension about the possibility of incongruity. On the other hand, it is to be noted that the dome, though a Renaissance product, is actually constructed around eight Gothic vaults,[14] and as such is an example of a Renaissance form depending on a medieval principle.

In northern Europe the use of classical features in Gothic church architecture was confined largely to decorations. An occasional tomb or chapel of classical design, some classical carvings on the screens, a Roman column or pilaster flanking an occasional door are the only Renaissance features that invaded the old churches.[15] In some Spanish churches this incorporation of the new with the old went further. The cathedral of Granada, for example, which Enrique de Egas began in 1520 as a Gothic structure, was given, under the succeeding architect, Diego de Silow, "classic bases, beautiful Corinthian capitals, [and] delicate variations of the classic entablature."[16] But on the whole, even in Spain this adaptation of the Renaissance style was not extensive, as the new dynastic connections with Burgundy opened Spain to a vigorous wave of Flemish Gothic art which tended to counter the invasion of Italianate style.

But while the embodiment of the new in religious buildings was limited, in secular architecture the invasion was bolder. The Gothic town hall of Bremen was renovated in 1612 with the addition of an arcade, producing a picturesque combination of a tall Gothic roof with regular ground-hugging Roman arches. The ducal residence at Heidelberg acquired a strong classical façade but retained on the façade the tiered top so characteristic of German and Dutch Gothic town houses.[17] The wing which Louis XII added to the *Château de Blois* (Plates 8 and 9) combined the high roof cut with dormers and topped by numerous large chimneys, the mullioned windows, pinnacles, spirelets, and lavish Flamboyant tracery — all Gothic — with strong horizontal lines, rhythmical spacing of windows, an impressive arched entrance, and some classical decorative motifs on the piers of the arcade — all classical. The result is a predominantly Gothic structure openly accepting the new style. The same may be said of the wing which Francis I added to the same Chateau, though the extent of the classical is greater.[18] Similarly typical is the Chateau of Azay-le-Rideau, one of the country residences popularly regarded as Renaissance. Renaissance are the orders that dress the entrance and the windows, and Renaissance is the horizontality that is suggested by the prominent stringcourses which run along the wall. Yet the towers, the dormers, and the high-chimneyed roof are Gothic. Gothic also is the want of plasticity of the wall treatment, and the prominence of the verticals caused by staggering the orders one on top of another from story to story.[19] Additional examples could be cited — Margaret of Austria's palace at Malines and the church *Zur schönen Maria* in Regensburg — but these few are enough to show us how the new style was being received and how late in the Renaissance the reception came.

Renaissance Style with Little or No Gothic

The second stage of development appeared when the new Renaissance style replaced the Gothic either completely or almost completely. In Italy this stage was simultaneous with the first stage just surveyed; in the remainder of Europe it followed the first stage and barely made its appearance as the Renaissance period came to a close.

CHURCH ARCHITECTURE In Italy the new style first appeared in the erection of numerous centralized churches. Brunelleschi's *Santa Maria degli Angeli* at Florence set the example. Alberti's *San Sebastiano* at

Mantua, and Giuliano da Sangallo's *Santa Maria delle Carceri* at Prato strengthened the trend. By the end of the fifteenth century it was well established, and thereafter "a real avalanche of centralized structures followed."[20]

Two illustrations of this second stage may be selected for closer examination: Giuliano da Sangallo's *Santa Maria delle Carceri* at Prato and Palladio's at Macer.

The first is in the form of a Greek cross so proportioned that the overlap of the two arms forms a square. On the arms of the cross rise flat-surfaced walls divided horizontally by an entablature, producing the effect of two stories, and decorated at all corners and at door frames with simple pilasters. Covering the structure are gabled roofs over the arms of the cross and a dome over the intersection. In the interior, broad, clean-surfaced arches, each pierced by a rectangular window, span the arms of the cross, and the dome, pierced by regularly spaced round windows, is fitted on these arches. The simple classical decoration of the outside is matched by equally simple pilasters and an entablature which runs around the entire structure. Beautifully proportioned, the whole is a play on two geometric figures, the square and the circle, and is in accord with the theories of the Neoplatonic architects.[21]

Palladio's church also belongs to the centralized type, but it differs from Sangallo's building in at least three notable ways. In form it is circular and is patterned after the Pantheon. It is elevated on a high platform to symbolize the detachment of God's temple from the mundane. Finally it is prefaced with an impressive classical portico in the fashion of *templum in antis*, with six Corinthian columns supporting an entablature and a pediment, and is reached by a monumental stairway extending along the whole breadth of the portico.[22]

Although the number of centralized churches was great, the traditional oblong church with pronounced nave and aisles was not wholly supplanted. The age-old meaning of the Mass and other religious rites did not change, and the old form, that of the Latin cross, was believed to accommodate itself more appropriately to them than the new round churches.[23] In consequence, the basilican type of church continued to be built. Such for example are Alberti's celebrated *Sant' Andrea* at Mantua, Brunelleschi's *San Lorenzo* at Florence, Biaggio Rossetti's

San Francesco at Ferrara, and Palladio's *Il Redentore* at Venice. But though these structures accent the nave, they have enough Renaissance properties to be recognized as new. They all have domes; their aisles are not prominent and often are even replaced by chapels; their supports, both piers and arches, are monumental and classic in style; their decoration is all classical; and their façades, sometimes double, with a large one superimposed over a broad one to cover effectively both the nave and the aisles, copy the elevations of the ancient temples.[24]

Resembling this type of church is the great *St. Peter's* at Rome. It was started by the ambitious Pope Julius II who wanted an edifice whose grandeur would symbolize the glory of God on high and the paramountcy of the Church of Rome on earth. Its original designer was Bramante, and his design called for a modified Greek cross, the modification consisting of the addition of a small replica of the whole structure in the angles between the arms and a square chamber at each of the two diagonal axes, and a powerful dome over the center. In this form it conformed to the centralized type. But while most of this design was retained, the masterbuilders who succeeded, Sangallo, Raphael, and Michelangelo, added three bays to one of the arms and so transformed the structure into a combination of a centralized church and a church with a nave. The result is a composite of the two Renaissance styles described above.

In accord with the new style, the basic elements of the church are classical. The huge Corinthian order, the tremendous coffered Roman vaults, the columnar drum which supports the dome, and, of course, the great dome itself are all classical. Also classical are the deployment of mass and the resulting monumentality (Plate 10). Yet the awesomeness of this monumentality combined with the dissolution of strict symmetry and with the extravagance of the interior decoration are Baroque in spirit. Intended to impress, the structure overwhelms; and such was never the intention of the temples of antiquity nor, indeed, of the true Renaissance churches.

The rest of Europe has far less to show in the way of Renaissance churches. Indeed, except for Spain, the other lands were in no position to embark upon extensive construction of churches. In Germany and England, the tension and conflict between the Catholic church and the rising Protestantism naturally precluded the erection of churches. France, although successful in stemming the Reformation movement, did so only after thirty years of bitter civil wars between the Huguenots and the Catholics, and so it, too, was in no position to engage in church-building during the era. Nevertheless, here and there, some churches were built in the new style.

In France only two or three such religious structures were erected. The Italian Primaticcio, in the service of the French royal family, designed the Chapelle des Valois, a two-storied mausoleum for Queen Catherine de'Medici and her family, in the circular form, with classical columns and arches and a Renaissance dome. The building, however, was never completed as designed, for its erection was abandoned when the second story was finished. Another example is the chapel which Philibert de l'Orme, who had spent three years in Italy studying architecture, designed for the Chateau of Anet. It, too, is circular in form — even the marble stones of its pavement are laid out in circular arcs — and is topped by a dome.[25] There are churches in France that conform to the Renaissance style but they were erected after 1600. In Germany two examples may be cited, the Chapel of the Fuggers in *St. Anna,* Augsburg, and *St. Michael's* at Munich, at least in the interior;[26] but in England, if the silence on this matter of John Summerson's recent work, *Architecture in Britain 1530–1830,*[27] is any indication, there is not a single significant example that belongs to the Renaissance years. To be sure, the churches of Iñigo Jones and Christopher Wren are Renaissance in style, but they are seventeenth-century structures and fall outside the Renaissance period proper. In Spain the examples are more common. Charles V's conquest of Italy naturally expanded the current of Italianate Renaissance style into Spain, and his personal predilection for it stimulated the flow still more. Some Italians received commissions in Spain, and Spanish artists worked and studied in Italy. With architects like Alonso Berruguete (he studied for some fifteen years with Bramante and Michelangelo) promoting the new style, it was bound to attain a notable expression. This it did in the famous Escorial which Juan Bautista and Juan de Herrera built for Philip II between 1563 and 1584.

Built in honor of St. Lawrence on whose feast Philip's army won a victory over the French at St. Quentin, the Escorial was a vast complex consisting of a monastery, church, college, and a palace each facing a court. The whole is enclosed by a flat wall punctuated by three tiers of regularly spaced windows and ending at the corners in rectangular towers. The result is severe and prison-like. But this is from the outside. On the inside the several buildings present a pleasanter aspect. Their style is wholly Renaissance. The church, 340 feet by 200 feet, is not quite of the centralized type but it conforms in its façade, dome, and arches to the late Roman style. The other buildings with their entablatures and rows of windows and simple uniform arcades emphasize the horizontal, in keeping with Renaissance Italian palaces. And the little, domed pavilion in the cloister imitates, on a small scale, the circular churches so dear to the humanist architects of Renaissance Italy. Finally, the simplicity of these structures and their symmetry could not have been improved upon by the Italians themselves.

SECULAR ARCHITECTURE In comparison with church architecture, secular architecture in the Renaissance style was more prevalent. Apparently the Renaissance society had enough old churches standing in good condition not to require many new ones, whereas it needed to replace the old, outmoded castles — which were no longer as useful as they were in feudal times — with more livable quarters, and so it built more residences. And this need to build provided an opportunity for the adoption of a new style. Even northern Europe showed considerable enthusiasm for it.

As in the case of church-building, Italy led the way in the construction of residences in the Renaissance style. The wealthy merchants, pretentious churchmen, and ambitions despots all called for new and impressive palaces and country villas, and Italy became dotted with secular buildings in the new style. It should be added further that many of these people were humanists and patrons of humanist artists and were therefore quite receptive to the style of antiquity.

To describe one of these palaces is to describe them all. True, there was variation, but it was mostly in the play of the façade and in the choice of classic dress. In fundamentals they were much alike (Plate 11).

In general, Renaissance palaces were built about the four sides of a courtyard like the Roman peristyle residences. In general, also, they were two or three stories high, with a heavily rusticated ground floor used for stabling horses, storing supplies, and housing servants and workshops, and with more smoothly surfaced second and third stories used for living quarters. These stories were further distinguished from each other by prominent stringcourses or entablatures separating them and by the difference in the classical dress with which the regularly spaced windows were framed. Finally, many of them were topped with large cornices. They all emphasized the horizontal axis, simplicity, proportion, and the pleasing deployment of mass. On the inside of the quadrangle there was an arcade in the Roman style. In the interior the rooms were usually simply appointed, the principal decorations consisting of wall frescoes.

As to the variations in the façades — other than the variations in, and the arrangement of, the orders used, and in the classic dress framing the windows — one noticeable difference deserves mention. Whereas some of these residences have their orders imbedded in the walls, others have, in addition, an impressive columnar portico in the style of classical temples and a single monumental staircase, or two smaller ones, leading to it. An examination of the pictures of Palladio's villas will convey the idea better than any lengthy description.[28]

Outside Italy, France led northern Europe in the use of Renaissance style for secular architecture. Francis I's enthusiasm for this style spread to his courtiers and to other nobility. Its popularity was further enhanced by the treatises which Serlio and Philibert de l'Orme prepared on the classical orders and by the buildings which they designed. The result was that by the middle of the sixteenth century secular architecture in France departed sufficiently from the Gothic to be classed as Renaissance. However, it should be noted that the buildings which were wholly in that style were relatively few, even as late as 1600.

Omitting the Chateau of Chambord which Francis I ordered in 1519 as essentially medieval — bastionlike round towers flanking its entrance and guarding its corners, a crowded and irregular skyline, and a moat, despite the arches, the double stringcourses running the whole length of the walls, and regularly spaced windows — we may examine three structures as representative of the Renaissance style: Serlio's Chateau of Aney-le-France, Lescot's Louvre, and Baptiste de Cerceau's Hotel Lamoignon.

Serlio's chateau is a combination of the medieval French Gothic and Italian Renaissance. The medieval features are the rectangular towers that project at each end of the building, the impression of verticality which results from the placement of pilasters one directly above the other and one for each of the three stories in the towers, and the prominence of the tall roof, the tall chimneys, and the dormer windows. Its Renaissance properties are the longitudinal axis of the main part of the structure, the prominent stringcourses that run the whole length of the building, towers included, and the varying classical dress of the windows. The symmetry and simplicity also stamp it as Italian. Furthermore, originally the wall of the ground floor was heavily rusticated, though the picture of the present building does not show this.[29]

Lescot's part of the Louvre is free from the medieval properties still noticeable in Serlio's chateau. All features of this court are classic, yet the total result lacks the monumentality of the Italian Renaissance palaces it imitates; instead, the structure appears to be overcrowded and florid. Certainly the carvings around the windows of the third story and on the face of the crowning arches at the ends and in the middle of the building are in excess. The building therefore shows signs of the approaching Baroque.[30]

Baptiste de Cerceau's Hotel Lamoignon is an example of a private town residence in the Renaissance style. No detailed description is necessary as in general the house conforms to the new style, but two features deserve to be pointed out. One of these is the use of huge orders that run the entire height of the two stories. This gives the façade a character of monumentality so lacking in the Louvre, and this is still further enhanced by the absence of pediments or arches over the windows in the first two stories. The other is an unclassical feature, the interruption of the entablature by dormer windows.[31]

East of France the Renaissance style in secular architecture was not as strong before the seventeenth century. Relatively few structures were erected wholly in the new style. However, a number of them adopted so much of the new as to justify their inclusion in this stage.

Among these, civic buildings were apparently in the majority, particularly in the Low Countries. Hendrick de Keyser's Town Hall at Delft and Cornelius Floris' Town Hall at Antwerp are especially good examples of an appreciative adoption of Renaissance architectural properties.[32] They are certainly more classical than the Town Hall at Bremen which was built later but which retained the tall Gothic roof.

In addition to these, other notable examples are the Plassenburg near Kulmbach, the Landhaus at Graz and Schloss Hartenfels zu Torgau.[33] However, though properly classed as Renaissance, they lack the chasteness of the true classic. Their use of decoration is excessive, and in this they point to the Baroque.

In England the new style in secular architecture was introduced by the leading courtiers connected with the promotion of Protestantism, especially the Lord Protector Somerset and the Duke of Northumberland, and their builder-protégés, like John Shute whom the latter sent to Italy to study architecture for three years. This style was continued by the courtiers of Elizabeth, some of whom built their country residences simply to be able to receive Elizabeth in high fashion when she went on her regular peregrinations.[34] Important county officials followed suit, and an occasional civic structure added to the total.

The movement found direction in the architectural treatise of Serlio,[35] and in that of John Shute — *The First and Chief Groundes of Architecture* — who drew heavily on the former. To be sure, Vitruvius was also known. But it also drew quite freely from contemporary architectural trends in France and in the Low Countries. Yet the style is not wholly borrowed from the Italian nor from the Italian as mediated through France and the Low Countries. It was given some national properties, such as the extraversion.

Although the structures differed from each other, they possessed some characteristics in common. They were generally two or three stories in height, with the stories clearly marked by prominent string-courses. Most of them made use of the classical orders, pilasters principally, but with greater reserve than did the French. They employed glass extensively, and their windows were heavily mullioned. Very often they employed bay windows, usually one row of rectangular bays on each side of the main entrance. Many of them had towerlike bays at the ends. Finally, most of those erected after 1550 were built to look out, rather than to look in, upon an interior court as were the Italian palaces, and this abandonment of the central court led to the "H" form of building. Then, as in France, many of them had the long hall or gallery.

Among the significant residences built in this style several deserve to be singled out. Somerset House in London (1547–1552) stands out as probably the first English house to be "composed altogether within classical discipline."[36] It also reveals the French influence in the superimposed orders in the gateway and the coupling of the windows in the end bays. Longleat Hall erected by Sir John Thynne is noted for its perfect symmetry, the rhythmical employment of the orders, the extensive fenestration, and the superb balustrade.[37] Sir Francis Willoughby's Wollaton Hall is an example of the combination of Italian through Serlio and of Dutch through DeVries. It has an air of surfeit pretension, while its elevated central portion with its cylindrical turrets and the pinnacled tops of its two side towers impart to it a castle-like appearance.[38] The House of the Elder Burley is distinguished by the polygonal towers that flank the entrance and the superimposed bay windows that top the entrance. The narrow slitlike windows in these towers are more suggestive of a castle than of a residence.[39]

Civic buildings in the Renaissance style are fewer, but one may be mentioned. Gresham's Royal Exchange stands out as the finest example of the new style as the Flemish cultivated it. Its builder was Henri de Pas of Antwerp, and much of the stone was imported from Flanders. Its distinguishing features were the Doric arcade — weak and effeminate looking — facing the courtyard, the Ionic pilasters of the second story, and the numerous little dormers one for each arch. To one authority this Flemish structure "shows that the classical or Italianate architecture, that was all the rage abroad, was not fully received into England."[40]

The style of these several structures has been called "new" and "Renaissance." It is "new" in the sense that it is quite different from Gothic, and it is "Renaissance" in the sense that it employed some "Renaissance" principles — symmetry, horizontality, simplicity — and classic orders. Yet to compare any of the structures built in this style with

Iñigo Jones's Banqueting House and the Queen's House or with the Lindsey House which were all built in the following century is to be struck by a great difference between true Renaissance style and a style which looks to the Renaissance but seems not to have quite forgotten the perpendicular Gothic. Perhaps, therefore, the designation "Renaissance" for the Tudor architecture is a bit previous. It certainly cannot apply to the architecture of the more modest manor houses and townhouses which continued to employ the traditional style.[41]

1. The most scholarly treatment in English of the evolution and the nature of the Gothic is Paul Frankl's *Gothic Architecture*, trans. Dieter Pevsner, vol. XIX of *The Pelican History of Art* (Baltimore, Maryland: Penguin Books Inc., 1962). He insists that the style evolved naturally as a result of attempts to meet certain structural problems arising out of the need to expand the churches to accommodate more priests and people and more elaborate rituals, and not as a by-product of scholasticism. For a brief analysis of the principles see John Ives Sewall, *A History of Western Art* (New York: Henry Holt and Co., 1953), 472–81.

2. This rationality is elucidated by Erwin Panofsky in his *Gothic Architecture and Scholasticism* (New York: Meridian Books, 1957). But cf. Frankl, *op. cit.*, 220–42, 260–70, and his *The Gothic; Literary Sources and Interpretations through Eight Centuries* (Princeton: Princeton University Press, 1960), 86–110.

3. Cf. Frankl, *Gothic Architecture*, 241.

4. See Fred H. Crossley, *English Church Design, 1040–1540* (London: B. T. Batsford, Ltd., 1945), 73–79 and plates 96–102.

5. Frankl, *Gothic Architecture*, plates 168–70.

6. *Ibid.*, 139 and plate 23.

7. For a revealing account of the erection of the cathedral of Milan see Frankl, *The Gothic; Literary Sources. . . .*, 63–83.

8. Talbot F. Hamlin, *Architecture through the Ages* (New York: G. P. Putnam's Sons, 1940), plate opposite p. 279.

9. For an excellent treatment of Alberti and Palladio consult Rudolf Wittkower, *Architectural Principles in the Age of Humanism*, no. XIX of *Studies of the Warburg Institute* (London, 1949), *passim*. On Serlio see Anthony Blunt, *Art and Architecture in France, 1500 to 1700*, vol. IV of *The Pelican History of Art* (Baltimore, Maryland: Penguin Books, 1954), 45–50.

10. For a brief analysis of this principle see Wittkower in *The New Cambridge Modern History* (Cambridge University Press, 1957), 129–30.

11. A stimulating interpretation of the Renaissance architecture which is at the same time a vigorous defense of it against the attacks of the Romanticists is Geoffrey Scott's *The Architecture of Humanism* (2d ed.; Garden City, New York: Doubleday and Co., Inc., 1954). This is a reprint of the 1924 edition.

12. For fuller explanation see Wittkower, *op. cit.*, 12–28. The reader might compare this with the symbolism of the Gothic cathedral as summarized in Henry Osborn Taylor's *The Medieval Mind* (4th ed.; London: Macmillan and Co., Ltd., 1938), II, 102–8.

13. Wittkower, *op. cit.*, plates 16a and c, and pp. 26–41.

14. See Sewall, *op. cit.*, 632, for a fuller description of the construction.

15. For some examples, see Blunt, *op. cit.*, 63, and plates 1, 2a, 4, 5, 12, 14, 15, 21, 36a. For examples of rural churches in France adding some classical features as a result of reconstruction see Yvonne Bezard, *La vie rurale dans le sud de la région Parisienne de 1450 a 1560* (Paris: Firmin-Didot et cie., 1929), 275–6.

16. Hamlin, *op. cit.*, 388.

17. For pictures of these see Hamlin, *op. cit.*, plate opposite 370.

18. Hamlin, *op. cit.*, 356–8, provides a fuller description of this mixture of the new with the old.

19. Over-all view in *ibid.*, opposite 360; a close-up view of the entrance in Blunt, *op. cit.*, plate 6.

20. Wittkower, *op. cit.*, 18. For an enumeration see nn. 7 and 8 thereon. Excellent photographs of several of these may be found in Julius Baum, *Baukunst und dekorative Plastik der Frührenaissance in Italien* (Stuttgart: Verlag Julius Hoffman, 1926), 2 ff.

21. Wittkower (*op. cit.*, plates 7 and 8) has pictures of the ground plan, interior, and exterior.

22. Pictures in *ibid.*, plates 9 and 10.

23. Wittkower (*op. cit.*, 27–28) cites the the names of the proponents of the cruciform church and reports their arguments.

24. For an analysis of these façades and their pictures see Wittkower, *op. cit.*, 80–87.

25. On these two examples see Blunt, *op. cit.*, 58, 60–61, and plates 32 and 36.

26. Pictures in Eberhard Hempel, *Geschichte der Deutschen Baukunst* (München: F. Bruckmann Verlag, 1949), 284, 308.

27. Published in 1954 as a volume in the *Pelican History of Art*.

28. Some of these can be seen in Wittkower, *op. cit.*, plates 22–25, 27–30.

29. Compare Serlio's design with the present structure as reproduced in Blunt, *op. cit.*, 49 and plate 28.

30. History of the building and its description in *ibid.*, 51–53. Picture on plate 29a.

31. *Ibid.*, plate 61B.

32. Pictures in Hamlin, *op. cit.*, plate opposite 371.

33. Hempel, *op. cit.*, plates 257 and 262.

34. Evidence for this is Summerson, *op. cit.*, 30–31.

35. See above, p. 127.

36. Summerson, *op. cit.*, 18. Picture in *ibid.*, plates 10 and 11.

37. *Ibid.*, plates 14 and 15.

38. *Ibid.*, plate 16.

39. *Ibid.*, plate 21b.

40. J. B. Black, *The Oxford History of England, The Reign of Elizabeth, 1558–1603* (Oxford: Clarendon Press, 1949), 256.

41. See, for example, the buildings represented in Summerson, *op. cit.*, plates 32 (A), (B), 35 (A), (B), 36 (A), (B).

IX

Sculpture

I N THE Middle Ages sculpture was an integral part of architecture. At first, indeed, it was carved out of the very stones used in the construction of the buildings. Only from the thirteenth century on did some sculptured pieces begin to free themselves, but seldom did they attain complete freedom with an aesthetic function of their own. But whether free or not sculpture simply served to add a symbolical vocabulary to the buildings of which it was such an intimate part.

Because of this integration sculpture passed through the same two developments as architecture. Until the twelfth century it was Romanesque, and from the latter part of the 1100's it yielded progressively to the Gothic style.

Romanesque and Gothic Styles and Their Properties

Since the Romanesque was not a living style on the eve of the Renaissance, a summary description of it will suffice. Its principal subject was Christ, either of the Apocalypse, or of the Ascension, or of the Last Judgment. It was thoroughly integrated into the structure of the buildings, and because its figures were adapted to the space available, license of form was common, particularly exaggerated elongation. In general, it possessed little realism but much fancifulness and symbolism, and was highly emotional. Finally, it was carved in bold relief but with unsophisticated craftsmanship. To be added to these characteristics is the fact that its source was not the immediate world of nature but the designs and descriptions of animals and peoples of the oriental fables as they found their way into medieval bestiaries, or the human models represented in the Carolingian manuscripts. It should be known also that the style spread to all western Europe through the widespread expansion of the Cluniac houses and through the increase of pilgrim traffic but that it attained its finest expression in southern France. For two outstanding examples the reader is referred to Giselbert's tympanum of St. Lazare at Autun and to the portal of the church at Moissac.[1]

Gothic-styled sculpture, on the other hand, was still in use on the eve of the Renaissance and requires a more comprehensive treatment.

In the first place, it was a steadily changing style, even though the changes took shape slowly and were not radical. In general, it passed through three stages. The first, called the Early Gothic and extending until the thirteenth century, is characterized by simplicity of design, formality, and idealization. Like the Romanesque, it is still very much a part of the architecture. When it freed itself a little more from the architectural lines, depicted action better, and admitted some individualization, of the heads at least, it reached the second stage, called the High Gothic. This lasted until the fourteenth century when the Late Gothic stage began. During this last stage, which continued into the Renaissance period, it acquired considerable freedom, in some cases even complete freedom, and tended toward elegance and mannerism or toward sensationalism and "the gift of tears," as the late Professor Mâle expressed it.

Although yielding to these changes, the Gothic was possessed of several significant lasting properties. One of these, almost as prevalent as in the case of the Romanesque, was its expository and didactic role in religion. In general, its themes were scriptural or hagiographical and its spirit devotional, though humanism was not unknown. Another was its obvious, though progressively decreasing, adaptation to the lines of architecture. The verticality of Gothic structures would not permit distracting elements, hence all parts, including sculptures, were given a linear axis and fitted smoothly into an integrated whole. A third property, and this was of great significance for subsequent development of art, was its tendency to be guided by nature, at least as to form if not as to scale or as to setting. Put another way, Gothic sculpture tried to be representational rather than imaginary. Fourthly, it was capable of narration and dramatic expression and was therefore less inclined to symbolism than the Romanesque.

Of these four properties the last two were really preparing the bases for modern art, particularly if realism of detail was added to them as sometimes happened. For attention to detail and adherence to nature, even if limited, could lead to an awareness of the reality of the subject as a whole. And once this was attained and regularly adopted as a basic principle, then the Representative Convention of modern art was born.[2]

For some fine expressions of Gothic the reader should examine the sculpture of the cathedrals of Chartres, Amiens, Paris, Rheims, Wells, and Bamberg.[3] Since all of these masterpieces were fashioned from a hundred to two hundred years before the Renaissance, we cannot take time here to examine them. It is the Gothic which persisted during the Renaissance that requires examination.

Gothic Style during the Renaissance

Pure Gothic in the late style continued in Italy until the second quarter of the fifteenth century and in the rest of Europe actually into the sixteenth century. Much of it retained the traditional properties described above, but some developed into two distinct genre.

REALISTIC GENRE One genre was that of realism, facial realism especially, somewhat similar to the realism of the contemporary Flemish painting. An excellent example is the statue of Charles V of France. Sovereign and of great renown though he was, Charles was not idealized but depicted in his natural appearance, hooked nose and all. Another is the effigy of that great savior of France, Bertrand du Guesclin.[4] In England many of the statues in Henry VII's chapel have the same powerful treatment.[5] Faces and personalities are strongly individualized, and drapery is heavy and adds to the sense of reality. In Germany this realistic genre had started a century earlier — in the thirteenth century — and is well exemplified in the statues of the German knight in the cathedral of Bamberg and of Margrave Ekkehard and his wife in Naumburg Cathedral (Plate 12). It continued into the Renaissance period and attained excellence in the works of Veit Stoss, who, like Copernicus, is claimed both by the Poles and Germans, and of Adam Krafft. Stoss is explosive with dramatic intensity which he attained in part by agitated forms and draperies, by rigorous realism, and deep modeling. His best creation is the *Death and Assumption of the Virgin,* in St. Mary's, Cracow.[6] Krafft's work is less agitated but for that reason less theatrical and therefore more sincere. Nevertheless, his realism is overdone as appears in his *Stations of the Cross*.[7] Burgundy has an unusually good representation in Clause de Werve's *pleurants* around the tomb of Philip the Bold,[8] and Flanders, in the *Nicodemus* of the Sepulchre of Solesmes by Michel Colombe.[9] With Italy and Spain offering little in this style, it may be concluded that the realistic genre of the Late Gothic after 1350 was quite widespread, but not in Mediterranean Europe.

Related to this genre in sentiment if not in form is the sculpture which is surcharged with emotion. The numerous examples of the Pieta are of this type.[10] The body of Jesus, freed from the cross, is represented as broken, lifeless, and shocking, and the Virgin and the attendants are depicted as suffering immeasurable grief. While the Romanesque preferred to treat Christ as the Lord, and the High Gothic, as the source of compassion and love, the Late Gothic, particularly after 1350, often depicted him as the Sufferer. The sombre and the pathetic were commingled to produce an image of crushing emotional reality (Plate 13).

Finally, combining the realism of appearance with appalling emotion were some tomb monuments. The bodies are represented as gaunt and mummylike, ravaged by death. Direful to the eye, they are equally shocking to the emotions.[11] It should be observed, however, that the nude tomb effigy was not common, the deceased being represented, according to custom, in their professional robes, with features idealized and hands clasped in prayer.[12]

INTERNATIONAL STYLE The other genre was the very opposite of the realistic style. It combined the cult of the aristocratic with the graceful and the tender and seemed to reflect the social graces of the fifteenth-century polite society. It is reputed to have originated when the canons of Late Gothic art were invaded by the gracility of Simone Martini's Sienese art. This was accomplished in the Mediterranean lands where the North met the South, and from there it spread throughout most of western Europe. From this widespread extension it has been given the name "International Style."[13]

More common in painting, the International Style did not produce many noteworthy pieces of large sculpture. One of the earliest examples, and illustrating the northern component which entered the composition of this style, is the *Notre Dame de Paris* (Plate 14). Although the statue represents the Madonna, the representation is defective, as the subject turns out to be a pretty girl regally draped and crowned and holding a doll-like baby. Lacking the spirit appropriate to motherhood and to godliness, and decoratively attired, the subject is really an expression of "prettied" elegance and social decorum. From France this type spread to Germany where it deteriorated into sheer attempts at prettiness.[14] In Italy it is represented by Nino Pisano's Madonna of the *S. Maria Novella*, Florence,[15] and by Giovanni di Balduccio's Madonna at Cremona.[16] But here it was early modified by local schools of art and by the infusion of classicism, though not completely, as the delicacy of Ghiberti's works is derived from it. In England there is the little-more human Alabaster Madonna of Flawford.[17] Only twenty-eight inches in height, the statuette is an example of the prevailing medium of the International Style, namely, small-sized reproductions for private use rather than large creations for public purpose.

Renaissance Style: Stages and Properties

While the Gothic was continuing, a new style began to make its appearance, namely, the "Renaissance" style. At first only a trickle and limited principally to Italy, in the fifteenth century this style grew in volume and began to exert influence beyond the Alps, and by the end of the next century it succeeded in displacing the Gothic. It is this style and its victory over the Gothic that has led to the conventional belief that sculpture in the age of the Renaissance was of the Renaissance style.

What then is the Renaissance style in sculpture? First, as in the case of Renaissance architecture, it is not a fixed style but one which changed with the times. In the fifteenth century its chief property was scientific realism, that is, as exact a reproduction of the subject as the knowledge of anatomy, of the materials, and of the laws of light would permit. As a corollary, this attention to reality naturally produced a second property, that of individualism. In the next century, with the mastery of form and representation at the command of the sculptors, realism gave ground to idealism. A mere reproduction of the form and even of its essential being seemed to the late fifteenth-century sculptors to be an insufficient function of art. What they desired was to employ form and representation as vehicles for their feelings and ideas, and, when they began to implement this philosophy of art, sculpture became idealized. This, of course, could be carried to excess, and the result may be sensationalism.

Although the Renaissance style was not static, it did have some properties which persisted throughout its life. One of these was classicism. Classical subjects (mostly mythological), classical heads and drapery, classical calm, classical proportions and broad modeling were constantly employed. Another property, also an element of classicism but so constant that it deserves to be recognized separately, was the use of the nude. So common was it that if Gothic sculpture may be considered as sculpture of drapery, the Renaissance sculpture well deserves to be called sculpture of the nude. A third property was humanism, which may be defined as the quality which reflects the worthiness and the grandeur of man per se. Man is made to appear significant in and by himself, rather than as a creature of God whose nobility is largely a function of his faith. Another property commonly attributed to Renaissance sculpture is that of secularism. While undoubtedly Renaissance sculpture is possessed of more secularism than medieval sculpture, the degree of difference is not so great as is generally asserted. Even a cursory examination of anthologies of Renaissance sculpture will reveal that a great percentage of the masterpieces represented old religious themes, while medieval sculpture on the other hand, even exclusive of the numerous effigies of princes, was not wholly given to religious themes.[18] It is possible therefore to overstress the secularism of Renaissance sculpture.

Renaissance and Gothic Styles Combined

Since the two styles, the Gothic and the Renaissance, overlapped in time, it was natural for the Renaissance style in its early stage to invade the prevailing Gothic and give rise to a hybrid style. It was also natural that in this composite the old style should be dominant with some sculptors and the new with others. And there are so many examples of this mixed style that it seems desirable to examine them country by country.

The new made its appearance in Italy first, and the sculptor who is credited with having introduced it on a significant scale was an Apulian who fashioned his masterpiece in Pisa and is therefore called Nicola Pisano (1205?–1278?).

Nicola's masterpiece is the pulpit in the Baptistry of Pisa. Its hexagonal panels are carved with scenes of the nativity, the adoration of the Magi, the presentation in the temple, the crucifixion, and the Last Judgment. The subjects then are scriptural and this, according to the conventional view, is medieval. But the figures are quite different from the traditional Gothic. The madonna is represented as Juno, and heads of male figures are copied after some antique model of Jupiter, and the angels look like Roman Victories. Even the horses are patterned after those of antiquity. Despite all this classicism, the crowded staging, the ampleness of drapery, and the lack of perspective are quite Gothic. The result therefore is a combination of the two styles with the antique elements predominating.[19]

Subsequent to this distinctive masterpiece, the role of the classic declined though it did not disappear completely. Nicolas' own second piece, the pulpit in the cathedral of Siena, shows this decline. The classic calm of the faces yields to Gothic emotionalism, the crowding is greater, and the narrative function is obvious. His son's work has more of the Gothic style. His façade of the cathedral of Siena has been recognized as perhaps "the finest bit of Gothic in Italy," and his pulpit in *Sant' Andrea* in Pistoja reveals his debt to the Late Gothic of France where he spent some ten years (1266–1277). Emotionalism and agitation are intensified, and the madonna with her mannered pose and her affectation resembles *Notre Dame de Paris*. Even more in line with the French Gothic is his pulpit in the cathedral of Pisa, so that he is charged with having "nipped his father's classical revival in the bud."[20] The works of Giovanni Balduccio in Milan; of the Campionesi, a family of marble-workers from Lake Lugano who sculptored for the della Scala family and reintroduced the equestrian statue; of Jacobello and Pier Paolo delle Messigne in Bologna and Venice; of Andrea di Ugolino in

Florence, who drew heavily on Giottesque form; of Lorenzo Maitani of Siena, particularly his designs for the façade of the cathedral of Orvieto; of the painter Andrea di Cione (Orcagna) — all reveal the same trend of intermingling the Gothic with some classic vocabulary, with the Gothic predominating, and all point to a growing mastery of the art. One has only to examine Orcagna's *Death of the Madonna* or the *Apostles* of Jacobello and Pier Paolo delle Messigne to see the advance and at the same time the persistence of Gothic properties.[21]

Following this group of workers in the hybrid style came a sculptor of first rank, Lorenzo Ghiberti (1378–1455), author of the famed Baptistry doors in Florence (Plate 15). His excellence lies in his superb craftsmanship, in his realistic management of space, and in his successful combination of Gothic charm and classical realism. Among his other Gothic properties may be mentioned the delicate linear movement, the attitudinized figures, the enveloping drapery, and narrational function. Together they give the impression of refined prettiness. Classical on the other hand are the nudes — in figure only, for the gracefulness is Gothic — the spaciousness which he employs to secure coherence, and the over-all restraint. He also employs some classical motifs in his decorations but only in the first doors, for the border of the second set is reported to have been derived from a Gothic book illumination. In general, then, Ghiberti is an exponent of the hybrid style, but one of superior merit. With him this style reaches its zenith in Italy. After him there could only be imitation or departure.

The imitators were of considerable merit, each emphasizing some particular properties. Luca della Robbia combined strong Gothic sentimentalism with classical simplicity; Andrea della Robbia emphasized illustration, elaboration, and wistfulness — all Gothicisms; Nino da Fiesole liked charm and daintiness; Agostino di Duccio subordinated realism to decorativeness, which, however, resembles Botticelli's beauty of line; while Giovanni Buon and his son Bartolommeo seemed to combine Venetian voluptuousness with Gothic mannerism.

In France the hybrid style was introduced by visiting sculptors from Italy. They brought classicism with them but allowed the French Gothic to invade their art. The result often turned out to be an unassimilated combination of the two styles. This is noticeable in the tomb for the

Duke of Orleans which Louis XII commissioned with Michele d'Aria and Girolamo Viscardi of Genoa and Donato di Battista Benti and Benedetto di Bartolommeo of Florence. The sarcophagus with its arcade is Italian, the recumbent body is French, while the French *pleurants* (official weepers) were replaced by figures of apostles whose ample drapes are Gothic.[22] A similar combination appears in the tomb which the brothers Giusti (they took the French name Juste) fashioned for Louis XII and Anne of Brittany. The kneeling figures, the *gisant* (recumbent effigy), the realism of the head of Louis' corpse are all French Gothic,[23] while the sarcophagus, the figure modeling, and the allegorical figures of the Virtues at the corners are classical though lacking in refinement. However, the spirit of the classic is more pervasive.[24] The tomb of the Amboise cardinals, directed by a native, Rouland de Roux, has only a minimum of classicism.[25] According to Blunt, "in its general form it is Gothic, in its wildness it is Flamboyant, in its detail it is Italianate."[26] Even Goujon who is generally regarded as a great exponent of the antique style could not wholly free himself from the persisting Gothic stream: his forms frequently take on the Gothic elongation, and his anatomies on occasion yield to the exigencies of monumental design.

Distinct from this group who worked in the hybrid style, in which the Gothic and classic components were inadequately assimilated, were two sculptors whose Gothic forms were infused with the spirit of Renaissance monumentality.

One, Michel Colombe, the probable creator of the Sepulchre of Solesmes, imparted to his work a breadth of concept and a feeling of reality only to be found in the monumental Renaissance masterpieces. The *Nicodemus*, for instance, though "Gothic in its homeliness," is "a truly Renaissance figure in its exaggerated personality."[27] Thus, with little classical vocabulary, Colombe achieved an ideal of power and grandeur that is usually associated with sixteenth-century Italian creations. Yet the same man, when he fashioned the *Relief of St. George* in the chapel of Gaillon, failed to attain an equally high standard. The dragon, as Morey describes it, is "a Gothic combination of imagination and homeliness," a picture-book beast without much reality, while St. George and his horse are engaged in a picture-book combat. The attempt at drama is inadequate, and the general result is weak. The difference between these two works illustrates clearly how ineffective the Italian influence was as yet.

The other was Claus Sluter, architect of the Carthusian monastery of Champnol, near Dijon, and sculptor of its several monuments, chief of which was the *Well of Moses*.[28] Although flourishing before the monumental style appeared, Sluter made his figures powerful and vital. And their accuracy has led a recent art historian to suggest that "no artist needs to know any more about anatomy than Sluter did."[29] Even his use of drapery as an enveloping mantle, though Gothic in tradition, helps to emphasize this substantiality of form. Moreover, except for some conventional details, such as the two small horns on the forehead of Moses and his long and handsomely curled beard, the representation is not symbolic. His Christ, for instance, is "a man who has met death bravely and in death found peace," while "the prophets are not creatures of celestial inspiration, but great men of this world, each one proclaiming his individuality in feature and gesture."[30] Thus, without a touch of the classic, he has brought out the power and reality associated with High Renaissance art, and it is this achievement which justifies placing him among the company of artists who mixed the medieval and the Renaissance styles rather than among the workers in pure Gothic.

As in France, the Gothic in Germany remained strong, so that the infusion of the Renaissance style during the first stage was superficial. Illustrative of this are the works of Peter Vischer, both father and son, of Nuremberg. The elder's tomb of Archbishop Ernest in the cathedral of Magdeburg has the classic only in the heads of the apostles and in the quiet planes. His masterpiece, the Reliquary of St. Sebaldus, Nuremberg, employs more Italianism in the details but this is overwhelmed by the opulence and virtuosity common to Gothic mannerist style. In addition, the superb self-portrait which he fashioned at one end of the base is in the style of Gothic realism.[31] His son's creations admitted more of the new, but it was more in subject matter than in form or spirit. Peter Flotner might he cited as one who employed the new style more freely and effectively but who, however, did not escape the Gothic. Leaving aside his *David* as an ineffective study of human anatomy in arrested motion,[32] we have in his numerous medallions respectable attempts at largeness of form and substantial reality. His *putti* are also quite Italian. Yet his women have German faces, their poses are mannered, and their robes superabundant[33] — all in good Gothic tradition.

England clung to her own traditional style more firmly than did the continental lands, but there, too, Italianism found some acceptance.[34] Henry VIII had invited Pietro Torrigiani to fashion the tombs for his parents, but Torrigiani's assistants were English workers. The resulting creations were naturally composite: the design was English, the modeling, particularly of the faces, and some of the decoration were Italianate. Although Torrigiani left England when Henry broke with Rome, the native sculptors who had worked with him on the tombs retained some of his Italianism. This influence is noticeable, for example, in the tombs of Henry Fitzroy (Henry's illegitimate son), of Thomas of Marney, and of Thomas, the Second Duke of Norfolk.[35] But most of this Italianism is confined to the decorations.

In Spain the invasion of Italian Renaissance style faced two opposing currents. There was the Spanish Gothic, colder and graver and stiffer than the Gothic of the remainder of Europe, and with its madonnas so obviously pervaded with Byzantine hieraticism. The other current was the Late Gothic of France, Burgundy, and Germany. This competed with the native style, but gained in popularity and therefore offered strong opposition to the Italian style. This victory of the northern Gothic is represented in Juan Pere de Vallfogona's retable for the cathedral of Tarragona and in another retable which he and master Hans of Gmund fashioned for Seo at Saragossa, but especially in Gil de Siloe's retable in the Carthusian church of Miraflores near Burgos and in his tomb for Don Juan de Padilla, Isabella's page. Sculptures on these are fundamentally Gothic, except for a few faces whose naturalism points away from the medieval.[36] In the sixteenth century came the hybrid style, and it came from Burgundy. Felipe Vigarni's Passion scenes on the screen behind the high altar of the cathedral of Burgos introduced "such Italianisms as elegance of attitude, interest in the nude, and greater tranquillity."[37] Damian Forment, in his retable at Saragossa, introduced Renaissance figure forms. Pietro Torrigiani who came to Spain from England brought his Italianism with him, but he yielded to the native here, as in England, and admitted some Spanish naturalism into his principal work. Other examples may be cited, such as Cardinal Mendoza's tomb in the cathedral of Toledo, with Mendoza's face particularly well rendered, and the tomb of Lady Elvira of Tendilla.[38]

From this survey of the mixed style in all the lands, with the Gothic component stronger than the Renaissance, it should be abundantly clear that the change in sculpture during the Renaissance period was slow and not extensive enough to justify any notion of a sharp break between the medieval and Renaissance styles.

Pure Renaissance Style

The last stage was, of course, that of the pure Renaissance. As may be expected, this style began in Italy, where it appeared about the middle of the fifteenth century. From Italy it passed to northern Europe, but not until the following century.

The initiator of this style in Italy, according to the conventional view, was Donatello. This view need not be disputed, for Donatello's contributions were of paramount influence. However, it would not be wrong to begin with the works of a sculptor whom Michelangelo deigned to follow, namely, Jacopo della Quercia.

Della Quercia was a Sienese artist, but he did not work in the "pretty" tradition which Simone Martini imposed on that city's art. His works are monumental, and this he achieved by modeling in broad planes and by the use of heroic nudes presented in elemental simplicity. Powerful but not forced, his figures possess grandeur without the theatrical display so common in the art of Italy's High Renaissance. Even the one mannerism which he retained from the late Gothic, the hip-shot pose of his women, does not detract from the figure, for he used it not to express grace but vitality. And the remarkable feature about his accomplishment is that it was attained without recourse to antiquity.

Among the creations which best illustrate this achievement are the tomb of Ilaria del Carretto in the cathedral of Lucca and the portal of San Petronio at Bologna whereon he fashioned his famous relief from Genesis and from the early life of Jesus. Both reveal nobility of conception and mastery of execution.

Donatello (*ca.* 1385–1466) is unquestionably one of the greatest Renaissance sculptors. His range is immense, extending from the human sweetness of a tender and girlish madonna to the forceful but natural realism of a powerful-minded *condottiere* and to the exaggerated and stark realism of a female cadaver. The same breadth holds true for his skill. He can represent a wisp of hair or the crease of a wrinkle in thin relief, or distance and space by recessive planes in the same relief, or a dynamic stallion in the round — all with the same expertness.

Among his many masterpieces four may be chosen as representative of his range and his skill. The equestrian statue of *Gattamelata*, although not the first of such monuments, is the first successful one in the Renaissance style (Plate 16). Viewed from a distance it may give the impression that the horse dominates the rider, but upon closer examination the powerful intelligence and will of the rider as depicted through a realistic face leave no doubt about the domination of the man. The final product is the result of a combination of Florentine realism and Roman antiquity suggested by the famous equestrian statue of Emperor Marcus Aurelius. Less monumental but superb in its peculiar way is his *Zuccone* (*Pumpkinhead*, because of the baldness). Probably intended as a representation of the Baptist, it depicts an old man with a thin, wrinkled face, a square jaw, and a gaunt body (Plate 17). But the age of the subject in no way suggests decrepitude; rather it reflects a dynamic spirit drawing vigor from experience. Not a pleasant figure to look at, its realism ever entrances. Realism carried to excess and yet without a whisper of sensationalism is represented in the *Repentant Magdalen*, a wooden statue in the Baptistry of Florence. It is a representation of a female cadaver draped in a shredded robe revealing fleshless neck, arms, legs, and feet. Probably a symbol of the awful prospect that awaits mankind at the end of life's journey — death and the subsequent spiritual suffering — it is the message rather than the macabre dialect that stands out. The very antithesis of this piece and of the former two is the Madonna done in light relief. She is represented as a lovely girl turned into an adoring and thankful mother, natural and not a picture-book being. Matching this warm human sweetness is the lightness of the veil that softly envelops her hair and one side of the face. Not even Botticelli's brush could have improved on the airy fineness of that filmy silken stuff, and yet so real that one can almost feel its touch.[39]

In none of these are there any Gothic traits, and this absence warrants placing Donatello among the foremost sculptors in the Renaissance style. Yet that is not a complete estimate of this great artist. His *St. George* copies the Gothic stance of feet set widely apart; and his *David*, "probably the first nude statue in the round in Italy for 1,000 years,"[40] is Gothic "in swing and proportions."[41] To be sure, retention of these Gothic features does not make him a representative of the hybrid style, but it is noteworthy that even so powerful a proponent of the Renaissance as Donatello had not fully succeeded in shaking off the medieval conventions.

After Donatello the pure Renaissance moved forward rapidly. Among the numerous cultivators of this style three may be mentioned as particularly significant. Antonio Pollaiuolo (1432–1498) is noted for his scientific realism of the body, for his exploitation of the nude, preferably in violent movement, both of which appear in his *Hercules and Antaeus* (Plate 18), and in realistic protraiture.[42] Andrea di Cione, called Verrochio (1435–1488), continued the realistic trend, but he was more responsive to the spirit of the antique and more sensitive to aesthetic appeal. Thus his equestrian statue of Colleoni, powerful in its realistic presentation, displays better balance between horse and rider than does Donatello's Gattamelata. His *Boy with the Dolphin* is a masterpiece of child anatomy in movement, but it is softer and warmer than Pollaiuolo's *Hercules and Antaeus* even allowing for the difference in the subject. His *David* is a wiry but a graceful youth. Lastly his *Madonna and the Child*, equal to Donatello in craftsmanship, is superior in naturalism. The mother and the baby are just that; the absence of adoration emphasizes the human and the natural.[43] Quite different in spirit from the works of the preceding were those of Andrea Contucci, otherwise known as Andrea Sansovino (1460–1529). Here the emphasis is less on human form than on the dramatization of sentimental themes,[44] and the work points to the affectation with which the Renaissance was to end.

Combining the realism, the nude, and the dynamic of the preceding works with the grandness of great conceptions were the creations of Michelangelo Buonarroti (1475–1564). Known to the popular mind for his powerful sculpturesque painting, Michelangelo was no less accomplished as a sculptor.

For the properties of realism and vigor and for the nude, Michelangelo could draw upon the models of antiquity and upon the works of some of his great predecessors. We have already mentioned his indebtedness to Jacopo della Quercia for the powerfulness of his nudes, and much of the rest came from Donatello through the latter's collaborator, Bertoldo, with whom Michelangelo studied sculpture, and from Ghirlandaio, his teacher in painting. But the largeness of conception, even though in keeping with the prevailing grandness of sixteenth-century Italian art in general, was fundamentally his own. Hence what he touched was transfused by his own personality and genius. These, it should be noted, were in part an expression of two tensions within him, that of Neoplatonism with its pagan cult of beauty and that of Savonarola's pietism.

Without attempting the difficult task of describing Michelangelo's sculptured works and of tracing the evolution of his style,[45] we might point out some of the more prominent traits that characterize his works. One of these traits is the depiction of many nudes in violent action. The bodies are fashioned in exaggerated poses with twisted torsos and throbbing muscles, and bursting, as it were, with the will and the power to act. The result is an essay in energy and action through the medium of the human form. This trait is particularly strong in his *Battle of the Centaurs* (Plate 19). Even a seated figure, such as his unfinished slave for the monument of Julius II, appears to be a vehicle for the same explosiveness.[46] Another trait is that of distortion. In a sense this property is present in the violence of the *contraposto* that he imposed on his figures. But its best illustration is to be found in his *Pieta*,[47] in which Mary is given larger bodily proportions than those of Christ, and at the same time she is represented as a young girl whereas her son is a mature man. Both are biological perversions, and, of course, Michelangelo knew this. He therefore violated physical realism to suit his purpose, whatever that may have been. It is probable that Mary was given an ample body to enable her to bear the weight of Christ normally, that is, without appearing to be burdened, and he wanted Christ in her lap to suggest the idea of overwhelmed motherhood. He actually represented her as a young maiden because he desired to recreate the power of her purity. "A woman of perfect purity," he is reported to have said, "would keep her youth forever."[48] The purpose of art for him, then, was not merely to represent the visible subject, but to convey his mental images. This is clearly obvious in the statues of bound slaves which he fashioned for the unfinished tomb of Pope Julius II. The bodies are representational to the degree that they do no violence to naturalism, but the bodies are not what captures the eye. Rather, the real attraction is the apparent helplessness of the bodies to break their bonds, representing perhaps the concept of a soul trying to free itself from the ties of earthliness. It is an allegory, then, an abstract idea in which he personally believed and which he tried to convey through the use of strained forms. Taken together, these properties reveal him as an abstractionist, more concerned, like Leonardo da Vinci, with the intent of the soul than with the outward man. Still another trait is his predilection for the monumental. This appears in the grandoise design he prepared for the tomb of Julius II. Everything about it was to be on a grand scale, the stability of the pyramidal pedestal, the size, the number of statues, and even the position of the effigy — Julius was to be represented as seated in the papal throne.[49] Indeed, it was so great and promised to take so much time for its execution that the impatient pope assigned him to another task — painting the ceiling of the Sistine Chapel — where progress might be more visible.

Where Michelangelo succeeded in making his sculptured bodies convey great ideas, the sculptors who tried to imitate him failed for lack of commensurate imagination. Their efforts led them into affectation, or into pretension and sensationalism, that is into Mannerism or Baroque.

Of the many imitators of Michelangelo two may be selected as a conclusion to this account of Renaissance sculpture in Italy. Jacopo Tatti, otherwise known as Jacopo Sansovino (1486–1570), possessed grace and perfection, but the first led him into affectation and the second into academic coldness. His *Bacchus*[50] may pass as an example of his finer creations with just a touch of mannerism. But his *Evangelist Mark* is weak.[51] There is a distinct disproportion between Mark's twisted body and his head, and the disparity fails to convey any inner message. On the whole it has the earmarks of exhibitionism. The other imitator is

Giovanni da Bologna (1509–1608), a Flemish master naturalized in Italy. In his hands Michelangelo's monumentality becomes elegantly colossal, and the dynamic and the powerful become mannered sensationalism. Although expertly done, the works are inwardly weak. His *Rape of the Sabine Woman* (Plate 20) is technically one of his best; it is a study of a female body, a youth's body, and a mature masculine body, and as such it is satisfying, but as a concept of kidnapping it is wholly theatrical. More powerful and closer to Michelangelo is his *Flussgottheit*.[52] Not a pleasant statue to view, it nevertheless succeeds in going below the surface and in bringing out the idea of terrific force without having to rely on a display of violence.

Pure Renaissance was introduced into France by visiting Italian sculptors, Giovanni Battista Rosso and Francesco Primaticcio of Bolonga. Both were engaged in decorating the palace at Fontainebleau, and tradition accords to them the credit of having introduced into France stucco sculpture in full relief and of being founders of a school — the Fontainebleau school — whence pure Renaissance style radiated throughout the country.

The style which they introduced can be observed in Rosso's decoration of the Galerie François I and in Primaticcio's Mantelpiece from the Queen's Chambre. In both of these, classical nudes are plentiful, too plentiful for that matter, and together with their arrangement and exaggerated posturing they give the impression of being sheer decorative designs. They are pretty to look at and their modeling is expert, but inwardly they are empty. The role of the ornamental is too patent.[53]

A third Italian, Benvenuto Cellini, author of the celebrated autobiography, added to the Renaissance influence. He spent the years 1540–1545 working in France and is known to have prepared models for a number of classical deities and to have completed a Jupiter, two bronze busts, a relief of a nymph, and the famous salt-cellar. While most of these creations, the selt-cellar excepted, are lost, in his day they served to inspire the French artists and to carry the Italian current further. What that influence was can be gathered from the salt-cellar. Its first striking feature is virtuosity of craftsmanship, and its second is the elegance of its nudes. Both features are marvelous, and in fact that is all they are in spite of the high esteem in which they are popularly held. Impossible to emulate, they could only lead to mannered works.

This Italian influence finally caught up with the French sculptors, and among these, two are of considerable merit.

Jean Goujon, about whose life little is known, represents the pure classic tradition in France at its best. In his *Tomb of Louis de Brézé* the classical elements appear to advantage in the Caryatids, particularly in their heads and drapery. The equestrian statue is in mannered Gothic, but is not by Goujon.[54] His *Pieta*, patterned after several Italian models, does justice to the bodies under the draperies in true classical manner, and the heads are quite Roman. However, its emotional intensity, no doubt required by the theme, is not in the best tradition of classic calm.[55] Equally close to the best in the classic tradition are the decorative reliefs of nymphs, tritons, and *putti* in his *Fontaine des Innocents* (Plate 21). It has been pointed out already that he allowed himself some elongation of the female bodies in the tradition of the Gothic, but, except for this, the reliefs in form and spirit have the classic stamp. One characteristic is his own, and that is the management of the drapery in prominent, closely repeated, parallel folds.[56]

Although his works reveal the influence of Primaticcio, Rosso, and Cellini, they are monumental and less decorative than any creations produced by these three men.

The second sculptor, Germain Pilon (1535–1590), represents more clearly the approach of the Baroque. One of his earlier works, the four *Virtues* at the corners of the tomb of Henry II and Catherine de'Medici, shows his modeling prowess and his adherence to a calmer style than was Primaticcio's by whom he was influenced. The three feminine figures (*Virtues*) which he carved for the monument of Henry II's heart have the classical idealism. His *Head of Cardinal Birogue* follows the canons of Italian realism. The *Virgin* is Michelangelesque in its abstraction of suffering motherhood. His *Deposition*, in relief, is Michelangelesque in its force but the voluminous agitated drapery and the emotionalism are overdrawn in the temper of the Baroque. But if Renaissance properties are paramount, he did yield to some non-Renaissance national traits. The effigy of Valentine Balbiani has Renaissance craftsmanship but the stark realism of Late Gothic, and the same applies to the *gisant* of Henry II.[57] But in comparison with his total output these few and partial Gothicisms are not sufficient to deny him a place as the last great French sculptor in the Renaissance style before it yielded to the Baroque.

The Renaissance style in the Low Countries had no Claus Sluter to carry it high. A number of lesser men spread it in the form of Italianism. Among these purveyors may be included Jacques du Broeucq, Lancelot Blondeel, and the architect Cornelius Floris de Vriendt (1514–1575). Their works reveal the fact that in the Low Countries the High Renaissance style was either accompanied by Late Gothic or leaned toward the Baroque.

In Germany the spread of the High Renaissance style is associated with Adolf Dauher of Ulm and his son Hans, with Konrad Meit of Worms, Hubert Gerhard, and Adriaen de Vries. In general this association is proper. However, what they employed was not pure Renaissance. The Dauhers, father and son, carved figures which were still quite Gothic, *putti* excepted. In addition, Adolf liked the pictorial function of sculpture in relief, and his *Triumph of Charles V* has the crowding and the agitation that are found in Late Gothic panel sculpture. Konrad Meit retained much of Gothic naturalism and of French *détente*. On the other hand, Gerhard and De Vries followed the style of Giovanni Bologna, that is, the early Baroque.[58] Nevertheless, with several cities — Nuremberg, Augsburg, Munich, Vienna — serving as disseminating centers of Italianism, the style of the Renaissance was apparently more widespread in Germany than in France.

England may be bypassed in this survey of High Renaissance sculpture, for the Italian influence departed with Torrigiani and the Dutch influence, some of it lightly Italianized, came in during Elizabethan days. The prevailing style generally followed the late medieval tradition with only a touch of the Renaissance. This can be gathered from the works of the most outstanding sculptor of the age, Nicholas Stone (1586–1647). His effigy of Dame Elizabeth Carey, at Stow-Nine-

PLATE 12 — *Margrave Ekkehard and His Wife, Uta*, Naumburg Cathedral. By permission of Marburg-Art Reference Bureau.

PLATE 13 — *Pieta*, Münster. By permission of Marburg-Art
Reference Bureau.

PLATE 14 — *Madonna, Notre Dame de Paris.* By permission of Alinari-Art Reference Bureau.

OPVS·DONATELLI

DAVID·REX

PLATE 17 — Donatello's *Zuccone*. By permission of Alinari-
Art Reference Bureau.

PLATE 18 — Pollaiuolo's *Hercules and Antaeus*. By permission of Alinari-Art Reference Bureau.

PLATE 19 — Michelangelo's *Battle of the Centaurs*. By permission of Brogi-Art Reference Bureau.

PLATE 20 — Bologna's *Rape of the Sabine Woman*. By permission of Brogi-Art Reference Bureau.

PLATE 21—Goujon's *Water Nymphs Fountain of the Innocents*. By permission of Art Reference Bureau, Inc.

Churches, Northamptonshire, exemplifies Renaissance workmanship, but the baby in the arms of Mrs. Arthur Coke is impossible as art.[59] Also medieval was the absence of the nude. The parties who contracted these tombs preferred to be represented with idealized but individualized faces and in their finest earthly raiments. The result is that the sculptured pieces are largely works on contemporary dress habits. The Renaissance, it should be recalled, gloried in the nude. The difference in the spirit could not be more clearly revealed.

As in architecture, so in sculpture, Spain admitted a strong current of High Renaissance style. Domenico Fancelli of Settignano (1469–1519) fashioned a tomb of Prince John after Pollaiuolo's tomb for Sixtus IV, and another for Ferdinand and Isabella in a mannered style. The Italians Leone Leoni (1509–1590) and his son Pompeo strengthened the Italianate trend through their tombs for Charles V and Philip II and their families. Bartolomé Ordóñez imitated his master Fancelli and tried emulating Michelangelo with whose works he came in contact while studying in Italy. A pupil of Michelangelo, Alonso Berruguete (*ca.* 1488–1561), added more of Michelangelesque traits and with them introduced some elements — elegance and agitation — of Mannerism (Plate 22). These were further intensified by the employment of Spanish religious emotionalism and ascetic-looking nudes. Even stronger in these traits were the executions of Gaspar Becerra (*ca.* 1520–1570).

From this survey of sculpture during the Renaissance period the obvious conclusion is that the Gothic style continued strong until about the middle of the fifteenth century; that a new style, the Renaissance style, was born; that this new style combined at first with the old to form a hybrid style; and that this new style did not displace the old and the hybrid styles wholly except in Italy.

1. Cf. Julius Baum, *Romanesque Architecture in France* (2d ed.; New York: B. Westermann Co., Inc., 1928), 234–8, 269. An excellent treatment is Émile Mâle, *Religious Art from the Twelfth to the Eighteenth Century* (New York: Pantheon Books, Inc., 1949), 17–57.

2. See Sewall, *op. cit.*, 539.

PLATE 22 — Berruguete's *St. Peter,* Toledo Cathedral. By permission of Ampliaciones y Reproducciones MAS.

3. For illustrations of some of these see Hans Karlinger, *Die Kunst der Gotik*, vol. 7 of *Propyläen Kunstgeschichte* (Berlin: Propyläen Verlag, 1926), 353–79.

4. Sewall, *op. cit.*, 511, figs. 13.24, 25, 26.

5. Arthur Gardner, *English Medieval Sculpture* (Cambridge: University Press, 1951), nos. 477–97.

6. George Henry Chase and Chandler Rathfon Post, *A History of Sculpture* (New York: Harper and Brothers Publishers, 1925), 261.

7. *Ibid.*, 262.

8. Otto Cartellieri, *The Court of Burgundy*, in the series *The History of Civilization*, ed. C. K. Ogden (New York: Alfred A. Knopf, 1929), 35.

9. Charles Rufus Morey, *Medieval Art* (New York: W. W. Norton and Co., 1942), 386.

10. Cf. Mâle, *op. cit.*, 116–9 and plates 26, 27.

11. *Ibid.*, plate 31.

12. See the great number of these in Gardner, *op. cit.*, 326–42.

13. Sewall, *op. cit.*, 532–3.

14. *Ibid.*, fig. 13.6.

15. Giuseppe Delogu, *Italienische Bildhauerei* (Zurich: Fretz and Wasmuth Verlag Ag., 1942), 46 and plate opposite it.

16. Constantine Baroni, *Scultura gotica lombarda* (Milano: Edizione d'arte Emilio Bestetti, 1944), plates 167, 168.

17. Gardner, *op. cit.*, fig. 590.

18. For some illustrations of secular sculpture see Gardner, *op. cit.*, figs. 165, 166, 196; Baroni, *op. cit.*, plates 1, 67–69; Mâle, *op. cit.*, plates 14, 15.

19. See Sewall, *op. cit.*, 515.

20. *Ibid.*, 546.

21. For the last two monuments see Delogu, *op. cit.*, plates opposite pages 53 and 54.

22. Blunt, *op. cit.*, plate 12 A.

23. These apparently were executed by Parisian masters (Henri Hauser and Augustin Renaudet, *Les débuts de l'age moderne* [3d ed.; Paris: Presses universitaires de France, 1946], 307).

24. Blunt, *op. cit.*, plates 13 and 14.

25. *Ibid.*, plate 15.

26. *Ibid.*, 17.

27. Morey, *op. cit.*, 386. But Hauser and Renaudet (*op. cit.*, 149) judge it "toute gothique de conception et d'exécution."

28. Pictures in Sewall, *op. cit.*, 552.

29. *Ibid.*, 541.

30. Professor Constable in *The Cambridge Medieval History*, VIII, 739–40.

31. Excellent picture in Gustav Glück, *Die Kunst der Renaissance in Deutschland den Niederlanden, Frankreich*, etc., vol. X of *Propyläen-Kunstgeschichte* (2d ed.; Berlin: Propyläen Verlag, 1928), 399.

32. Ernest Friedrich Bange, *La piccola scultura in legno e pietra del rinascimento tedesco*, trans. Giuseppe Delogu (Milano: Edizioni d'arte, 1937), plate 81.

33. *Ibid.*, plates 82, 83.

34. Gardner, *op. cit.*, figs. 587–9. Cf. also Katherine A. Esdaile, *English Church Monuments 1510–1840* (London: B. T. Batsford Ltd., 1946), introduction (by Sacheverell Sitwell), 12–57 and plates 41–43.

35. *Ibid.*, plates 5, 40, 45, 46.

36. For some examples see August L. Mayer, *Mittelalterliche Plastik in Spanien* (München: Delphin-Verlag, 1922), plates 30–32, 37–40.

37. Chase and Post, *op. cit.*, 366.

38. Mayer, *op. cit.*, plates 34 and 40.

39. Pictures in Sewall, *op. cit.*, figs. 15.9–18.

40. Morey, *op. cit.*, 343.

41. Constable in *Cambridge Medieval History*, VIII, 770.

42. Delogu, *op. cit.*, 120, 123.

43. *Ibid.*, 127, 128, 131; Sewall, *op. cit.*, figs. 16.7–9.

44. Delogu, *op. cit.*, 171–2.

45. For a brief analysis see David M. Robb and J. J. Garrison, *Art in the Western World* (4th ed.; New York: Harper & Row, Publishers, 1963), 379–81.

46. Delogu, *op. cit.*, 183.

47. *Ibid.*, 176 and Sewall, *op. cit.*, fig. 16.21.

48. Sewall, *op. cit.*, 738.

49. For a brief description of the tomb and its imaginary reconstruction see Erwin Panofsky, *Studies in Iconology* (Torchbook ed.; New York: Harper & Row, Publishers, 1962), 187–8 and plates 131–2.

50. Chase and Post, *op. cit.*, fig. 190.

51. Delogu, *op. cit.*, 215.

52. Delogu, *op. cit.*, 231.

53. For pictures see Blunt, *op. cit.*, plates 22, 23, 41.

54. *Ibid.*, plate 52.

55. *Ibid.*, plate 55 A.

56. *Ibid.*, plates 53, 55 B.

57. For pictures of the several pieces here mentioned see Blunt, *op. cit.*, plates 63–68.

58. Bange, *op. cit.*, plates 1–14, 60–66.

59. Pictures in Esdaile, *op. cit.*, 21 and 62.

CHAPTER **X**   *Painting*

L IKE ARCHITECTURE and sculpture, painting during the Renaissance
  period underwent a great transformation. It broke away from the
medieval styles; discovered and accepted new techniques and different ideals; and upon mastering these it gave expression to new and
consummate art. Since this whole process of transformation is the real
history of painting during the Renaissance, clearly each phase of this
evolution needs to be explored. A description of just the end product,
the High Renaissance style, is not enough.

Painting on the Eve of the Renaissance and during the Early Renaissance

BYZANTINE-GOTHIC STYLE Two styles determined the nature of painting during the later Middle Ages. One was the Byzantine style, with
its properties of hieraticism, iconographic vocabulary, artificial balance,
colored backgrounds in gold or in luminous hues, flatness — that is, absence of three-dimensionality — and little or no feeling for the realities
of nature and human anatomies. The other style was the Gothic, with
its properties of elegance, delicateness and linearity, visual reality, and
naturalism. Although the places of origin of these two styles were far
apart — Byzantium and France — and although one style predominated
in the Mediterranean lands and the other in the remainder of western
Europe, by the thirteenth century they were more or less combined.
Thus in the Gothic north, the iconography and the backgrounds of rich
cloth and deep colors remained Byzantine. On the other hand in Italy
and Spain, the severity of the Byzantine was softened by the grace and
humanism of the Gothic.

Whether the style was Byzantine, Gothic, or Byzantine-Gothic, the
prevailing subjects were religious and the function was spiritual edification and inspiration. Secular themes were less common, but more
numerous than popular tradition would have it, especially in the Gothic

lands. The illuminated manuscripts, for example, drew on chivalric activities, on animal lore, and on bird and flower life. Sometimes seasons were depicted, and occasionally — this more in Italy than in the north — allegories of social and moral virtues.

Another general characteristic common to these pre-Renaissance styles was the anonymity of the productions. There are not many signed or identifiable works, say, before Giotto's day in Italy or before Van Eyck's time in the Netherlands. Some illuminated manuscripts can be traced to their creators, but by and large anonymity remained the prevailing custom.

INTERNATIONAL STYLE Out of these styles there emerged in the fourteenth century the International style of painting. Until recently it was believed that this style originated in Avignon where the Italian painters and the northern artists who flocked to the papal court fertilized each other's styles and that from there, because of widespread papal connections, it radiated throughout most of Europe.[1] Now, however, the traditional view is challenged, and the origin is attributed to the intermingling of the Gothic and the Italo-Byzantine stylistic streams at several places.[2] Gothic style traveled to Italy, Lombardy in particular, and Italian style moved northward with the numerous Italian business representatives in Paris, Bruges, Ypres, and elsewhere. Spain received both currents, Italian by way of the Mediterranean and Gothic by way of the merchant and crusading routes through France. Thus the International style was in the stage of formation even before the popes established themselves in Avignon. Hence all that the papal residence in Avignon contributed to the movement was to facilitate its expansion.

The reason for the widespread acceptance of the International style was the prevalence of overrefined chivalry. Elegant airs, fashionable dress, social formality, exaltation of the feminine world, and fastidiousness became chivalric standards and found acceptance not only among the nobility which cultivated these properties with the view of preserving their social pre-eminence, but also among the wealthy commoners who aspired to social equality with the nobility and therefore aped their conduct. Hence the affectation of the romances, hence the preciosity of the *rhétoriqueur* poetry, hence also the International style. This, of course, presumes that painting found a new clientele, that is, the rich secular society.

From the description of the cultural milieu in which the International style developed, its main properties can be readily surmised. Panofsky details them as "amazing sophistication and extravagance in manner, dress and appurtenances; thin, nervous hands and wasplike waists; choking collars; childlike delight in everything that glitters and tinkles."[3] To these should be added calligraphic linearity, fastidiousness of detail, inadequate plasticity, and ineffective perspective. Combined, these resulted in ornamental "prettiness," artificial and idealized, a sensitive craftsman's art rather than great painting.

Europe-wide as the style was, it had numerous practitioners, many of them known and deserving of recognition. But only a few need be examined in this short survey.

In Italy the foremost representative and formulator of this style was Simone Martini of Siena. Although a contemporary of Giotto, Simone remained untouched by the Giottesque monumentality.[4] He retained the Gothic and the Italo-Byzantine properties, enlivened them with inner animation, and softened them with a mood of delicate charm and pensiveness. His *Annunciation* in the Uffizi of Florence is illustrative of this prim and sentimentalized art (Plate 23). Yet it is not wholly shallow art for all its decorativeness, for the lovely forms, the coy poses, the delicate details all seem to underscore the beauty and the burden of the unexpected message. When Martini's style came to Florence, it retained its general properties but yielded somewhat to the demands for realism of form and space. This is illustrated in the works of Gentile da Fabriano (*ca.* 1370–1427). In his *Adoration of the Magi*[5] the "curse of the fashionable" and the display of decorative detail are prominent, but at the same time there is an attempt at depicting individualized faces and strong bodies, and at representing the scenes in space. Between these two styles, that of Simone and Gentile, ranged much of the rest of Italy's painting in the International style, and it continued strong into the fifteenth century. One has only to examine the works of such painters as Bartolo di Fredi, Andrea da Firenze, Antonio Veneziano, Lorenzo Monaco, Francesco d'Antonio, Maestro del Bambino Vispo, and Stefano de Giovanni (Sassetta) to realize how prevalent this style remained in Italy, and this, despite the powerful influences of Giotto and Masaccio.

In northern Europe this International style retained more of the Gothic elements and was further influenced by the calligraphy of miniaturist art. The technique of the illuminator entered widely, imparting sharpness of line and in general the doll-like mannerism so prevalent in most illuminated pictures.

As might be expected the International style in northern Europe first appeared in the works of the illuminators. One of the earliest great practitioners of this art was Jean Pucelle of Paris (*fl.* 1319–1324). His illuminations in the Prayer Book for Jean d'Evreux, Queen of France, and in the *Breviarie de Belleville* show a remarkable "concentration on the effect of plastic forms,"[6] but at the same time the doll-like houses in which he places some of his people, so out of proportion with them, the elegant posture of some of the subjects, the airy gracefulness of the birds, butterflies, and the dragonflies (his signature really) leave no doubt about the fairylike aristocratic tradition to which these exquisite illuminations belong.[7] To the same tradition belong the works of Jacquemart de Hesdin, illuminator for the Duke of Berry, and of the master of the *Hours of the Marchel de Boucicaut*, though the latter redeems his work by incorporating naturalism and aerial perspective, namely, the principle which recognizes that color tone varies with the distance. And topping all were the works of Paul, Herman, and John Malouel (Paint-well), known popularly as the Limbourg brothers.

The Limbourgs were from Guelders, and their reputation as illuminators carried them from the service of the court of Burgundy to that of Duke of Berry for whom they began the *Très Riches Heures.* All together they completed seventy-five pictures for the manuscript and brought the International style in the art of illumination to its highest peak. For, while they retained all the properties associated with this style, they imparted more realism to their figure types and established the landscape as a popular genre.[8] But their forte is the combination of the microscopic with the telescopic, the proximate with the distant, and the homely with the fashionable, without incongruity. So much of it is doll-like and yet at the same time, with only an occasional exception, quite real. In this sense their work is at once traditionalist and forward looking.

Although the Limbourgs were probably the finest illuminators, illumination in France and in the Netherlands in the International style did not stop with them. It continued even into the sixteenth century. Thus Jean Bourdichon's (*ca.* 1457–1521) illumination of the *Hours of Anne of Brittany*, as Blunt informs us, "still followed the Late Gothic tradition."[9]

Elsewhere in northern Europe the art of manuscript illumination did not attain the excellence it reached in France and the Netherlands, but, wherever it was more than mere shopwork, it tried to emulate the International style. In England, where it came with some Italian influences[10] and Franco-Flemish artists, it is to be seen in the *Book of Hours* which Herman Scheere decorated, probably for John of Beaufort.[11] Inferior to the continental works in representation of space, it has the delicate drawing, the meticulous detail, the sentimental aristocratic air associated with the International style. Others imitated his mode and thus prolonged the style. But common as the style was, it had some competition from a combined native-Italianate style represented in the creations of Siferwas, which, while weaker in the representation of bodies and gestures, were superior in the depiction of dramatic action.[12]

From manuscript illuminations the International style passed to panel painting, and with the transfer went most of the traditional properties. A few examples may suffice to illustrate the fact. In England the finest representation is the Wilton Diptych which depicts the presentation of a young Richard II to the infant Jesus. Richard, on his knees, is presented by Edmund (Black Prince), Edward the Confessor (Edward III), and John the Baptist; Jesus is in the arms of the Virgin; and the two are surrounded by eleven angels.[13] Showing very little naturalism and some Italianate modeling, it has the grace, delicateness, and conventionalism common to the International style. In France the Maître de Moulins, in his *Assumption and Nativity*,[14] copied the delicate idealism of the late Gothic miniaturists. Although decorativeness is reduced in favor of bodily and spatial realism, some trademarks of the mannerist style, pictorialism especially, are still extant. Closer to the Gothic tradition is the *Aix Annunciation*[15] by an unknown master, but even here the use of receding arcades to capture the sense of space suggests the approaching Renaissance style. In Germany, one of the more accomplished representatives of this style was Stephan Lochner of Cologne. In his *Virgin of the Rose Trellis, Madonna of the Violet,* and *Epiphany*[16] are to be seen the decorativeness, the gilded tracery, the gold and brocaded backgrounds, the gracious postures, the stagelike atmosphere — all an "experiment in prettification" which seems to have been the *raison d'être* of the International style. To be sure, his work has a peculiar personal touch manifest in the representation of the Madonna which, though made full-bodied, seems to transcend the merely human, and the eerie texture of her raiment adds to that mystic quality. Spain had several schools of the Riviera style, as the International style is called there, but, though each had some peculiar property, they all possessed some characteristics of that style. The works of Jacomart, of Jaime Huguet, and of Luis Borassá's followers, with emphasis on the courtly, the decorative, and the detailed, provide the evidence.[17]

From the few examples cited the reader should not get the impression that the International style had only a limited following. On the contrary, it was the prevailing style during the first century of the Renaissance. And recognition of this fact is important, for, inasmuch as the heart of this style was late medieval Gothicism, it means that the break between medieval painting and Renaissance painting was not abrupt.

The Development of the Renaissance Style

Although the International style predominated until the middle of the fifteenth century, the Renaissance style appeared during the same period and later supplanted it. Since this new style passed through several evolutionary stages, a description of each of its stages of development is desirable. Moreover, since its development was not uniform, the description will need to be given country by country.

Italy

THE NATURALISTIC STAGE The first stage in the development of Rennaissance style in Italy may be called the stage of naturalism. People are not doll-like, nor are they epitomes of chivalric grace passing in an everlasting parade. They are substantial beings moving about in space. They have volume, and space is three-dimensional. To capture this in painting became the prime objective, and when that was attempted the first step was taken in the direction of Renaissance art.

Credit for this significant achievement is given to a Florentine named Giotto (1266–1337). Although surrounded by the Italo-Byzantine style with its symbolism, hieraticism, formalism, and flatness, he broke with tradition and started an innovation.[18] If an examination is made of any collection of his frescoes, such as that edited by Jean Leymarie and published by Librairie Plon, several new characteristics will be noticed readily. One of these is the "bulkiness" of his people. Even if their anatomies cannot be seen because he drapes them in heavy robes, the impression is conveyed that underneath these garments there is real flesh and bone. By this massiveness he imparts substantiality to his subjects and so makes them appear naturalistic. Another new feature, and it strengthens this naturalism, is the absence of formalism and symmetry. His subjects are not posed in equal numbers on both sides of a central axis nor in identical postures. They are so arranged in the scene as if they had assembled naturally. Thirdly, there is no pictorialism and no diffusion; the drama of the episode catches the eye at once and holds it, and this imparts a reality to the situation that no formal arrangement of the actors can achieve. The fourth feature is the employment of natural background. Although he still uses the solid-colored backgrounds at times, and although his representation of the objects of nature — rocks, trees, buildings — is defective for lack of perspective, the fact that he uses them at all is significant, as it initiated a break with tradition. Fifthly, there is masterful depiction of the emotional message without a surplus of dramatics and sentimentality. Finally, everything is elemental and fundamental; there is no toying with minutiae (Plate 24).

On closer examination some limitations become apparent. Because particulars are subordinated to the totality of the picture, the faces — of womenfolk particularly — are not individualized. This is as true of such quiet scenes as that of *Mary and Joseph Returning from the Temple* as of more dramatic situations such as *The Descent from the Cross*[19] or the *Massacre of the Innocents*.[20] For the same reason proportions are occasionally violated. Thus the children climbing the trees in the *Entry into Jerusalem*[21] are far too big for the trees, as indeed the people are in relation to the city walls. The same disproportion between the people, the trees, and the two rocks is present in the famous *Flight to Egypt*. Another limitation is his inability to delineate human anatomy. Having captured the essence of reality as to the whole human bulk, he cannot represent the corporeal details realistically. Thus his hands have a waxen appearance, and those of the shepherd in *Joachim among the Shepherds* or of the maidens in *The Return from the Temple*[22] are particularly bad; thus his eyes, olive shaped, seem to have a conventionalized treatment.[23] Then there are the retention of solid-colored backgrounds and faulty foreshortening of the angels flying in the air.[24]

As to the merits and the defects of his productions, the latter, it is important to recognize, are noticeable only upon close scrutiny whereas the first capture the eyes at once and hold them fixed. And it is this capacity to communicate that makes his style commanding.

Giotto's style was beyond his contemporaries,[25] as, later, Michelangelo's was beyond his contemporaries. Except for two or three men who had more than a modicum of success imitating him, such as Agnolo Gaddi and Spinello Aretino,[26] the others could not emulate his principal innovations. While they tried to copy his naturalism, they were not disposed to accept the monumentality by which he achieved this. It seemed to be quite alien to the taste of the age, and so they continued in the suave and sentimental Gothic tradition and merely tried to incarnate it with some of the Giottesque naturalism. The result was the Florentine school of the International style, and of this we have already taken note.

The painter who finally attained Giotto's standard and then improved upon it was the short-lived Tomaso Guidi, better known as Masaccio (1401–1428). According to one critic, Masaccio followed Giotto "in simplicity, economy of gesture and detail, and in the momentum which he [gave] to whatever he want[ed] to express by the solid bulk and monumentality of his figures," but he added the technique of chiaroscuro (modeling of forms from "a construction of light and shade") and the science of aerial perspective (clarity of objects varies inversely with the distance).[27] It should be added also that he used the nude more freely and with greater realism and that he increased the secular note in religious pictures. The combination of these innovations with the Giottesque elements resulted in his initiating what is called the "Grand style," which thereafter was to remain as the ideal style of painting.[28]

To examine this style we might turn to two of his masterpieces, *The Tribute Money* and *The Expulsion*. In the first,[29] in the center of the picture, we see the publican meeting Jesus and the apostles and asking for tax money; on the left, Peter securing the coin from the fish's mouth; and on the right, handing it to the same tax collector. The picture is therefore arranged in narrative sequence, and in this respect it is in keeping with the Gothic mode. But all else is non-Gothic. The individual members of the company are fashioned in Giottesque style; they are real personages and their substantiality is secured by their "bulkiness," by the ample robes, and by their occupying space. Actually, in the last property they excel anything that Giotto could have done, and the reason lies in the fact that their forms are modeled with light and shade. Indeed, the most striking feature of the picture is the *chiaroscuro* and its use to impart the sense of space. This effecting of space is further improved by the employment of an architectural design, on the left side of the picture, which recedes in conformity with the laws of perspective, and by the rendering of the distant trees and hills more vague as they are more distant from the first plane of the picture. Finally, there is that short-frocked publican with his legs bare, whereby the nude is made to appear, confidently and without any apology. We might also note the secular and unemotional tone which prevails in spite of the fact that the scene is taken from the life of Jesus.[30] The whole is full of promise of High Renaissance art.

In *The Expulsion* (Plate 25) the same powerful style and techniques are employed. But here two new features are added: the use of the nude body, simply molded but elemental, as a vehicle for emotion; and secondly, the successful rendering of the inner feelings of man. Adam is overwhelmed with shame and Eve with pangs of grief and remorse, and the heavy gait and the postures magnify this sense of ignominy and guilt. It might be observed that Adam's right leg and Eve's left forearm and hand are crudely represented, yet, since the bodily forms are not an end in themselves, these defects are not serious. Emotion is what Masaccio wanted to paint, and who is there to say that he did not succeed in his objective?

MODIFIED INTERNATIONAL STYLE Following Masaccio two schools evolved. One may be described as a modified form of the International style, and its foremost representative was Fra Giovanni of Fiesole (1387?–1455) called Angelico in affectionate recognition of the pretty angelic types that he painted. The old in his works consists of his delicate line, decorativeness, richness of color pattern, and deficiency of realistic emotions; and much of this because his "imagination created a world remote from all the passions of mankind, a mystic's ecstatic vision of a perfect state in which earthly events took on a heavenly significance."[31] The new in his style — and this grew upon him progressively as a result of the influence of Giotto and Masaccio — is the reality that he tried to impart to his space by the use of perspective. Moreover, when he painted for the imperialist Pope Nicholas V, he even imparted some monumentality to his subjects. But in the combination of the old and the new, the old appears to have prevailed.[32] Since Angelico painted in this style by choice, it would appear that the public still preferred the International style as improved by the incorporation of some naturalism to the "speculative" mode of Masaccio.[33]

THE "SCIENTIFIC" STAGE The second school may be described as the "scientific" school. Although designated by the single name, actually it had two branches. One preoccupied itself with the science and technique of perspective, and the other with the mastery of the human anatomy, its internal construction as well as its outward form.

The first branch in general may be described as a school of geometricians who employed all kinds of physical props to secure the impression of receding space. Long arcades, often inappropriate to the scene and sometimes actually distracting, were perhaps the most common device.[34] Sometimes long and winding roads disappearing in the far distances, frequently crowded with knightly processions, were used.[35] Often also, there were deliberate displays of foreshortening. The most accomplished practitioner of all this "science" was the eccentric artist Paolo di Dono (1397–1475), called Uccello because of his love of birds, and his masterpieces are scenes of the *Battle of St. Romano* (Plate 26) in which the Florentines defeated the Sienese in 1432. What he accomplished in these paintings is a study in foreshortening, for as battle scenes they are devoid of drama. They have all the appearance of a mechanical engagement between two sets of toy soldiers on toy horses moving in opposite directions and colliding. There is hardly any realism. But as an experiment in a technical problem they show some scientific competence.

The second branch, that of corporeal realism, has two notable representatives. One was Antonio Pollaiuolo (1429–1498). According to Vasari, Pollaiuolo "dissected many human bodies to study the anatomy, and was the first [painter] who investigated the action of the muscles in this manner, that he might afterwards give them their due place and effect in his works."[36] That he succeeded in his aim, and with vengeance at that, is to be seen in his *Hercules and Antaeus* and *Hercules Slaying the Hydra of Lerna* (Plate 27). These may be characterized as successful experiments in the art of painting powerful nudes in violent action. At the same time the use of the meandering river in the background of the second picture to create the illusion of distance marks him as a follower of the first branch. The other was Luca Signorelli (1441–1522). In his *The Descent of the Damned into Hell*[37] there is an even more flagrant display of nudes in every conceivable position, all so postured as to bring out the musculature in the most revealing way. Although a religious theme, it lacks the proper atmosphere. Thoroughly mundane and "scientific," it fails to evoke the awe and horror that may be expected of the final scene on earth. It certainly is inferior in this respect to Michelangelo's *Last Judgment*, though Michelangelo was an admirer of Luca's works and actually used this particular one as a model for his own masterpiece.[38]

Closely related to this second branch were those artists who combined the bodily realism with classic themes and pagan spirit. As an illustration we may name Andrea Mantegna (1431–1506). With him the cult of antiquity was a veritable passion, and in such scenes as *Parnassus, Minerva Expelling the Vices, Triumphs of Julius Caesar,* and *Triumphs of Scipio,* he not only reproduced the themes of antiquity but also captured the heroic spirit associated with them.[39] Even though they were intended as allegories on morality — virtue over vice and chastity over love, for example — what stands out is not the moral lesson but the form and spirit of antiquity. Indeed, he could not escape from this spirit even when he painted religious subjects.[40]

While these several schools were developing, there were eclectic artists who drew upon them all, mingling the naturalism of Masaccio with the bodily realism of "scientific" painters, with some properties of the International style. Among this group the notorious Carmelite friar, Fra Lippo Lippi (1409–1469), deserves notice. In his *Funeral of St. Stephen*,[41] the spirit of Masaccio is alive again. There is bodily monumentality, and a corresponding grandeur of the setting. Faces are naturalistic, and characters are strong. On the other hand, his pictures of the Virgin — *Nativity* and *The Virgin and the Infant*[42] — represent her as a lyrically pretty girl with the tenderness customarily found in pictures belonging to the International school, while the filamentlike veil that covers her head is reminiscent of the light-handedness of Fra Angelico. There is however a difference: the saintliness of Angelico's Virgins or the courtliness of the Virgins of the International school is replaced by the sensuousness of a sweet maid. His *bambini*, on the other hand, are his inimitable trade mark; they are urchins, human in every respect but for their conventionally rendered hair. The one new property, then, that he emphasizes is "the irreligious ideal of sensuous beauty."[43] The other prominent representatives of this school who may be mentioned are Piero della Francesca (1416–1492), Andrea del Verrocchio (1435–1488), and Domenico Ghirlandaio (1449–1494). Thus Piero, although interested in perspective to the extent of writing a treatise on it — *De perspectiva pingendi* — and although yielding to the demands of naturalism and realism, did not wholly surrender expression and feeling to these "scientific" interests;[44] thus Andrea, although a student of Pollaiuolo and an imitator of the latter's realism, sentimentalized his madonnas;[45] thus Domenico, by representing the characters of antiquity as contemporary Florentines, admitted not only the facial realism associated with the scientific school but also the social elegancies which were current at the time and which found expression

PLATE 23 — Simone Martini's *Annunciation*. By permission of Anderson-Art Reference Bureau.

PLATE 24 — Giotto's *Flight to Egypt*. By permission of Anderson-Art Reference Bureau.

PLATE 25 — Masaccio's *Expulsion*. By permission of Alinari-Art Reference Bureau.

PLATE 26 — Uccello's Battle of St. Romano. By permission of Alinari-Art Reference Bureau.

PLATE 27 — Pollaiuolo's Hercules Slaying the Hydra and Hercules and Antaeus. By permission of Alinari-Art Reference Bureau.

PLATE 28 — Botticelli's *Birth of Venus*. By permission of Alinari-Art Reference Bureau.

PLATE 29 — Leonardo da Vinci's *The Last Supper*. By permission of Alinari-Art Reference Bureau.

PLATE 30 — Raphael's *Disputa*. By permission of Alinari-Art Reference Bureau.

PLATE 32 — Giorgione's *The Sleeping Venus*. By permission
of Alinari-Art Reference Bureau.

PLATE 33 — Titian's *Bacchus and Ariadne*. By permission of
Anderson-Art Reference Bureau.

in the International style. All three however, contributed to the shaping of Renaissance painting by their emphasis on classical themes and on mundane spirit.

THE STAGE OF IDEALISM Following the "scientific" stage came the stage of idealism. Having mastered the science of space, of anatomy, of modeling, and the other techniques of painting, the artists could achieve further progress only if they combined this mastery with largeness of vision, that is, if they admitted idealism as a determinant. This does not mean that further experimentation in the science and in the techniques ceased, but rather that all the extant knowledge of them plus any additional discoveries that were made in the art were employed in the service of idealism.

It is customary to attribute this shift in objective from representation to idealization to the parallel shift in philosophy from Aristotelianism to Neoplatonism. Whereas, according to Aristotle, reality did not exist apart from the particular, the revived Platonism maintained that true being existed outside the objects of nature, in the idea which the physical object merely embodied. Applied to painting, this necessarily meant depicting not what the physical eye saw but what the mind's eye could conceive;[46] and since the mental conception was more important than the visual image, it was deemed proper to depart from the physical actualities if by doing so the idea could be represented more accurately. One has only to visualize the thunderous nudes of Michelangelo or the elongated ones of El Greco to recognize the nature of this shift. Yet, lest it be assumed that "deformation" was the principal way by which a depiction of the ideally real was achieved, it should be pointed out that Leonardo da Vinci attained this end by adhering to the realities of the physical world and discovering in them the spiritual potency that actuates them.

The artist who is generally credited with initiating the shift was Alessandro Filipepi, popularly known as Botticelli (1444–1510) which is Italian for "little barrel." Apprenticed first to a goldsmith, he acquired the light touch of a technician. Subsequently he studied painting under Pollaiuolo, and from him he acquired the "sense of movement." From his association with the Medici court he acquired a taste for the refined. Here also he may have come under the influence of Neoplatonism.

Lastly, in 1491, he joined the followers of the mystic Savonarola whence came the deep emotionalism that appears in some of his later pictures. Hence, by training and by association he was fitted to lead the change.

As may be expected, his earlier works show the influence of Pollaiuolo and of Gherlandaio, but they illustrate little that is new and may be disregarded. His later works, such as *The Birth of Venus* (Plate 28), *The Primevera*, and *The Theological Virtues*,[47] represent the change. In them the element of idealism is paramount. The themes are allegorical, the human forms are represented generically and not realistically, the compositions are rhythmical, and the atmosphere lyrical. All things are so rendered as to suggest the ideal of beauty.[48]

In a more somber mood and reflecting the spiritual anguish that the revivalist preaching of Savonarola aroused in him is the picture *The Bewailing of Christ*. Using little of the macabre effect which the northerners employed in their *Pietas*, he yet succeeded in depicting the sense of utter grief, which indeed was his aim.

Before going on to the next exponent of the school of idealism, we might glance at the work of an Umbrian, the fascinating Pietro Vanucci, known as Perugino (1446–1523). Although a rogue and a cheat, defaulting on obligations without qualms, Perugino as a painter was refined and serene. In this he was in step with the International style, although he imparted more naturalism to his bodily forms than was customary with the Internationalists. His landscapes are particularly felicitous. They have an idyllic character and are so painted as to give the illusion that they are enveloped in air and bathed by light. They may well reflect the peace and charm of the Umbrian countryside; but at the same time they seem to transcend the particular and to suggest, by their warmth and vista, the communion of heaven and earth, that is, the oneness of Creation. This is well represented in *The Crucifixion*,[49] a detail of the larger subject *St. Bernard's Vision of the Virgin*. Here the serenity and the magnitude of the valley have an enveloping effect; and the crucified Christ at its head, represented sentimentally rather than tragically, seems to sustain that impression; for it is by his death that man can once more find comfort and peace in the embrace of his maker. Thus the old iconography and a new way of rendering spatial atmosphere and light are combined to register an appealing message.

If there is a question about the propriety of including Perugino among the idealists, how then can we classify that universal genius Leonardo da Vinci (1452–1519)? On the basis of the 120 notebooks which he compiled on things natural and philosophical and on the repeated advice therein to learn from nature,[50] one might be inclined to include him among the practitioners of the scientific mode. Certainly the numerous drawings of human and animal forms in a great variety of poses reveal him to be a searcher for the realities of anatomy and of motion.[51] The same may be concluded from the equally numerous drawings of mechanical contrivances. But scientist though he was, it would seem that he studied anatomy as he experimented with painting techniques and with the use of chiaroscuro, not merely to reproduce the physical realities obvious to the eye, but primarily to bring out the inner significance of the object or of the scene. In his own words, a painter should paint not just the physical man but the "intention of his soul" also; and that is what he himself strove to capture. This, of course, is something other than representation.

Two pictures may be chosen to study this property, the *Mona Lisa* and *The Last Supper*. In the first there is a naturalistic representation of a lady,[52] sufficiently individualized to be accepted by some art critics as an actual portrait. But it is obvious that the portrayal of the physical woman is not the picture's chief merit. Something else is more attractive: it is undefinable, and each spectator may well read his own meaning into it. We might suggest the idea of "the eternally feminine," but the suggestion seems to be inept as it carries with it a connotation of frailty and sensuousness, neither of which applies to the lady in the picture. "The mystery of womanhood?" No, even though she has the "mysterious" smile, and even though the background with the serpentine waters and the broken crags and the vapory, greenish atmosphere is enigmatic. Could it be just an ideal of beauty defined through "a strange quintessence of brooding dreams and intellectual detachment"?[53] Whatever label we should invent, it will certainly fail to convey the full meaning of the picture. All that can be said is that Leonardo succeeded in depicting a woman at once humanly warm and intelligent, but wistfully meloncholy as if to say that she knows the pains and joys of being a woman, and is a little tired and wants to dream.[54] The telling point is that one's mind does not stop at the physical reproduction but is attracted toward the imagined inner being. Perhaps we can say that Leonardo idealized by "psychologizing" his subjects. What techniques he employed to achieve this end is of course his secret, but two or three stand out prominently. One is the superb modeling with light and shade; another, the employment of a background that contributes to the mood of the subject;[55] and the third is the placement of the subject in the front plane of the picture.

The second work is *The Last Supper* (Plate 29) which he painted in the refectory of Santa Maria at Milan. Here he distills not the inward being as much as the essence of a dramatic situation. Christ has just declared that one of his colleagues would betray him, and the shock of the revelation has electrified the assemblage.[56] There is alarm and dismay and shocked conscience on the part of each apostle, and the calm of Christ by contrast actually intensifies the charged atmosphere. That is what Leonardo wished to convey, and his mastery of the human form, chiaroscuro, composition, and perspective is merely a means to an end which may be defined as "the soul of a dramatic occasion."

The third picture, *The Virgin of the Rocks*,[57] does not possess any quality that has not been observed in the two preceding masterpieces, unless it is the pyramidal arrangement of the principals. But it has been selected to illustrate the fact that, though artistically Leonardo is decidedly unmedieval, he yet retains some medievalism. The setting of rocks and caverns is an obvious departure from the medieval type of background if we were to consider it merely as a naturalistic background. But if we notice the inappropriateness of such a cold setting for two naked babies, we are at once struck by the possibility that the background is symbolical, and indeed it appears to be just that. Professor D. W. Robertson, Jr., has recently pointed out that "the openings in the rock are refuges for the faithful in Christ, [and that] the caverns are vacancies in the wall of the Lord's Vineyard," and he has traced the popularization of this interpretation back to the twelfth century.[58] Another feature, also reminiscent of medieval habits, is the attribution of mature religious feelings to the infants Jesus and John the Baptist.

Who could imagine a baby's head and upraised hand so pregnant with the message of its future mission? The medieval custom had generally cultivated this characteristic, and Leonardo here followed tradition even though he improved immeasurably on the depiction of a baby's body.

To move from Leonardo to the next notable artist, Raphael, is to move from a profound psychologist to a painter with a predilection for the sweet and the grand. For Raphael's sweetness the reader may turn to his earlier madonnas. Leonardesque in form and Peruginesque in their tranquil setting, they are warm and motherly and sweet, but they are wanting. Mary was not an ordinary mother but a woman who bore the Savior and saw him die on the cross; and this, his early madonnas do not convey. He failed to impart that sense of mission, for he only saw a good mother fondling her child. Only some of the later ones, like *Madonna di Foligno* and *Sistine Madonna* (Dresden) by their visionary signification saved the genre from this limitation. For the grand there are his *Disputa* (Plate 30) and the *School of Athens* in the Vatican.[59] Both are regarded as the finest creation in the High Renaissance style of painting. Nothing is lacking in them as to mastery of form, perspective, composition, or balance. They even have profundity, the first symbolizing the genesis of the miracle of transubstantiation, the second, the genesis of worldly knowledge in the philosophers and scientists of Greek antiquity — an accepted medieval idea, incidentally[60] — and the two together, the Renaissance culture as a synthesis of Greek learning and Christian faith. Yet, they look like grandiose illustrations, the work of an artist who had big ideas but could not quite translate them by his artistry.

Not so the next artist, the poet, sculptor, architect, and painter Michelangelo Buonarroti (1475-1564), a small and misshapen man with a touchy disposition, sensitive soul, and unexcelled powers of imagination. His training under Ghirlandaio and under Donatello's student Bertoldo inclined him to the monumental and the vital, and this inclination was strengthened by his admiration for the simple but powerful sculptures of Jacopo della Quercia. At the same time, he acquired somewhere — perhaps from the Neoplatonist circle in Florence and perhaps from observing the futile crash of high ideas on the sordid realities of

Italian politics — an attitude of mind which seemed to combine contrasts: hope with despair, and impotence with frenzied power. From thence, too, came his admiration for man as the grandest creature of God who yet is helpless without him,[61] a feeling which is so keenly reflected in his cry "Lord, what shall I do unless thou visit me with thine ineffable grace?"[62] From the combination of these two, the elemental and monumental with a passion torn between opposites, came forth the powerful creations that have always kept the world in awe.

The masterwork where all this can be studied is, of course, his celebrated decoration of the ceiling in the Sistine Chapel. In it the vehicle which conveys his message and his mood is the nude, and the means is *démesure*. Bodies are heavy, disproportionate, and twisted, but they proclaim a humanity that is heroic and dynamic. Everywhere is grandeur, but it is potential rather than actual and dependent on the engendering power of the mighty Creator. What would happen if this gift of greatness were misused can be seen in one of his later pictures, *The Last Judgment* (Plate 31), also in the Sistine Chapel. God appears titanic, his wrath inexorable, while man, though big, is both graceless and helpless, and his fall abysmal. This is a message which demands more than mere mastery of art; it requires exalted imagination and deep passion; that is, it requires Michelangelo.

Obviously Michelangelo was inimitable, and yet his influence was overpowering, and many tried to emulate him. But lacking his vision, they could only produce hollow dramatics. The forms they might copy, but the spirit was beyond them. The result was Mannerism, a post-Renaissance style which falls outside our period.

THE VENETIAN SCHOOL Most of the above artists who helped to guide the Renaissance style from naturalism to scientific realism and to ideal ism were from Florence, either by birth or by training, and are generally regarded as representatives of the "Florentine school" of painting. Those like Raphael and Michelangelo who labored in Rome, for the papacy especially, and who emphasized the properties of grandeur are said to belong to the "Roman school." Between them, these two schools formulated most of the great principles of Renaissance painting. Some lesser schools had also made their contributions. That of Perugia, for example, contributed to the mastery of space; that of Padua, to the cults of humanism and antiquity; that of Ferrara, elegance and impersonality; and so on. But there was one school whose contribution was great enough to win for it a place beside the "big two," namely, that of Venice.

The school was a product of several influences. From the Byzantine world, with which Venetian economic fortunes were closely entwined, came the predilection for deep colors. This was strengthened by the city's marine location: the dampness precluded much fresco painting and so diverted the painters to the use of oils, a more brilliant medium; at the same time the rich coloration of the waters and clouds which prevails there was bound to evoke a love for color. From the artistic and cultural centers of Italy came the various aspects of Renaissance style, such as, naturalism of form and movement, the science of perspective, and the cult of antiquity. From the commercial wealth and from the political and social constitution enshrining it came the glorification of earthly splendor and of the aristocratic. Combining these several influences into a harmonious one and breathing high spirit into it, Venice produced its own peculiar style.

In the formulation and expression of this style there were many painters. While a surprisingly large number of them had more than average competence, only a few of the most influential can be considered here.

The Bellinis came first in time. Jacopo (*ca.* 1400–1470), the father, represents the stage of transition from the International school led by his master Gentile da Fabriano to the Renaissance style. Gentile, the first son, tried to convert painting into a mirror of Venetian social life. The second son, Giovanni (1430–1516), brother-in-law of Andrea Mantegna and teacher of Giorgione and Titian, cultivated color.[63] Together they tended to make of painting a pictorial art, rich and attractive but not impressive.

The trend started by the Bellinis was carried on by Vittore Carpaccio and improved upon by Giorgione of Castelfranco. Carpaccio's works pay more attention to facial realism, but that is lost in the emphasis on the panoramic and the aristocratic.[64] Giorgione (*ca.* 1475–1510) may have excelled his predecessors in the use of color,[65] but his unquestioned contribution consisted of the introduction of Arcadian settings and mood, of a warm humanization of his subjects, and the admission of the sensuous. Through such pictures as *The Sleeping Venus* (Plate 32) or *The Picnic* he "established the female nude as a subject in its own right."[66] Its physical beauty is admitted and depicted warmly, but not exploited or vulgarized. In another of his works, *The Concert*,[67] he approaches idealism. What one sees in it is not just three people trying to work out a tune, but the idea of the problem of concertizing when some members are unequipped for the task intellectually or vocally.

All the foregoing developments were climaxed by the works of Titian. This versatile artist who lived to be almost a hundred years old (1477–1576) improved upon the art of composition. Not interested in mere verisimilitude, he made his composition serve as a stimulus for holding the viewer's interest. This he accomplished by balancing two opposites on the canvas, a clearly visible and a beckoning vista in one corner against a heavy mass darkened and pregnant in another corner. How this principle of composition evokes the viewer's interest and his powers of analysis can be seen from two of Titian's masterpieces, *Bacchus and Ariadne* (Plate 33) and the portrait of Charles V.[68] Another influential contribution of his consisted in the establishment of a widely accepted canon for portraiture. The portrait was to represent the subject as "a person of superior, physical, moral and intellectual power"[69] and to make the viewer look up to the subject with respect and admiration.[70] The third influence was the popularization of the female nude. Such works as *Sacred and Profane Love*, the *Bacchanale*, *The Offering to Venus*, *Venus and the Organ Player*, *Venus and Adonis*, *The Toilet of Venus*, and others can hardly be said to reflect a deep interest in the cult of antiquity. They must be taken for what they are, a sensuous glorification of the physical woman whose attraction derives almost wholly from her flesh. Finally, he influenced Venetian religious painting to assume a visually objective function, as if religion were a matter-of-fact habit. Such creations as *Noli me Tangere,* or the *Assumption*, or *The Virgin and the Infant*, or the *Madonna of the Pesaro Family* fail to evoke a religious feeling. They are attractive but they are not spiritually convincing. If his later works, such as *Crowning with Thorns*, and *Entombment*, were done in a more tragic mood,[71] they did not exert as much influence on the future painters as his earlier works and may be regarded as out of accord with the world-liness of the Venetian society.

What Titian left undone in the way of making painting great but earth-bound, Paolo Caliari of Verona (1528–1588), known as Veronese, completed. What he accomplished may be seen from his allegory *Venice Governing the World with Justice and Peace*.[72] Venice is a round-faced, youngish woman, buxom, resplendently robed, and seated on a throne covered with ermine. There is no sense of power and responsibility. Veronese merely dressed one of the lovely aristocratic ladies of the day, of ample proportions and dignity, and seated her on the throne. The result is obviously wanting in spiritual or symbolic significance. His saints are perhaps even more shallow. Saint Justina in the picture of her martyrdom or Saint Helena having a vision[73] are contemporary Venetian women displaying their resplendent robes and vaunting their bodily beauty. That was his role in shaping the Venetian style, namely, "idealizing prosaic magnificence," as Symonds puts it.[74] We might add that by resorting to exaggeration to accomplish this end, Veronese, more than Titian, prepared the way for Mannerism.

The last stylist of Renaissance painting in Venice was Jacopo Robusti, popularly known as Tintoretto (1518–1594). Following his own slogan "the color of Titian and the drawing of Michelangelo," he naturally gave great intensity to his work, which he still further accentuated by a deft use of light. Instead of employing illumination in accordance with the laws of light, he used it arbitrarily, as spotlights are used in the theater, to enhance the dramatic language of the scene.[75] This is illustrated in *The Presentation of the Virgin* (Plate 34). According to the staging of the scene, light falls on the stairs up which the little girl ascends in awe and adoration. Yet, though the light should bathe her clearly, she is barely touched by it; instead it is made to fall in an oval which seems to follow her. Even more glaringly in violation is the light that whitens the robes of the aged man in the lower left-hand corner of the picture. He descends the stairs in the shade of a tall wall; the stairs at his side are shaded, but his robe in the back and his leg are illuminated. Still, it is because of this manipulation of light that the dramatic effect is heightened. Another way in which he employed light is to be seen in *The Last Supper*.[76] Here it is represented as splashes of brightness streaming through darkness and creating an eerie impression — a method which El Greco later exploited so effectively to evoke a feeling of mysticism. In this picture, however, the note of the factitious is unmistakable. Perhaps this is partially due to the fact that the picture lacks spiritual significance, for what in it captures the eye and the mind are the mechanics of the art — unusual angles of vision, encompassment of the viewer into the space of the scene, impulsive movements and actions of the subjects — and not the intended message. Even such themes as *Christ Washing the Feet of the Apostles* and *Christ on the Road to Calvary* suffer from this defect — too much manifest skill and Tintoretto.[77]

With Tintoretto the High Renaissance style in Italy came to an end and Mannerism declared itself, and so the survey may be terminated with him.

Painting in the Netherlands during the Renaissance

In the Netherlands, which was second only to Italy in the art of painting, the Renaissance style passed through two stages. The first may be called the native or the Flemish stage, as it continued in an improved way the late Gothic style of the Flemish illuminators. It held the field unchallenged until about the end of the fifteenth century, with only a minimum admission of Italianisms. Thereafter it yielded steadily to the invading Italian style just studied, and this transformation may be regarded as the second stage of the Renaissance style in the Netherlands.

THE NATIVE STYLE The first stage, referred to as a continuation of the late Gothic style, was naturally possessed of the usual Gothic properties. Affectation and stylization are written over much of it. Madonnas are frequently represented as elegant, circumspect young ladies dressed in rich apparel. Robes and carpets and thrones are luxurious. Male subjects look as if they had just stepped out of the knightly parade of the order of the Golden Fleece; and Gothic castles dot the backgrounds. Gothic also is the iconography, especially the representation of the baby Jesus as a tiny man with a mature-looking face. But balancing these Gothicisms and saving the works, there was the property of visual realism. The photographic eye of the painter caught every detail and imprinted it exactly on the canvas: the fine and intricate designs in the cloth and the rugs, every hair in a fur collar, every wrinkle in the face of a man, and so on. This attention to exactness in facial appearance made for individualism and saved the paintings from excess of artificiality. Moreover, where simple folk were introduced into the scenes, they were represented with the smell of the earth still clinging to them, and this led to genre painting. It is this combination of the late Gothic stylization and realism which distinguishes the art of this stage from that of the International style and identifies it with the Renaissance style.

The first eminent artists who worked in this style were the Van Eyck brothers, Hubert and Jan. Until Hubert's death in 1426 (?) they collaborated in their work, apparently without revealing their respective hands; and since their common creations do not differ significantly from Jan's signed works, they might be treated as Jan's.

To select any one creation of Jan's as most exemplary is hardly possible. Three of his paintings therefore might be chosen as illustrative: *The Adoration of the Lamb* (known as the *Ghent Triptych*),[78] *Giovanni Arnolfini and His Wife* (Plate 35), and *The Madonna of Chancellor Rolin* (Plate 36). All combine stylization with realism as described in the preceding paragraph. The luxurious raimant of God the Father and the Virgin, the elegance of the cavalcade of knights and judges, and the trim, idyllic-like trees in the first picture, and an equal display of resplendence of dress in the third picture stamp the works as traditionalist. At the same time the facial realism of Adam and Eve in the first picture and the utter realism of the face of Chancellor Rolin in the last mark the works as new. The picture of Arnolfini and his wife represents similar characteristics, but there the spirit of the bourgeois replaces the aristocratic atmosphere of the other two. At the same time the subject, perhaps a ceremony of a marriage agreement, reveals another significant trait, namely, admission of the intimate and the folksy. In all three there is an obvious absence of emotion and the figures seem to be immobilized.[79] The pictures therefore look severe. On the other hand, their colors are deep and warm, their brilliance being due to the luminosity of the oil medium upon which he improved and with which he built his pictorial world. One additional phase of Jan's work, which is prominent in all three of the paintings listed but which should be emphasized, is his portraiture. It is difficult to discern his secret in portraiture. Panofsky suggests that it is his emphasis on the individuality, which is another way of saying that it is a product of visual realism; but at the same time, and this is indeed on the level of genius, the likeness which he attained through realism is not a surface likeness but one which also reflects the realities of the inner man.[80] Thus, without psychologizing his subjects, he yet succeeded in getting them to declare themselves.

Another influential exponent of the Flemish style was Rogier van der Weyden (*ca.* 1400–1464) of Tournai, known also by the name of Rogier de la Pasture. He retained most of the characteristics developed by Jan van Eyck; but whereas Van Eyck emphasized descriptiveness, Rogier heightened the emotional content, made his figures more dynamic, and the pictures warmer.[81] His achievement, represented in such works as *St. Luke Painting the Virgin, Bladelin Nativity*, and the *Deposition*,[82] consisted, as Mather suggests, in following "the way of progress without sacrificing the precious heritage of the Gothic past."[83]

Deviating from the photographic realism of Van Eyck and the pretty pietism of Rogier were the creations of Petrus Christus and of Dirck Bouts. Christus' *A Carthusian* and *St. Eligius and a Couple*[84] reveal the deviation to be in the direction of a "homely idiom . . . humbly human rather than heroic."[85] Dirck's *The Last Supper* and the *Beheading of the Innocent Knight*[86] show an inclination to rigidity in the vertical axes and a noticeable impassivity.

With Hans Memling (*ca.* 1433–1494) came the return to Van Eyck and to Rogier van der Weyden. Any of his pictures of the Madonna or his *Mystic Marriage of St. Catherine*[87] contain all the *agréments* of Van Eyck and the form and grace of Rogier. His own mark on them consists in the general sweetness with which he invests these pictures and the obviousness of his symmetry. His predilection for the sweeter and the warmer expressed itself in portraiture in softer realism than that of Van Eyck, or, as Panofsky puts it, in "a genuine synthesis of stylization and verisimilitude."[88]

While Memling was painting almost wholly in the refined Flemish tradition, his contemporary from Ghent, Hugo van der Goes (1430–1482), and his fellow citizen from Bruges, Gerard David (d. 1523), began to depart in the direction of the Italian style. Basically they were still following the mode of Van Eyck and Rogier, but they added to it greater plasticity of form, imparted more humanity to their people, tried their hand at Leonardesque *sfumato*, and introduced monumentality to their portraits and dramaturgy to their compositions. That they attained considerable success may be judged from the fact that, whereas the earlier Flemish works were judged by Michelangelo to be "painting . . . of stuffs — bricks and mortar, the grass of the fields, the shadows of trees, and bridges and rivers which they call landscapes, and little figures here and there,"[89] the works of Van der Goes, particularly the *Nativity* which he painted for the Florentine Tommaso Portinari, served as models for two generations of Italian painters, Ghirlandaio most of all.[90]

The principal paintings in which the two Flemish painters reveal themselves as traditionalists with only a slight admission of Italianism are David's *Marriage of St. Catherine, The Virgin among Virgins*, and Van der Goes' *David and Abigail*.[91] David's *Judge Sisamnes Accused* has more dramatic power than is usual for the Flemish style, and Van der Goes' *Nativity* and *Death of the Virgin* have some monumentality.[92] The *Nativity* has captured the spirit of awe and adoration combined particularly well.

With Gerard David and Hugo van der Goes the first stage of Flemish Renaissance style was moving into the second stage. However, before the Italianate stage is examined, a glance at the eccentric painter Jerome Bosch and the great genre artist Peter Bruegel is in order.

Jerome Bosch (*ca.* 1450–1516) defiies understanding. Mather refers to him as "a sinister visionary," "a spokesman of the terrifying belief in sorcery, witchcraft and all manner of diabolism," and "a satirist and a cynic."[93] Sewall regards him as a social psychiatrist who delved into "the nether reaches of the mind, that realm more-real and yet not real, before whose gateway all men pause in dread."[94] Mather is of the opinion that he obtained his grotesque forms from the carved decorations in the cathedrals, while Panofsky calls them archaisms and suggests that they came "from the fantastic and often Rabelaisian humor of the drolleries in the fourteenth and early fifteenth century manuscripts, English as well as Continental . . . from the physiognomical overstatements — crass by a very excess of veracity — of the *réalisme* pre-Eyckian," and from "the illustration of such allegorical treatises and poems as the *Pèlerinage de vie humaine*."[95]

Done in exaggerated realism and caricature but not fantastically is his *Christ before Pilate* (Plate 37). Christ is shown as a little "preacher, hopelessly trapped, and resigned to his fate."[96] The difference in the power between him and the hard and cruel officials who surround him is of telling effect,[97] and one wonders if the picture does not hint at the failure of Christianity. *The Prodigal Son*[98] may be taken as an illustration of Flemish genre painting and so one of his saner pictures. But the type of picture by which he is known to the world is represented by such works as the *Hay Wagon* or the *Garden of Delight*.[99] The first is a rendition of the Flemish proverb "the world is a mound of hay, each one takes what he can grasp." It shows a huge wagon of hay on which lovers dally and which all humanity, represented by popes, emperors, princes, and commoners, follow in equanimity, while other folk press about its wheels, engage in brawls, and are helplessly crushed. The load is drawn by demons and is headed straight for the Inferno, which is depicted in the form of yawning mills amid a burning and fuming landscape. The second, *Garden of Delight*, is more complicated. In the foreground there is a conglomerate multitude of nudes, tiny and lithesome, mostly in pairs, and generally in provocative poses. Higher up, around a fountain of youth — really a circular pool in which doll-like nudes wade knee-high in obvious pleasure — humanity, represented by a myriad of little, naked people, mounted on various animals — horses, oxen, tigers, bears, boars, camels, etc. — rides everlastingly in an orgy of passion. Above this central theme is a pond whence rise fantastic shapes and where other lithe people, oblivious of their fate, continue with their incredible activities. On the sides are the Earthly Paradise and the City of Hell. Both pictures apparently are satires on man's earthly folly and on his unconcern for anything else but the passions of the flesh, but the moral messages are considerably obscured by the excessive grotesqueness which provokes sheer amazement rather than awe.

To achieve the most telling effect he resorted to a variety of artistic devices. He used light and shade expertly to bring out volume, to create the sense of space, or to capture the mood of the atmosphere as occasion demanded;[100] but generally his pictures have a hazy overcast that dulls the colors. He used mere outline or silhouette to suggest form, but in the case of arboreal scenes he sometimes resorted to the illuminators' techniques. His *St. John the Baptist in the Desert*, particularly as to trees and shrubs, is unmistakably Eyckian.[101] He employed elegance, but he was superb in caricature. Finally, while some of his work is narrative, it does not stop with narration but attempts to psychologize it. This is well illustrated in the *Prodigal Son*.[102]

Greater than Bosch because he was less given to phantasmagorias was Peter Brueghel the Elder (*ca.* 1528–1569). During his twenties he was an etcher for an engraving shop and often prepared reproductions of some of Bosch's work, so that Bosch's influence naturally carried over into his own work. This is reflected, for example, in *The Triumph of Death*, *The Fall of the Rebel Angels*, and in the *Mad Meg*,[103] where such Boschian devices as toadlike fishes, kettle-topped beings, fire-belching horizons, cadavers, transparent globes enclosing little people, etc., are quite conspicuous. However, his temperament was more serene; his outlook on the world, saner; and Italian influence on him, particularly as to composition, greater. These made his pictures more natural and more logical. But the greatest influence on him was his love of the Dutch people and their countryside. He painted the folk in small groups, and he painted them in mulititudes; he painted them at work, at sport, and at festivities. With them he painted their homes and towns and their countryside. This concentration on ordinary reality won him high regard as a genre painter.

Pictures which represent him best as the exponent of the Dutch scene are the five extant of the series of the *Seasons*.[104] In them he captured the climate as well as the mood: thus the sunlit grainfield, heavy with calmness, creates the impression of harvest sultriness; on the other hand the blanket of snow over a valley interspersed with large splashes of gray ice, the dark leafless trees, the heavy-coated hunters trudging, and the ambling pace of the hounds give an impression of a numbing cold. Both pictures seem to suggest nature's supremacy over struggling man who appears to be unaware of the struggle. Pictures which reveal him as an admirer of countryfolk are his *Peasants' Dance* (Plate 38), *The Wedding Dance*, and *Country Wedding*.[105] Without sentimentalizing, with only a touch of the caricature, he succeeds in establishing an intimacy between these country people and the viewer. There is a casualness and a naturalism that is infectious. Also in the genre style but proverbial in content and moralistic in purport are such pictures as *Misanthrope, The Land of Plenty, The Birds' Nester, The Unfaithful Shepherd*. In the same spirit but larger in conception are his *Nativity* and the *Slaying of the Innocents*,[106] both of which are probably satires on Spanish outrages against the Dutch.

His style is that of Bosch, only superior. Capable of rendering in the precise Flemish style, he however eschewed the stylized delicateness of the Eyckian school and preferred to block out his subjects with masses of color. His forms are therefore heavy and monumental, and this characteristic is managed with telling effect in the silhouette. With this style he combined the principle that "the world is a vast universe of space, the human population a detail, and the single person insignificant,"[107] and the combination resulted in elemental naturalism.

THE ITALIANATE STYLE With Brueghel the survey of the native stage of Netherlandish painting during the Renaissance period may be terminated and the second stage, the Italianate stage, turned to. Appearance of the Italianate style was noted in the works of Hugo van der Goes and David. After them the Italian stream grew larger until it overwhelmed the native style.

Among the number of artists who expanded the stream two may be noted. Jan Gossart introduced the nude (*Adam and Eve*),[108] big and muscular like Michelangelo's though somewhat ignoble in treatment. He also employed the chiaroscuro in which he used light as Tintoretto was to use it later (*The Agony in the Garden*).[109] His portraiture imitated the Leonardesque style (*Jean Carondelet*).[110] Quentin Massys (1465–1530), whom Thomas More saluted as "*veteris novator artis*," added still more to the stream. Monumentality and composition after Leonardo and Raphael were two of his principal contributions. Next came his use of color dramatically and the humanization of the portrait. These can be observed in his *Deposition, The Choirmaster*, and *Aegidius*.[111] However, they were not purely Italianate, for the facial realism of the subjects and the macabre-looking body of Jesus in the *Deposition* are definitely Flemish. Almost wholly in the Flemish tradi-

PLATE 34 — Tintoretto's *The Presentation of the Virgin*. By permission of Alinari-Art Reference Bureau.

PLATE 37 — Bosch's *Christ before Pilate*. By permission of
Art Reference Bureau, Inc.

PLATE 38 — Brueghel's *Peasant Dance.* By permission of Art Reference Bureau, Inc.

PLATE 39 — Van Orley's *The Virgin and Child with Angels.* By permission of The Metropolitan Museum of Art, Bequest of Benjamin Altman (1913).

tion also is Massys' celebrated *Banker and Wife*,[112] which he copied from Van Eyck, where he employs much of the Flemish vocabulary and re-captures the bourgeois spirit generally associated with such Flemish genre paintings. Hence it is fitting to regard these two painters, espe-cially the latter, as cultivators of "a genuine synthesis between the indigenous tradition and the Italian High Renaissance."[113]

The elimination of this "indigenous tradition" was the work of four men. One was Bernard van Orley (1493–1542), who studied at Rome, where the works of Raphael and Michelangelo were already attracting wide attention, and became painter to the court of Burgundy. He imitated Raphael's ideal of beauty and grandness of concept and achieved measurable success therein. His *Madonna* (Plate 39), somewhat heavy headed, has some of the sweetness and loveliness for which Raphael's madonnas are noted. His *Last Judgment*[114] has the cast of a grand illus-tration, but the angels floating in the sky lack grandeur and resemble in beauty those in Raphael's *Ascension*. Second was Jan van Scorel (1495–1562), canon of Utrecht cathedral. He studied under various masters, including Dürer, and spent two years at Rome. His works, according to Mather, imitate Raphael's bodies and Titian's landscapes.[115] The *Bap-tism of Christ*[116] is regarded as one of his maturer creations. What it reveals is a somewhat sentimentalized Raphaelism. Franz Floris (1516–1570), sometimes called the "Flemish Raphael," was probably the fore-most of these Italianizers. He tried to imitate Michelangelo's rendering of the nude, but succeeded only in introducing the style of the "scien-tific" school. This is illustrated in his *Fall of the Rebel Angels*[117] where the display of the muscularity of the tumbling nudes is closer to Signo-relli than to Michelangelo. Finally, Marten de Vos (1531–1603), student of Floris and of Tintoretto, tried to introduce the latter's style of organi-zation and management of light. If he was only partially successful in this attempt, still his works have very little of the Flemish style left. *The Tribute Money*[118] illustrates both facts.

PLATE 40 — El Greco's *Saint Andrew*. By permission of The Metropolitan Museum of Art, Bequest of Stephen C. Clark (1960).

Our conclusion would be challenged by those who would include Rubens and Van Dyck in the history of Netherlandish Renaissance painting. But chronologically both men did their work in the seventeenth century, which is generally not included in the Renaissance period, and stylistically, according to the accepted canons of classification, they belong to the Baroque. Hence even if they do represent the culmination of the Italian style in the Low Countries, it is not the High Renaissance style that culminates in them, but the Italian Baroque. We are justified, therefore, in closing our survey of the Italian Renaissance style in the Netherlands with Marten de Vos and so with second-rate artists at best.

Painting in Germany during the Renaissance

As in the Netherlands, so in Germany, Renaissance painting had two phases, the native and the Italianate. But the relative merits of the two were reversed: in Germany the native phase, always weak, yielded to the superior excellence of the so-called Italianate.

THE NATIVE STYLES: "SMALL TOWN" ART To discern some characteristics common to the native phase throughout the land is rather difficult. There was no Van Eyck in Germany to command wide acceptance of one style, and so a number of local schools developed each with its own characteristics. Still, some generalizations may be ventured.

One property more or less common is the apparent kinship of this art with Flemish miniature art, but with the gracefulness reduced and the homeliness increased. Noticeable also are the narrative style and a tendency toward emotionalism. The combination of these three traits with regional characteristics and with a certain lack of competence on the part of the artists resulted in, what Mather calls, "small-town" art.[119] No wonder one of the painters of this type of art was driven to inscribe on one of his pictures:

> Cry aloud, Art, and mourn bitterly, for no one now desires you! Alas! Alas! 1431. Lucas Moser of Weil, Master of this work; pray God for him.[120]

As representatives of this native tradition three or four artists merit some notice. The author of the above lament, Lucas Moser, is one of

these. His pictures on the subject of St. Mary Magdalen[121] reveal him
as a folksy narrator with a touch of the illuminator and the Flemish
realist. Conrad Witz (d. 1448) of Geneva and Basel is another. His
St. Mary Magdalen and St. Catherine and *Annunciation* illustrate his
lack of imagination but reveal his proficiency in the use of light and
shade; while his *Deliverance of St. Peter* shows him as a storyteller.[122]
More deserving of recognition is Michael Pacher of Bruneck in Tyrol.
In general, his conceptions were nobler and his modeling more substantial. He seems to have come under some Italian influence: his nude
Trajan in *St. Gregory and Trajan*[123] is believed to be a direct study of
Mantegna. A better work is one of the scenes from the legend of St.
Wolfgang, namely, *St. Wolfgang and the Devil*.[124] The saint, for exam-
ple, has a largeness of body and of character generally lacking in Ger-
man painting before the time of Dürer.

Far superior to any of the above was Mathis Gothart-Neithart, known
popularly as Matthias Grünewald (*ca.* 1468–1528). Because of his general excellence, and because of the difference in the character of his work
as compared with that accomplished in the "small-town" tradition, he is
at times included among those who painted in the High Renaissance
style. This classification is questionable, for he lacked the essentials of
the latter style, that is, humanism and classicism, while he was strong
in the mysticism and emotionalism of the late Middle Ages. Perhaps,
therefore, he should be included with the Native school but recognized
as exceptional.

His masterwork is the Isenheim altarpiece now at Colmar. It consists of ten panels on which are painted the great events in the life of
Jesus — *Annunciation and Nativity, Crucifixion, Deposition,* and *Resur-
rection* — and scenes from the experiences of the anchorite St. Anthony.
A general examination of these[125] will reveal some traits of the native
style. In the *Temptation of St. Anthony* are to be found the diabolic
monstrosities; in the *Annunciation* and *Nativity*, the domestic-type features of the Virgin and the angels, and the practical but ideally inappropriate utensils of tub, pot, and crib; in the *Crucifixion*, the macabre of
Christ's body and extravagant emotionalism; and in *The Meeting of
Holy Erasmus with Holy Mauritius*, the excessive attention to dress
ornamentation. In the weird wildness of the backgrounds in the

Anthony pictures and in the exaggeration of the sinister coarseness of the mockers of Christ in *The Derision of Christ* there is also some Boschianism. These features are more in the tradition of the native school than in that of the High Renaissance. On the other hand, the prevailing dynamism and the use of color arbitrarily to accent the intended emotions are Italianate. However, they do not transform his style into High Renaissance style.

THE ITALIANATE STYLE The High Renaissance style, or what passes for that in Germany, was the accomplishment of four notable artists: Albrecht Dürer (1471–1528), Lucas Cranach (1472–1553), Albrecht Altdorfer (*ca.* 1480–1538), and Hans Holbein (1497–1543). Their contemporaneousness raises the question of the apparently sudden burgeoning of the Italianate — and to this, two reasons may be offered and a note of caution appended. One reason undoubtedly was the focusing of attention on Italy as a source of culture by the German humanists and artists. This is illustrated, for example, in Dürer's report to his humanist friend, Willibald Perkenheimer, that in matters artistic Italy is to Germany as the sun is to cold.[126] The other reason is the political success of the Holy Roman Emperor Charles V in thwarting the French claims to Milan and in converting Italy to an imperial protectorate. This naturally led to greater intercourse between the two lands and to increased influence on the art of painting, particularly since it was the very age — the first half of the sixteenth century — when Italian painting was at its highest. Yet, while these two circumstances exposed German painting to increasing influences of the Italian High Renaissance style, the resulting transformation was not complete. This is the word of caution, for, as shall presently be seen, the German High Renaissance style retains several characteristics of the native tradition.

Dürer, one of eighteen children of an immigrant Hungarian goldsmith, began his training in his father's shop. There he learned how to use the graver, and the skill remained with him throughout his career. Subsequently he was apprenticed to a painter who operated a shop where books were illustrated, and there he learned the art of woodcutting. In 1490 he began a four-year tour which took him to a number of German painters, to Venice, and to Basel where he gained a reputation as a designer for woodcuts. In 1505 he visited Italy again and lived with

Giovanni Bellini in Venice. In the meantime he had established a firm friendship with the great humanist of Nuremberg, the celebrated Willibald Perckenheimer, who introduced him to the classics and mythology. In 1515 he was honored by Emperor Maximilian with a pension of 100 florins a year, and in his endeavor to have this grant confirmed by the future Emperor Charles V he traveled to Flanders and there learned to appreciate the works of the great Flemish masters.

From these few facts about his career one would conjecture that Dürer's works would contain both influences, the native and the Italian, and indeed this is so. The native tradition appears in several traits. One is the use of "idiomatic homeliness." Particularly strong in his engravings, as may be seen in the *Knights of the Apocalypse* and in *Anne and Joachim*,[127] it is also present in his finest paintings. The faces and heads of his madonnas, for example, look like inadequately idealized heads of German women,[128] while the faces of the superbly rendered apostles, although suggesting strong-spirited men, look like some faces that he may have seen on the streets of his city.[129] The same is true of his St. George in the Paumgartner altar.[130] The subject's face is rendered idiomatically in keeping with the facial realism so dear to the Netherlandish painters, except that Dürer has toned down the microscopic detail. Two other traits are his realistic rendition of details[131] and the use of heavy robes which are made to fall in monumental folds. Then there is the use of medieval symbolism and iconography. His engraving of the *Knight, Death and Devil* represents a Christian faced with the problems of daily life; *Saint Jerome in His Study* is an allegory on the contemplative life, Jerome symbolizing the Christian scholar who secludes himself to contemplate; *The Revelation of St. John the Divine* and the illustrations for his *Apocalypse* reflect a mood of fear and apprehension, his own as well as the public's, due to the belief of an impending doom at the midmillennium (1500), a mood similar to that which prevailed five hundred years earlier when the populace became alarmed at the prospect that the world would end in the year 1000;[132] and *Melancholia* probably stands for the inadequacy of the creative faculty.[133] It is well known that, in spite of his pride in his workmanship and his search for some rational principles behind beauty, he believed "that the power of artistic creation was a mystery not to be taught, not to be learned, not to be accounted for except by the grace of God and influences from above."[134] Perhaps the *Melancholia* symbolizes this concept, and if the interpretation is correct, then it would testify to Dürer's limited acceptance of humanism.

The High Renaissance characteristics in his work are no less notable. One is his empiricism, a combination of his concern for the science of space, distance, and light, for figure construction, and for objective realism. This is clearly represented in such works as *Knight, Death and Devil*, the *Army Beleaguering a City*, and his *Self-Portrait as a Journeyman*.[135] Another is the grand style of composition. This is successfully accomplished in the *Adoration of the Trinity*, and somewhat less well in the *Madonna of the Rose Crowns* where the overcrowding detracts from the attempt at largeness.[136] Closely related to this characteristic is the property of idealism. Present in some of his grander compositions, it is strongly present in several of his self-portraits[137] and in his *Adam and Eve*,[138] now at Madrid, which is, however, quite ineffectual. A third trait is the admission of classical form. This is amply illustrated in the difference between his engraving of Minerva, symbol for philosophy, and that of his master Wohlgemut:[139] whereas Wohlgemut's is Gothic, Dürer's is classic organically as well as in pose. A similar contrast is to be found in his illustration of the *Death of Orpheus* and in *Ovide Moralisé* done ten years earlier.[140] With the classic form came the classic theme, hence such pictures as his mermaids, Venuses, and Graces. But many of these lack refinement and look merely like pictures of corpulent nudes.[141] This emphasis on the corporeal structure of the human form probably derives from Mantegna, some of whose mythological engravings Dürer copied in 1494. This Mantanesque influence may be seen in the nudes in the *Bathhouse*.[142] Perhaps the strongest Italianate trait is the modeling in light and shade. In this technique he was superb.

On the whole it would appear that in Dürer's works the High Renaissance style predominated over the native. However, in view of the persistence of the native elements in them, particularly in the engravings, he cannot be classified purely as a High Renaissance painter. Rather, he belongs to both schools, with the Italian having a commanding role.

The next two representatives of the High Renaissance style, Cranach and Altdorfer, were less influential in shaping the history of German painting and may be dealt with briefly. They retained many of the characteristics present in Dürer and, in general, did not improve upon them. Cranach actually lacked largeness of conception and expanded his efforts on the simulation of prettiness, in which case, it would seem, he was looking backward to the International style. When applied to his female nudes this "prettification" resulted in unclassic, lascivious forms, made the more provocative sometimes by being dressed in big hats or necklaces.[143] In general, his pictures are defective in emotion, but strong in affected sentiment. Altdorfer had the tendency of de-etherealizing religious subjects and of bathing them in a fairytale atmosphere. A romantic, he found inspiration in nature's vastness and tried to reproduce that fascination in his paintings. How he combined the power of nature with man is excellently shown in *St. George* and the *Battle of Issues*.[144] In the first, St. George on his well-mannered horse has come upon a beast, but both man and beast are dwarfed by the immense forest, not weird nor foreboding, but fairylike. On the other hand, in the second the mightiness of the impending battle is suggested by the huge massing of the martial host on land and an equally portentous massing of the storm clouds above. One mass reinforces the other, and the two intensify the portent of the message. The whole is fantastic but in an entirely different spirit from that in St. George. In either of these, as in most of his pictures, there is little that is Gothic, unless it be the property of elegance rather than of vigor in St. George's horse or in the idyllic stamp of his trees or in the rich caparison and the pricking gait of the horses in the Issus scene.

Hans Holbein is difficult to assess. In his portraiture, which was his greatest achievement, he could be Italianate or German as he wished. His *Bonifacius Amerbach*, *Erasmus* (Basel), and *Sir Thomas More* were all modeled broadly in the Italian manner, but his later portraits, especially for his English patrons, such as that of Jane Seymour or of Anne of Cleves, are done in the Flemish technique.[145] There is at the same time a comparable distinction in characterization. Those done in Italian style bring out the inner state of the persons; those done in line are surface likenesses, depicted expertly but without sympathy. In his religious pictures there were some German traits. His *Madonna of the Meyer Family*[146] combines the ideal with the idiomatic and thereby suffers in majesty. On the other hand, the naturalism of the face of the donor in devout prayerfulness could hardly be improved upon. Similarly German was the macabre realism of his dead Christs, but the decorations which he fashioned for the house façades of some people at Lucerne and again at Basel were in the high classical mode, derived from Mantegna. He was also capable of the monumental style as appears from his design *Samuel Denouncing Saul*.[147] Thus, expert beyond experts, he could work in whatever style he pleased or his patrons desired. Still he can hardly be classified as wholly Italianate. Mather calls him a cosmopolitan stylist, and this appraisal may well be accepted.

Painting in France during the Renaissance

THE FLEMISH SCHOOL Following the epoch of the grand illuminators and of the International stylists, France did not have a distinguished era of painting as did Italy, Flanders, or Germany. There was no influential native school, and so foreign styles prevailed, principally Flemish and Italian, and a little German. The Flemish school was represented by a number of known artists, but only a few deserve mention and then mainly for their portraiture. One of the first workers is this style was Jean Fouquet (*ca.* 1415–1480), a miniaturist who spent two years in Italy and eventually became Louis XI's painter and "illuminator." He attained considerable renown as a realistic illuminator, and the technique naturally carried over into his paintings. In the two acclaimed works, *The Virgin and the Child* and the portrait of Charles VII,[148] the Gothic and the Flemish manners are paramount. The first is an impossible rendition of a great theme, unless one should find satisfaction in its hieratic formalism, in its red-and blue-colored angels or in the fact that it is an undevotional representation of Mary — the model reputedly being Charles VII's mistress Agnes Sorel. The second by its realism succeeds in bringing out the neurasthenic character of the subject. With an inconstant sovereign like that to head the state it is no wonder that destiny had to find a savior of the nation in the person of Joan of Arc. A more effective portrait known as *The Man with the Glass of Wine*[149] and painted by an anonymous artist is also done in Flemish style. Bypassing Simon Marmion, whose scenes from the life of St. Bertin[150] are fashioned in miniaturist style, and Jean Perréal, or Jean de Paris, as the probable painter of Louis XII,[151] also in the Flemish tradition, we come to the finest exponent of the northern type of portraiture, the noted François Clouet (*ca.* 1510–1572). François' father, Jean, was also a portraitist, but the son abandoned his father's more substantial modeling[152] for the northern mannerist style. The *Lady in Her Bath*[153] combines portraiture with domesticity in the tradition of the Flemish school. His *Pierre Quthe*[154] is posed after the style of Florence and follows the canons that Titian established for portraiture, but his portrait of Charles IX[155] as to "stance of figure [and] flat, almost heraldic treatment of the elaborately embroidered dress" shows German influence and conforms to the "international mannerist style."[156]

THE ITALIANATE STYLE The High Renaissance style was a deliberate import and as such did not establish solid roots in French soil during the period of the Renaissance. Although Italian influences were constantly asserting themselves from the time the International style appeared, they were mainly those of Milan, which were themselves conditioned by northern influences, and not of sufficient hauteur to displace the northern styles. This may be observed in Nicholas Froment's *Moses and the Burning Bush* or Fouquet's *Pieta*.[157] This remained the situation until Francis I, the man who reportedly claimed that he had "inspected all the best works and by the greatest masters of Italy,"[158] determined to bring the High Renaissance style at one sweep. He collected works of Leonardo da Vinci, Raphael, and Titian and tried to induce the great Italian painters to work for him. Leonardo responded and actually spent the last three years of his life attached to the court, and Andrea del Sarto spent one year (1518–1519). But when the foremost artists were not to be had, Francis accepted those not so great, among them Rosso and Primaticcio.

Giovanni Battista de Guasparre, known as Rosso, was a Florentine painter and designer who worked in Rome between 1523 and 1527, moved about in Italy after the sack of the city, and in 1530 accepted Francis' invitation to supervise the decoration of the palace at Fontainebleau. Francesco Primaticcio was a Bolognese associate of Giulio Romano, the artist who employed the Raphaelesque style of combining sculptured stucco and painting in decorating the Gonzaga palace at Mantua. He brought Romano's style to France when he joined Rosso in 1532 at Fontainebleau. Neither man had real depth, with the result that the Grand style of Rome which they introduced at Francis I's favorite palace turned out to be merely an affected imitation.

What it became in their hands may be gathered from their stucco decorations and from several extant paintings or designs for the same.[159] Clearly it is a mannered style. The nudes aspire to classical form, but turn out to be fashioned copies of the Hellenistic ideal style. This is particularly true of Primaticcio's work, and his was the greater influence. His body forms are softened structurally, are sinuous, elongated, and are given calculated traits; the profiles are prettily classic; the air is that of graceful but artificial staging. In general, to use Mather's phrase, the mark of a "consciously willed elegance"[160] is patently all over them.

What these two artists started others carried to excess. Niccolo dell' Abbate of Modena, who had joined the staff at Fontainebleau by 1552, carried this style to idyllic heights as illustrated in his *Orpheus and Eurydice*,[161] and in doing so made landscape painting fashionable. Antoine Caron (*ca.* 1520–1600) pandered to the neurotic tastes of the aristocracy with his renditions of *fêtes galantes* and of classical mythology, all in a highly mannerist style.

Francis I had wished to make France of his time a center of the Grand style of the Renaissance. But, when his artistic protégés brought the Renaissance style to his court, affected gracefulness replaced grandeur. France therefore failed to develop a distinguished Renaissance style of painting as it had failed to cultivate a strong native style.

Painting in England during the Renaissance

England had its style of painting in the Middle Ages, and there were one or two English artists — John Siferwas, for example — who painted competently in the International style; but it had no native school of painting during the Renaissance. With the repudiation of the Roman Catholic church went also rejection of its art, and no new school of painting was born to replace that art. What painting there was, was mostly portraiture, and practically all of it was done by foreign artists. Since most of these were from Netherlands or Germany

— Holbein, Gerlach Flicke, Hans Eworth, Guillim Scrots (Stretes), Antonio Moro[162] — their style was that of Netherlands or Germany, and that we have already studied.

In the course of Queen Elizabeth's reign two native artists appeared, George Gower, a merchant turned painter who became Elizabeth's Sergeant Painter, and Nicholas Hilliard (*ca.* 1547–1619), her limner and goldsmith. There is nothing distinctive about Gower's work[163] except that it is not done in line as were the works of the visiting continental artists. Hilliard's, on the other hand, has the distinction of not only copying the Mannerist style of the contemporary court of France but also of bringing out the subject's character.[164]

With these few remarks, we have said enough that needs to be reported about Renaissance painting in England.

Painting in Spain during the Renaissance

The first stage of painting in Spain during the Renaissance has been mentioned but not examined. It was the stage of the invasion of the late medieval Italian and Flemish styles, separately and blended in the International style. Subsequently, from the time of Ferdinand and Isabella when Burgundy and Naples were tied to Spain, there was another, more intense influx of both these streams, but with the Italian influence stronger. This later invasion may be considered as the second stage in Spanish painting during the Renaissance. The last stage came in the late sixteenth century when the native influence reasserted itself over the foreign styles.

FLEMISH AND ITALIAN SCHOOLS: THE FIRST AND SECOND STAGES In the early part of the first stage the Flemish current seemed to predominate. Works of such Netherlanders as Rogier van der Weyden, Dirck Bouts, and Gerard David were in vogue. Flemish painters worked in various centers in Spain, and Spanish artists went to Flanders to study with the great masters themselves — Luis Dalmáu, for example, studied in Van Eyck's studio. Out of this stream there issued several notable representatives. Bernardo Martorell (?–1453) combined the Flemish interest in realistic detail with northern pietism and Byzantine hieraticism into a fascinating style.[165] Luis Dalmáu (?–1460) followed the Flemish style also, and in addition reduced the devotional content. In his *Madonna of the Councillors*,[166] for example, the two donors are represented as typical northern *bon bourgeois* both stylistically and in characterization. Admittedly, however, his color has not the brilliance of the Flemish works. Jorge Inglés continued the trend in his retable for the Hospital of Buitrago. In the pictures of the donors, the Marquis of Santillana and his wife, the color has the brilliance common to Flemish painting.[167] Perhaps his characterization is deeper than that customary in Flemish works. The greatest of these representatives was Bartholomé Bermejo. In such works as *Santa Engracia* and *St. Michael*[168] he shows himself strictly a follower of the International style. His *Santo Domingo de Silos*[169] is reputed to be his best work, equal to the Flemish in color, but the formalism of the throne and the flat background is Gothic rather than Flemish. What he could create however is best illustrated in the *Pieta*[170] he painted for Canon Luis Despla. It is not pure Flemish but combines the Flemish body form and Flemish interest in the microscopic with the composition of the Italians and with effective manipulation of light and dark. The unshaven, woeful face of the donor, the macabre realism of the dead Christ's body, as well as the deep anguish of the Virgin are fully in the tradition of the north. The delicate rendition of the herbs and leaves is also Flemish. But the organization of the whole, canopied by a threatening storm, is full of dramatic portent and reflects the large spirit of Italian artists. With this masterpiece the era of the Primitives came to end, and that of the Italian Renaissance style began.

Italian influences operated contemporaneously with the Flemish, and early traces can be found. One Gherardo Starnina, a Florentine, painted the Chapel of St. Bloise in the cathedral of Toledo. Another Florentine, Dello di Nicola, was responsible for the *Last Judgment* in the apse of the old cathedral of Salamanca. Some of these influences began to affect the native artists: Ferrer Bassa (?–1348), court painter to Pedro IV of Aragon, for example, followed the monumentality of Giotto, and like Giotto he was interested in bringing out the psychological significance of his scenes;[171] Luis Borassá (?–*ca.* 1424) of Barcelona employed simple but powerful natural backgrounds;[172] and Bermejo, as was seen above, began to follow the Italians in his composition. But on the whole this early Italian influence was less pervasive than the Flemish stream.

The big wave of Italianate influence started in the second half of the fifteenth century and began to overwhelm most of the local styles. One of the first notable purveyors of this style was Pedro Berruguete (*ca.* 1450–1504) who learned his Italian art from Pierro della Francesca and from Signorelli. His paintings in the church of Santo Tomás of Avila and in the cathedral of Toledo[173] have the "scientific" properties of his masters — mathematical schematization, display of perspective, monumental bodies, and diversity of personalities. However, he still reveals some Flemish traits. Alejo Fernandez (?–1545) used the device of classical architectural settings to bring out spaciousness. Hernando Llanos and Hernando Yañez de la Almedina brought from Italy, where one worked with Leonardo da Vinci, monumental effect, classical disposition of drapery, and even an attempt at Leonardo's enigmatic style. Peter de Kempener, known in Seville as Pedro de Campaña, a Flemish artist who studied with Bernard van Orley and drew upon Raphael and Michelangelo, introduced "the attempt to express pathos with reserve and nobility [and] the simplification and concentration of design along lines of monumentality."[174] After these imitators came the full flowering of the High Renaissance. Juan de Juanes (1523–1579) of Valencia tried to emulate Raphael's cult of beauty, but in doing so achieved a sentimentalized version of it.[175] Luis Morales (*ca.* 1509–1588), also a follower of Raphael, even exceeded the sentimentalization of Juan de Juanes and fell into Mannerism. Known to his contemporaries as *El Divino,* he employed "always the same gracile contours, the same diaphonous bleached-out carnations, the same exaggerated and woebegone pathos, always the same pallid Christs and sentimental Madonnas."[176] Juan Fernandez de Navarrete (1526–1579), known as *El Mudo* because of his muteness, and sometimes called the "Spanish Titian" for his handling of light, sought to save the new style from oversweetness by bolder rendition and by use of naturalism and of scenes of everyday life. Alonso Sanchez Coello (1531/2–1588), the great portraitist, although a Romanist and Mannerist, is best known for his portraits in the Cosmopolitan style made famous by his teacher, the Dutchman Moro, and by Hans Holbein. His *Philip II*[177] is a good illustration of this realistic rendition garnished with aristocratic accoutrements. On the whole, then, the Italianate stage produced works that were sweet and elegant and affected but not truly powerful or great.

THE "NATIVE" SPANISH STYLE   Even as this Italianism was dying from surfeit of sweetness and beauty, the "native" Spanish began to assert itself. It is not wholly "native," for it retained many of the canons and techniques of the Flemish and the High Renaissance styles. But it breathed the Spanish spirit into these and transmuted them into something different, something which can be found nowhere else but Spain. Hence the designation.

The nature of this transmutation is to be observed in the paintings of several men who did their work after the middle of the sixteenth century. Francisco Ribalta (1551–1628), known as the "patriarch of the Spanish classical school," broke with the Italian formalism, as his *San Bruno*[178] and *Vision of St. Francis*[179] clearly show. In these two pictures his forms are not idealized but, modeled after the bold style of Tintoretto, they stand strong in their own true dignity, while the masculine religious ardor about them enhances their sincerity. Ribalta's contemporary Juan de las Roelas (1558–1625) still clung to some of the Raphaelesque beauty, but in his *Martyrdom of St. Andrew*[180] are to be seen heroic proportions and dramatic atmosphere. If it were not for the sweet grace of the heavenly host, the picture would be overwhelmingly realistic. Greater than either was Francisco de Herrera (1576–1656). Abandoning the Italianate completely, he painted as he saw, but he saw powerfully. Mather says "his pictures are full of the savage dignity and fanatical ardor of the national character." Moreover, to bring this vitality out he "invented a coarsely effective handling, loading the paint on and pulling it about so that the light splintered from it as it does in nature."[181] In his picture *St. Bonaventura Received as a Franciscan*,[182] for example, there is no sentimentalizing. The men are big and real — in the elemental sense rather than in the pictorial sense — and the spirit of the theme is commensurate. There is the strength that is associated with simplicity and honesty. Culminating this stage was El Greco, but his excellence and uniqueness require that he be given separate attention.

El Greco (1541–1614), whose real name was Domenikos Theotokoupolos, grew up in Crete, lived about ten years in Venice, and spent two years at Rome before coming to Spain in 1572. Each place left its mark on his art. In Crete, where the Byzantine tradition was strong, he acquired the spirit of hieraticism[183] and such techniques as the forward posting of his subjects and starting his pictures with a uniform ground. In Venice he learned the mastery of the brush stroke from Titian, the use of light without reference to its source from Tintoretto, and from Veronese, full-bodied forms as well as the practice of painting from wax models prepared beforehand. In Rome he developed a dislike for the Grand style. He failed to appreciate the nudes of Michelangelo and was prepared, according to reports, to undertake the repainting of the latter's *Last Judgment* "in a decent, seemly manner, and of quality equal to that of the original."[184] Apparently he could not accept what he believed to be the glorification of the naked man. He brought these skills and attitudes with him to Spain where they came under the influence of the rising native style of painting. Moreover, he himself yielded to the strong religious spirit of the Spaniards. The result was a change from his Italianate style to his Spanish style.

The style he developed bears his personal stamp of deep mystic spiritualism. Many of the themes are expressive of the mystic communion of the man with the spirit of the divine. In the *Virgin and Apostles Receiving the Holy Ghost*,[185] the bewilderment and the ecstasy of the electrified company suggest the wonder of this participation. *St. Peter's Tears*[186] is a portrayal of a yearning for such an experience. The celebrated *Burial of Count Orgaz*,[187] showing the rite of interment here on earth, God with his heavenly host on high, and the passage of the deceased's soul from earth to heaven, is a graphic symbolism of this act, and the steady pious gaze of the attendants at the mysterious process seems to animate the symbolism into a living experience. His numerous renderings of St. Francis invariably represent the saintly friar as a pious, strong-spirited ascetic whose mastery over body lifted him above the earthly. Other themes denote the overwhelming power of the other world. His *Christ on the Cross*[188] (Zumaya), or even the more earth-bound *Toledo*,[189] for example, seem to disembody the spirit, expose it to the ominous spectral firmament above, and lead it to self-purgation.

Other traits which mark his style as distinctive are really devices he employed to evoke this mystic spiritualism. But whether a means to an end or the end itself, they are indelible marks of his style. One is the distortion of the human forms: he elongated them, twisted their postures, and charged them with animation or nervous movement. Then, he eschewed detail and often merely suggested the forms so that they had an apparitional aspect (*Vision of the Apocalypse*,[190] *St. Andrew*, Plate 40). Another is the depiction of the atmosphere as electric, foreboding (*Christ on the Cross, St. Andrew, Virgin and Apostles Receiving the Holy Spirit*). Still another is the arbitrary and daring use of light and dark to accentuate the strange and the spectral (*The Virgin Mary* and *St. John*, details from the *Crucifixion* and *Toledo*).[191] Combined with the religious themes, these devices produced a style which emphasized the spiritual rather than the material and the visionary rather than the concrete.

One additional characteristic of his painting, but in a different mood from the preceding traits, is the physical and spiritual refinement with which he endowed the Spanish grandees. Whether in their portraits, as in that of *Julian Romero de las Azanas*, or in some idealized version of them, as in *The Burial of Count Orgaz*, these aristocrats are all represented as gentlemen of breeding and intelligence, with spiritual stature to match. Their features, their beards, their white ruffled collars, and their refined hands — all are suggestive of their strong internal grace. But although aristocratic to their fingertips, they are not prim like those of the International style, nor sensuous and carnal like those of the Venetian school.

This uniqueness of El Greco's style raises some difficulties as to where to classify him. The bodily deformations and the intense emotionalism point to the Mannerist style. On the other hand, the absence of superficiality and the sincerity of the religious spirit reflect the earlier classic tradition. At the same time his employment of the elemental is also Renaissance. Perhaps therefore he could still be considered with the Spanish Renaissance school, but as one with whom Renaissance painting in Spain was approaching its end.

Looking back over the survey we find that Spain accepted the High Renaissance style of Italy at the beginning of the sixteenth century, tried it for some fifty years, and then repudiated its forms and spirit in favor of a spiritually severe style, more in keeping with the nation's religious soul, which reached its culmination in El Greco.

1. So Sewall, *op. cit.*, 533, and Constable in *Cambridge Medieval History,* VIII, 760.

2. E. Panofsky, *Early Netherlandish Painting* (Cambridge: Harvard University Press, 1953), 24, 67.

3. *Ibid.*, 67.

4. See below, p. 195.

5. Frederick Antal, *Florentine Painting and Its Social Background* (London: Kegan Paul, 1947), plates 105, 106.

6. Panofsky, *Early Netherlandish Painting*, 29.

7. See figs. 13.10 and 11 in Sewall, *op. cit.*, 504–5.

8. Sewall, *op. cit.*, figs. 13.14–15, p. 507.

9. Blunt, *op. cit.*, 18.

10. This is traced briefly in Margaret Rickert, *Painting in Britain: The Middle Ages*, vol. V of *The Pelican History of Art* (Baltimore, Maryland: Penguin Books, 1954), 166–8.

11. *Ibid.*, plate 166.

12. *Ibid.*, plate 166.

13. *Ibid.*, plates 152–3.

14. Frank Jewett Mather, Jr., *Western European Painting of the Renaissance* (New York: Henry Holt and Co., 1939), figs. 89, 95.

15. *Ibid.*, fig. 99.

16. *Ibid.*, figs. 103, 111, 112.

17. See Mather, *op. cit.*, figs. 124, 125, 127, 130–2, 134, 135, and Jacques Lassaigne, *Spanish Painting from the Catalan Frescos to El Greco,* trans. Stuart Gilbert (Geneva: Éditions Albert Skira, 1952), 56, 60, 63.

18. Concerning the change consult Cesare Gnudi, *Giotto*, trans. R. H. Boothroyd (Milan: Aldo Martello Editore, no date), introduction.

19. See reproductions in Yvon Taillandier, *Giotto*, trans. Lucy Norton, "Hyperion Miniatures" (New York: The Macmillan Company, no date), 26, 27.

20. *Ibid.*, 30–31, 37.

21. Jean Leymarie, *Giotto Fresques*, in series "Collection Iris" (Paris: Librairie Plon, 1950), plate VIII.

21. *Ibid.*, plate VI.

22. *Ibid.*, plates I, V.

23. Cf. the eyes of the followers of Jesus in the *Entry into Jerusalem* in *ibid.*, plate VIII.

24. *Ibid.*, plates VI, X, XI.

25. Cf. Leonardo da Vinci's statement "after Giotto art again declined, because all were imitating paintings already done," Edward McCurdy, *Leonardo da Vinci's Note-Books* (New York: Empire State Book Co., 1935), 164.

26. For examples of their work see Antal, *op. cit.*, plates 66, 146, 147.

27. Morey, *op. cit.*, 338. But on Masaccio's role with respect to aerial perspective see Sewall, *op. cit.*, 629.

28. On this point see *ibid.*, 626–7.

29. *Ibid.*, fig. 15.21.

30. Antal, *op. cit.*, 307–8.

31. *Cambridge Medieval History*, VIII, 770.

32. For some reproductions see André Blum, *Les maitres du Quattrocento*, in *Éditions de clairefontaine pour le France* (Paris: Intercontinentale du livre, 1949).

33. Sewall, *op. cit.*, 645.

34. For one example see Masolino da Panicale's *Salome before Herod* reproduced in Blum, *op. cit.*, plate 13.

35. Cf., for example, Mantegna's *The Martyrdom of St. James, The Crucifixion, The Agony in the Garden*, and *St. George* reproduced in Giuseppe Fiocco, *Paintings by Mantegna* (New York: Henry N. Abrams, Inc., no date), plates 5, 9, 20, 23, respectively.

36. Giorgio Vasari, *Lives of Seventy of the Most Eminent Painters, Sculptors, and Architects*, eds. E. H. and E. W. Blashfield and A. A. Hopkins (London: George Bell and Sons, 1897), II, 200–1.

37. Blum, *op. cit.*, plates 58, 59.

38. Vasari, *op. cit.*, II, 361.

39. Blum, *op. cit.*, plates 83–85.

40. *Ibid.*, plate 82.

41. *Ibid.*, plate 20.

42. *Ibid.*, plates 21, 22.

43. Morey, *op. cit.*, 341.

44. See in Blum, *op. cit.*, plates 52–55.

45. *Ibid.*, plates 33–35.

46. For an illuminating treatment of this subject see the chapter "Neo-platonism and the Arts" in Nesca A. Robb, *Neoplatonism of the Italian Renaissance* (London: George Allen and Unwin Ltd., 1935), 212–38.

47. Clear, easily accessible reproductions in Gabriel Rouchés, *Botticelli*, "Collection des Maitres" (Paris: Les éditions Braun & cie., 1950), plates 23–25 and 45–46.

48. For a detailed explanation of the allegory and of the idealism in one of these, *The Birth of Venus*, see Edgar Wind, *Pagan Mysteries in the Renaissance* (New Haven: Yale University Press, 1958), chap. viii: *The Birth of Venus.*

49. Blum, *op. cit.*, plate 76.

50. For an English edition of some of the extant parts see Edward Mc-Curdy, *Leonardo da Vinci's Note-Books*, 1935.

51. For this see the reproductions in Adolphe Basler, *Léonard de Vinci*, "Collection des Maitres" (Paris: Les éditions Braun & cie., no date), plates 32–46, 53–60.

52. Basler, *op. cit.*, plates 27, 28.

53. Robb, *op. cit.*, 231.

54. Cf. the characterization in Antonina Vallentine, *Leonardo da Vinci*, trans. E. W. Dickes (New York: The Viking Press, 1938), 356.

55. On this see Robb, *op. cit.*, 233–4.

56. Cf. the description in Vasari, *op. cit.*, II, 385–7.

57. Sewall, *op. cit.*, plates 16.13–14.

58. For a full treatment see his article "In Foraminibus Petrae: A Note on Leonardo's 'Virgin of the Rocks,'" *Renaissance News*, VII (1954), 92–94.

59. For an analysis of the picture see the reproductions and their diagrams in Sewall, *op, cit.*, plates 16.17–20.

60. On this see Harry B. Gutman, "The Medieval Content of Raphael's 'School of Athens,'" *Journal of the History of Ideas*, II (1941), 420–9.

61. An excellent analysis of Michelangelo's idealization of the beauty in the human form is to be found in Anthony Blunt, *Artistic Theory in Italy, 1450–1600* (2d ed.; Oxford: Clarendon Press, 1956), 59–64.

62. Cited in Sewall, *op. cit.*, 750.

63. For reproductions of the works of all three see Blum, *op. cit.*, plates 90–95.

64. *Ibid.*, plates 96–101.

65. See his *Madonna with Saint Francis and Saint George* (in color) in Helen Gardner, *op. cit.*, plate III, 418.

66. Sewall, *op. cit.*, 759.

67. *Ibid.*, plate 16.33.

68. Reproductions in René Huyghe, *Le Titien*, "Collection des Maitres" (Paris: Les éditions Braun & cie., 1949), plates 24 and 42. For an analysis of this principle see Sewall, *op. cit.*, 762–3.

69. Sewall, *op. cit.*, 765.

70. For some examples see the many plates in Huyghe, *op. cit.*

71. The two types may be seen in *ibid.*, plates 20, 21, 27, 32–34.

72. In Gabriel Rouchés, *Paul Véronèse*, "Collection des Maitres" (Paris: Les éditions Braun & cie., 1950), plate 55.

73. *Ibid.*, plates 13, 15, 16.

74. *Op. cit.*, I, 758.

75. For an analysis see Sewall, *op. cit.*, 752–5.

76. *Ibid.*, fig. 16.41.

77. See Bernard Berenson, *Italian Pictures of the Renaissance, Venetian School* (New York: Phaidon Publishers, Inc., 1957), II, plates 1272–3, 1298–9, and others.

78. In Paul Gay, *Van Eyck*, "Collection des Maitres" (Paris: Les éditions Braun & cie., no date), plate 20.

79. On this matter see Panofsky, *op. cit.*, I, 182, 183.

80. *Ibid.*, I, 194–5.

81. Cf. *ibid.*, I, 249–50.

82. In Mather, *op. cit.*, figs. 34, 41, 42.

83. *Ibid.*, 77.

84. *Ibid.*, figs. 43, 44.

85. Panofsky, *op. cit.*, I, 309.

86. Mather, *op. cit.*, figs. 47–49.

87. Paul Fierens, *Memlinc*, "Collection des Maitres" (Paris: Les éditions Braun & cie., no date), plates 15, 29, 44, 46, 53, 56–58.

88. Panofsky, *op. cit.*, I, 348.

89. Cited in Horace Shipp, *The Flemish Masters* (New York: Philosophical Library, Inc., 1954), 23.

90. Sewall, *op. cit.*, 616.

91. Pictures in Mather, *op. cit.*, figs. 63, 64, 51.

92. *Ibid.*, figs. 65, 50, 53.

93. *Op. cit.*, 145, 146.

94. *Op. cit.*, 772.

95. *Op. cit.*, 357.

96. Mather, *op. cit.*, 148.

97. For details see F. M. Godfrey, *Jerome Bosch*, "World Masters" (New York: Authentic Publications, Inc., no date), plates 94–95.

98. *Ibid.*, plates 100–1.

99. *Ibid.*, plates 23–33, 63–71.

100. See the colored plates in *ibid.*, 27, 61, 81, 97.

101. *Ibid.*, plate 61.

102. Cf. *ibid.*, introduction, xi.

103. André Leclerc, *Brueghel the Elder*, "Hyperion Miniatures" (New York: The Hyperion Press, no date), plates similarly named.

104. *Ibid.*, plates 42, 41, respectively.

105. *Ibid.*, plates 13, 15, 20.

106. Large reproductions of these and others may be seen in the popular magazine *Life*, December 27, 1954, 28 ff.

107. Sewall, *op. cit.*, 784.

108. Mather, *op. cit.*, fig. 76.

109. *Ibid.*, fig. 79.

110. *Ibid.*, fig. 78.

111. *Ibid.*, figs. 69–71.

112. *Ibid.*, fig. 72.

113. Panofsky, *op. cit.*, I, 353.

114. Mather, *op. cit.*, fig. 170.

115. *Ibid.*, 308.

116. *Ibid.*, fig. 168.

117. *Ibid.*, fig. 172.

118. *Ibid.*, fig. 173.

119. *Ibid.*, 191.

120. Cited in *ibid.*, 203.

121. *Ibid.*, figs. 116, 117.

122. *Ibid.*, figs. 118, 120. For a colored reproduction of the *Annunciation* see Otto Fischer, *Geschichte der Deutschen Malerei*, band III of *Deutsche Kunstgeschichte* (München: F. Bruckmann Verlag, 1942), 144.

123. Mather, *op. cit.*, fig. 121.

124. *Ibid.*, fig. 122.

125. *Ibid.*, figs. 146–8. Others in Fischer, *op. cit.*, plates between 230 and 245.

126. E. Panofsky, *Albrecht Dürer* (3d ed.; Princeton: Princeton University Press, 1948), I, 9.

127. Georges Noel, *Dürer*, "Collection des Maitres" (Paris: Les éditions Braun & cie., no date), plates 37, 45.

128. *Ibid.*, plate 15; Mather, *op. cit.*, fig. 144.

129. Fine reproductions in Fischer, *op. cit.*, 227–9.

130. Noel, *op. cit.*, plate 20.

131. *Ibid.*, plate 4.

132. On Dürer's belief in miracles and eschatology, a state of mind generally associated with the medieval man, see Otto Benesch, *The Art of the Renaissance in Northern Europe* (Cambridge: Harvard University Press, 1947), 9–11.

133. For a treatment of these see Sewall, *op. cit.*, 775–8. Pictures in Noel, *op. cit.*, plates 49, 52, 51, respectively.

134. Panofsky, *Albrecht Dürer*, I, 12.

135. Benesch, *op. cit.*, plates 6 and 9.

136. Fischer, *op. cit.*, 224, and Noel, *op. cit.*, plate 21.

137. Noel, *op. cit.*, plates 14, 16, 19, 33.

138. *Ibid.*, plates 24–26.

139. Panofsky, *Albrecht Dürer*, II, figs. 44, 46.

140. *Ibid.*, II, figs. 49, 50.

141. Noel, *op. cit.*, plates 34, 46.

142. *Ibid.*, plates 36, 54.

143. Gabriel Rouchés, *Cranach L'Ancien*, "Collection des Maitres" (Paris: Les éditions Braun & cie., 1951), plates 12, 41, 42, 44, 46, 54.

144. Fischer, *op. cit.*, 256, 261. Cf. the other plates in between.

145. For these see Mather, *op. cit.*, figs. 150, 152, 153, 156 and Fischer, *op. cit.*, 299, 301.

146. Mather, *op. cit.*, fig. 151.

147. Fischer, *op. cit.*, 295.

148. Colored reproductions in *French Primitives of the XVth Century*, "Museum of Masterpieces" (Paris: Éditions du Chêne, 1950), plates II, III.

149. *Ibid.*, plate V.

150. Basil Taylor, *French Painting* (London and New York: Thames and Hudson, 1951), plates 33, 34.

151. Blunt, *Art and Architecture in France, 1500 to 1700*, plate 17B.

152. *Ibid.*, plates 25A–B, 26, 27.

153. *Ibid.*, plate 48.

154. *Ibid.*, plate 49.

155. *Ibid.*, plate 47.

156. *Ibid.*, 69.

157. B. Taylor, *op. cit.*, plates 22, 18, respectively.

158. Cited in *ibid.*, 16.

159. See Blunt, *Art and Architecture in France, 1500 to 1700*, plates 22A–B, 23, 41–44.

160. *Op. cit.*, 340.

161. Blunt, *op. cit.*, plate 45. For a colored reproduction of his *The Rape of Proserpine* see *Art Treasures of the Louvre* (New York: Henry N. Abrams, Inc., 1951), plate 22.

162. They are studied in Ellis Waterhouse, *Painting in Britain, 1530 to 1790*, vol. V of *The Pelican History of Art* (Baltimore, Maryland: Penguin Books, 1953), 1–18.

163. Self-portrait in *ibid.*, plate 15a.

164. *Ibid.*, plate 19.

165. For pictures see Lassaigne, *op. cit.*, 50–51.

166. *Ibid.*, 59.

167. *Ibid.*, 68, 69.

168. Mather, *op. cit.*, figs. 134, 135.

169. *Ibid.*, fig. 133.

170. Lassaigne, *op. cit.*, 73–77.

171. *Ibid.*, 38–44.

172. *Ibid.*, 46.

173. *Ibid.*, 85.

174. Mather, *op. cit.*, 360.

175. Lassaigne, *op. cit.*, 91.

176. Mather, *op. cit.*, 365.

177. Lassaigne, *op. cit.*, 95.

178. *Ibid.*, 97.

179. Mather, *op. cit.*, fig. 203.

180. *Ibid.*, fig. 201.

181. *Ibid.*, 362.

182. *Ibid.*, fig. 200.

183. See, for example, *The Saviour* in Leo Bronstein, *El Greco*, "The Library of Great Painters" (New York: Harry N. Abrams, 1950), 105.

184. Lassaigne, *op. cit.*, 106.

185. *Ibid.*, 119.

186. *Ibid.*, 110.

187. Bronstein, *op. cit.*, 50–55.

188. Lassaigne, *op. cit.*, 107.

189. Bronstein, *op. cit.*, 111.

190. Lassaigne, *op. cit.*, 118, 121, 122.

191. *Ibid.*, 108, 109; Bronstein, *op. cit.*, 111.

XI

Summary
of Significant Innovations
in Literature and Art
during the Renaissance

Literature

A NY ATTEMPT to be precise on the extent and nature of the innovations in literature during the Renaissance is, of course, out of the question. But some notion of what happened may be obtained by balancing the more obvious innovations against the equally obvious continuations from the Middle Ages.

As to the continuations there were some which underwent but little change, and others which were modified noticeably but not substantially.

To begin with, the vernaculars, which had begun to take shape in the later Middle Ages, became national in extent and gained in standardization and in literary sophistication. The degree of change naturally varied from country to country. In Italy it was the Tuscan of Dante and Petrarch, that is, the vernacular of the late Middle Ages, which was adopted nationally. Likewise in Spain, it was the vernacular of the thirteenth century that eventually prevailed. On the other hand, the English vernacular dates from Chaucer's time, and the German appeared even later, so that both may be said to have shaped themselves more or less during the Renaissance.

In the realm of literature proper, relatively little change occurred in religious drama, *novelle*, farces, and folksongs. Other than increased elaboration there is no substantial difference, for example, between a late fifteenth-century morality and its thirteenth-century counterpart. Nor is the late Renaissance folksong significantly different from an early Renaissance or a late medieval folksong. Greater changes appeared in the romance and the lyric. The romance, made popular by the press, dropped the poetic and adopted the prose form, except in Italy, and heightened storiology at the expense of epical properties; while the lyric put on a classical dress. But these changes, while noticeable, were really not substantial: the romance, as to theme, spirit, and aristocratic airs, remained medieval; and the lyric still revealed its dependence on troubadour compositions.

But side by side with these continuations, little changed or modified noticeably but not substantially, there were some real innovations.

In the field of romance two new forms developed, the pastoral romance and the romantic epic. The first, it will be remembered, was largely the creation of Sannazaro whose *Arcadia* served as a model throughout Europe. It combined poetry with poeticlike prose, treated of love in a mood of sweet melancholy, and generally moved on an elevated spiritual plane. Sydney's *Arcadia* testifies to the extent and the depth of this influence. The second, also born in Italy, combined the structure of Vergilian epic with much matter from the medieval romance and the spirit of both. Its popularity was impressive, *Orlando Furioso*, *Lusiad*, and *Faerie Queen* being its most successful examples.

In the lyric field the innovation that captured the literary world was the sonnet. The form itself was not new, but the gathering of sonnets together into a sequence, if Dante is excepted, was new; and this, together with the great increase in the number of sonnets written in the course of the Renaissance period, justify the inclusion of the sonnet among the innovations in Renaissance literature.

Also new was the secular and religious drama based on classical models, comedy on Plautus and Terence, and tragedy on Seneca. One outcome of this imitation was the provision of form and structure for the drama, something it had lacked before. Another consequence was a decided elevation of the style, due in part to the necessity of adapting the language to the high status of the characters involved in the plays and in part to the fact that drama in the Renaissance came to be regarded as a form of literature. Less the result of direct classical dramatic heritage but still influenced by it was the very important innovation of characterization. In a steadily increasing number of plays the *dramatis personae* ceased to be representations of allegorical abstractions and became persons, or they ceased to be types and became real people whose character shaped itself with the progress of the story. Of course, an obvious innovation was the formation of companies of professional actors and the erection of permanent theaters, both lacking in the preceding age.

In connection with the innovations in drama, the case of the romantic comedy is unique. In structure and in language it followed the classical models; for action, story, and people it drew on the medieval romantic tradition; for its rationale it depended upon the social and religious ideals current in the Middle Ages. Thus as a literary form it was new, but in much else it adhered to the old.

In the field of prose, the novel was an important new development. Based on the medieval *novelle*, for the story was the essence of both, it departed from its precursor by assuming greater length, by subordinating anecdotes to one principal plot, by employing characters which develop with the story, and by trying to be a mirror of society as well as a form of literary entertainment.

In addition to these developments in the several separate fields of literature there were at least three developments of considerable consequence which affected the field of literature as a whole.

One major development was the classicization of literature. This took at least three forms. One was the investment of literature with form and structure, and this applied to drama, romantic epic, pastoral romance, lyric to some extent, and history. Another was the refinement of vocabulary and of expression in general. The third combined excessive Latinizing of style with an exhibition of classical learning verging on pedantry. All three tended to elevate the general tone, but when carried to excess they threatened to make literature stylized and artificial.

The second development was the emergence of individualism. This is generally attributed to the humanistic influence of the classics. Medieval lyricists sang impersonally to impersonal maids, and dramatists spoke of and to every man rather than of and to some individual person. The Renaissance writers began to do otherwise, to write as if their feelings were personal and the subjects of their address real individuals. To some extent this is true, but only to some extent, for such characterizations as Petrarchism, Euphuism, Gongorism, Ciceronianism certainly imply that much of Renaissance literature was imitative and therefore weak in individualism.

The third development, a significant one, was the great increase in prose. Literature was being conceived as something to be read rather than to be recited, and, with the help of increasing literacy and of an expanding press which made books cheaper, more and more prose literature came into being. This was an impressive index pointing truly toward the modern age.

By way of summary, then, we can say that Renaissance literature, while retaining many medieval characteristics, assumed a steadily increasing number of modern properties.

Art

At the outset of the Renaissance period the prevailing style of painting in western Europe was the International style, a combination of Byzantine and Gothic styles. It was done in line, and looked formalistic, graceful, and painterly. Even as this style was gaining in popularity, the Renaissance style appeared in Italy. The new style began when painters started depicting their subjects naturalistically, and it advanced as the artists gained greater knowledge of perspective and anatomy, replaced tempera with oils, and adopted chiaroscuro. It finally flowered as the High Renaissance style when idealization was added to the mastery of the above essentials. Thereafter, toward the end of the sixteenth century, it became mannered and moved toward the Baroque.

This is the history of painting in Italy. In other lands the story is largely the fusion of the Italian Renaissance styles with the competing Flemish style and with native traditions. In the Low Countries it was joined with the native miniaturist school of art; in Germany, with the Flemish and the two together with the native "idiomatic" traits; in Spain, likewise with the Flemish and with the native spiritualism; and in France and England, with the Flemish again, but with no distinctive national traditions, as these were lacking.

In addition to these changes in style, several other notable developments occurred. One was the appearance of portraiture and of landscape and genre painting, all of which reflect a trend toward the mundane. Another development was the increasing secularization of religious pictures. And still another was the disappearance of anonymity and the simultaneous elevation of the artist professionally and socially.

To discover and to describe these changes is relatively easy. But to account for them is a more difficult matter. At best only some generalizations can be suggested. One factor which fostered the change was undoubtedly the cult of antiquity. There is no question that it forced its way into the subject matter, for paintings of classical themes are numerous. Presumably, in consequence of this infusion, the interest in the nude was stimulated and largeness of spirit and monumentality promoted. As part of this cult but deserving of separate notice was the factor of humanism with its predilection for Neoplatonism — Christianized Neoplatonism, that is. What this promoted was the subordination of the material to the ideal on the assumption that true reality is of the spiritual order. Another reason for the changes was the patronage of art by wealthy laymen. Whether these people undertook to be patrons because of their appreciation of art or because they felt that such support added to their social prestige, their patronage was bound to have some influence on the art. They seem to have preferred portraiture — scenes from antiquity or of contemporary social occasions in which they had a part, country scenes, that is, secular themes in general — and the artists obliged. However, this increase in worldly themes should not blind one to the fact that religious themes still predominated. A third factor was the growth of science. Depiction of surface appearances, which may be regarded as a qualitative treatment of the subject, yielded to rendering of the fundamentals in accordance with the principles of anatomy, of the laws of light and of proper composition, which in turn may be considered as a quantitative treatment. Such a change, it will be recalled, actually took place in formal science itself. Still another factor, and one which is too often ignored, was simply the natural growth that occurs in trades without the benefit of intellectual movements and academic cults. Painters as apprentices rather than as scientists learned the "trade" from their masters, and some, impelled by ambition or curiosity rather than by formal science or philosophy of art, experimented with their masters' techniques and media with the view of equaling or surpassing them. To the extent that they succeeded they were clearly introducing improvements and change; and as this was repeated from one generation to another, the final result turned out to be significantly different from the initial stage. This explanation may sound too simple, but its simplicity should not be held against it. Studies of the relations between artists and their pupils who in turn became teachers provide confirmation to it. Indeed, that is what some of the Renaissance artists actually asserted in the handbooks which they prepared on their art. Thus Cennini in his manual on painting (*ca.* 1400), and Roriczer in his handbook on architecture (1486), and Dürer in his work on the employment of geometry and perspective, all pay tribute to their predecessors for their contributions and then describe their own improvements or inventions.[1]

1. On this see Edgar Zilsel, "The Genesis of the Concept of Scientific Progress," *Journal of the History of Ideas*, VI (1945), 332–6.

Bibliography

Works on Renaissance art and literature come in one unending wave, beyond control even if limited to publications appearing in English. Obviously only a sample selection of some of the more recent writings can be presented here.

Some Current Bibliographical Aids

To keep abreast of the new publications in these two areas, the student may consult:

Renaissance News, 1948–, a quarterly published by the Renaissance Society of America.

Studies of Philology, the annual April issue.

Publications of the Modern Language Association (*PMLA*) the annual May issue.

The Journal of the Warburg and Courtauld Institutes, published by the Warburg Institute of the University of London.

General Works on Art and Literature

Some classics and some challenging general works dealing with both of these areas, with which students should become familiar, are:

Burckhardt, Jacob. *The Civilization of the Renaissance in Italy*. Various editions.

Huizinga, J. *The Waning of the Middle Ages*. In the series *Anchor Books*. Garden City, New York: Doubleday and Company, Inc., 1954.

Symonds, John Addington. *Renaissance in Italy*. Various editions. The 2-volume work published by the Modern Library of New York in 1935 is as good as any.

Sypher, Wylie. *Four Stages of Renaissance Style. Transformations in Art and Literature, 1400–1700*. In the series *Anchor Books Original*. Garden City, New York: Doubleday and Company, Inc., 1955.

Works on Literature

Abbé, Derek van. *Drama in Renaissance Germany and Switzerland.* Victoria: Melbourne University Press, 1961.

Atkins, J. W. H. *English Literary Criticism: The Medieval Phase.* New York: The Macmillan Co., 1943.

Atkins, J. W. H. *English Literary Criticism: The Renaissance.* 2d ed.; London: Methuen & Co., Ltd., 1951.

Auerbach, Erich. *Dante, Poet of the Secular World.* Translated by Ralph Manheim. Chicago: University of Chicago Press, 1961.

Baker, Ernest A. *The History of the English Novel.* 2 vols. New York: Barnes and Noble, Inc., 1929.

Baldwin, Charles Sears. *Renaissance Literary Theory and Practice.* New York: Columbia University Press, 1939.

Baugh, Albert C. *et al. A Literary History of England.* New York: Appleton-Century-Crofts, Inc., 1948.

Bradner, Leicester. "The Latin Drama of the Renaissance (1340–1640)," *Studies in the Renaissance,* IV (1957), 31–54.

Bradner, Leicester. "The Rise of Secular Drama in the Renaissance," *Studies in the Renaissance,* III (1956), 7–22.

Brenan, Gerald. *The Literature of the Spanish People from Roman Times to the Present Day.* Cambridge: University Press, 1951.

Bush, Douglas. *Classical Influences in Renaissance Literature.* Vol. XIII of *Martin Classical Lectures.* Cambridge: Harvard University Press, 1952.

Bush, Douglas. *Prefaces to Renaissance Literature.* Cambridge: Harvard University Press, 1965.

Chambers, E. K. *English Literature at the Close of the Middle Ages.* Vol. II, Part 2 of *The Oxford History of English Literature.* Oxford: Clarendon Press, 1945.

Clark, Barrett H. *European Theories of the Drama.* New York: D. Appleton-Century Co., Inc., 1936.

Closs, August. *The Genius of the German Lyric. An Historic Survey of Its Formal and Metaphysical Values.* London: George Allen & Unwin, Ltd., 1938.

Craig, Hardin. *English Religious Drama of the Middle Ages.* Oxford: Clarendon Press, 1955.

Crane, Ronald S. *The Vogue of Medieval Chivalric Romance during the English Renaissance.* Menasha, Wisconsin: George Banta Publishing Company, 1919.

Crane, William G. *Wit and Rhetoric in the Renaissance.* Columbia University Studies in English and Comparative Literature. Gloucester: Smith P., 1964.

Darmesteter, Arsène and Hatzfeld, Adolphe. *Le seizième siècle en France: Tableau de la littérature et de la langue.* 7th ed.; Paris: Librairie Ch. Delagrave, 1901.

Donovan, Father Richard B. *The Liturgical Drama in Medieval Spain.* No. 4 of *Studies and Texts.* Toronto: Pontifical Institute of Mediaeval Studies, 1958.

Entwistle, William J. *The Spanish Language together with Portuguese, Catalan and Basque.* London: Faber and Faber, Ltd., 1946.

Farnham, Willard. *The Medieval Heritage of Elizabethan Tragedy.* Berkeley: University of California Press, 1936.

Gardner, E. *Arthurian Legends in Italian Literature.* London: J. M. & Dent Sons, Ltd., 1930.

Green, Otis H. *Spain and the Western Tradition. The Castilian Mind in Literature from El Cid to Calderon.* Madison, Wisconsin: University of Wisconsin Press, 1963.

Herrick, Marvin T. *Italian Comedy in the Renaissance.* Urbana, Illinois: University of Illinois Press, 1960.

Jackson, W. T. H. *The Literature of the Middle Ages.* New York: Columbia University Press, 1960.

Kristeller, Paul Oskar. "The Origin and Development of the Language of Italian Prose," in his *Studies in Renaissance Thought and Letters.* Rome: Edizioni di Storia e Letteratura, 1956, 473–93.

Lewis, Clive Staples. *English Literature in the Sixteenth Century.* Vol. V of *The Oxford History of English Literature.* Oxford: Clarendon Press, 1954.

Lewis, D. B. Wyndham. *François Villon.* New York: The Literary Guild of America, 1938.

Mason, H. A. *Humanism and Poetry in the Early Tudor Period.* New York: Barnes and Noble, Inc., 1960.

Muscatine, Charles. *Chaucer and the French Tradition.* Berkeley: University of California Press, 1957.

Nicoll, Allardyce. *World Drama from Aeschylus to Anouilh.* New York: Harcourt, Brace and Co., 1950.

Nicoll, Allardyce. *The Development of the Theatre.* New York: Harcourt, Brace and Co., 1927.

Northup, George Tyler. *An Introduction to Spanish Literature.* Revised by Nicholson B. Adams. 3d ed.; Chicago: University of Chicago Press, 1960.

Priebsch, R. and Collinson, W. E. *The German Language.* New York: The Macmillan Co., 1938.

Sells, A. Lytton. *The Italian Influence in English Poetry from Chaucer to Southwell.* Bloomington, Indiana: Indiana University Press, 1955.

Smith, Winifred. *The Commedia dell'Arte.* New York: The Columbia University Press, 1912.

Spaulding, Robert K. *How Spanish Grew.* Berkeley: University of California Press, 1948.

Taylor, Archer. *Problems in German Literary History of the Fifteenth and Sixteenth Centuries.* New York: Modern Language Association of America, 1939.

Tilley, Arthur. *The Literature of the French Renaissance.* 2 vols. Cambridge: University Press, 1904.

Tilley, Arthur. *François Rabelais.* Edited by A. Jessup. Philadelphia: J. B. Lippincott Co., 1907.

Tillyard, E. M. W. *The English Renaissance, Fact or Fiction.* Baltimore: The Johns Hopkins Press, 1952.

Vittorini, Domenico. *The Age of Dante.* Syracuse: Syracuse University Press, 1957.

Wilkins, Ernest Hatch. *A History of Italian Literature.* Cambridge: Harvard University Press, 1954.

Wilkins, Ernest Hatch. *Life of Petrarch.* Chicago: University of Chicago Press, 1961.

General Histories of Art

Students lacking background in art may begin by consulting general histories on the subject. Among the better ones are:

Gardner, Helen. *Art through the Ages.* 4th ed.; New York: Harcourt, Brace and Co., 1959.

Robb, David M. and Garrison, J. J. *Art in the Western World.* 4th ed.; New York: Harper & Row, Publishers, 1963.

Sewall, John Ives. *A History of Western Art.* New York: Henry Holt and Co., Inc., 1953.

Works on Social Backgrounds of Renaissance Art and on Artistic Theory

Alberti, Leon Battista. *On Painting.* Translated with Introduction and Notes by John R. Spencer. New Haven: Yale University Press, 1965.

Antal, Frederick. *Florentine Painting and Its Social Background. The Bourgeois Republic before Cosimo de'Medici's Advent to Power: XIV and Early XV Centuries.* London: Kegan Paul, 1947.

Benesch, Otto. *The Art of the Renaissance in Northern Europe.* Cambridge: Harvard University Press, 1947.

Blunt, Anthony. *Artistic Theory in Italy, 1450–1600.* 2d ed.; Oxford: Clarendon Press, 1956.

Frankl, Paul. *The Gothic; Literary Sources and Interpretations through Eight Centuries.* Princeton: Princeton University Press, 1960.

Panofsky, Erwin. *Gothic Architecture and Scholasticism.* New York: Meridian Books, 1957.

Wittkower, Rudolf. *Architectural Principles in the Age of Humanism.* Vol. XIX of *Studies of the Warburg Institute.* London: The Warburg Institute of the University of London, 1949.

General Works

Baum, Julius (ed.). *Romanesque Architecture in France.* 2d ed.; New York: B. Westermann Co., Inc., 1928.

Berenson, Bernard. *The Italian Painters of the Renaissance.* Revised edition. Oxford: Clarendon Press, 1930.

Berenson, Bernard. *Italian Pictures of the Renaissance, Venetian School.* London: Phaidon Press, 1957.

Blum, André. *Les maitres du Quattrocento,* in the series *Éditions de clairefontaine pour le France.* Paris: Intercontinentale du livre, 1949.

Blunt, Anthony. *Art and Architecture in France, 1500 to 1700.* Vol. IV of *The Pelican History of Art.* Baltimore, Maryland: Penguin Books, 1954.

Chase, George Henry and Post, Chandler Rathfon. *A History of Sculpture.* New York: Harper and Brothers Publishers, 1925.

Evans, Joan. *English Art 1307–1461.* Vol. V of *The Oxford History of English Art.* Oxford: Clarendon Press, 1949.

Fischer, Otto. *Geschichte der Deutschen Malerei.* Band III of *Deutsche Kunstgeschichte.* München: F. Bruckmann Verlag, 1942.

Frankl, Paul. *Gothic Architecture.* Translated by Dieter Pevsner. Vol. XIX of *The Pelican History of Art.* Baltimore: Penguin Books, Inc., 1962.

Freedberg, Sydney Joseph. *Painting of the High Renaissance in Rome and Florence.* 2 vols. Cambridge: Harvard University Press, 1961.

French Primitives of the XVth Century. In the series *Museum of Masterpieces.* Paris: Éditions du Chêne, 1950.

Gardner, Arthur. *English Medieval Sculpture.* New ed.; Cambridge: University Press, 1951.

Hamlin, Talbot F. *Architecture through the Ages.* New York: G. P. Putnam's Sons, 1940.

Lassaigne, Jacques. *Spanish Painting from the Catalan Frescos to El Greco.* Translated by Stuart Gilbert. Geneva: Éditions Albert Skira, 1952.

Mâle, Émile. *Religious Art from the Twelfth to the Eighteenth Century.* New York: Pantheon Books, Inc., 1949.

Mather, Frank Jewett, Jr. *Western European Painting of the Renaissance.* New York: Henry Holt and Co., 1939.

Morey, Charles Rufus. *Medieval Art.* New York: W. W. Norton and Co., 1942.

Panofsky, Erwin. *Early Netherlandish Painting, Its Origins and Character.* Vol. I. Cambridge: Harvard University Press, 1953.

Puyvelde, Leo Van. *La peinture flamande au siècle de Bosch et Breughel.* Paris: Elsevier, 1962.

Rickert, Margaret. *Painting in Britain: The Middle Ages.* Vol. V of *The Pelican History of Art.* Baltimore: Penguin Books, Inc., 1954.

Shipp, Horace. *The Flemish Masters.* New York: Philosophical Library, Inc., 1954.

The Writings of Albrecht Dürer. Translated and edited by William Martin Conway, with an Introduction by Alfred Werner. New York: Philosophical Library, Inc., 1958.

Summerson, John. *Architecture in Britain, 1530 to 1830.* Vol. III of *The Pelican History of Art.* Baltimore: Penguin Books, 1954. Fourth edition of this work appeared in 1963.

Taylor, Basil. *French Painting.* London and New York: Thames and Hudson, 1951.

Vasari, Giorgio. *Lives of Seventy of the Most Eminent Painters, Sculptors, and Architects.* Eds. E. H. and E. W. Blashfield and A. A. Hopkins. London: George Bell and Sons, 1897.

Waterhouse, Ellis. *Painting in Britain, 1530 to 1790.* Vol. V of *The Pelican History of Art.* Baltimore: Penguin Books, Inc., 1953.

Wind, Edgar. *Pagan Mysteries in the Renaissance.* New Haven: Yale University Press, 1958.

Wilenski, R. H. *French Painting.* Boston: Hale, Cushman and Flint, Inc., 1936.

Works on Specific Artists

There are several series of reproductions of the works of artists with which students of art should be familiar.

Collection des Maitres. Paris: Les éditions Braun and cie.

Hyperion Miniatures. New York: The Hyperion Press.

World Masters. New York: Authentic Publications, Inc.

"The Taste of Our Time," *Biographical and Critical Study.* Directed by Albert Skira. Lausanne: Imprimeries Réunis S.A.

The first three are inexpensive paperbacks, but they contain usable reproductions. The Skira series is more costly, but its reproductions are in color. No references to specific artists published in these series need be made here.

For more comprehensive studies of some of the individual artists, the following are valuable:

Bronstein, Leo. *El Greco.* New York: Henry N. Abrams, 1950.

Cecchi, Dario. *Titian.* Translated by Nora Wydenbruck. New York: Farrar, Straus and Cudahy, Inc., 1958.

Clark, Sir Kenneth M. *Leonardo da Vinci; An Account of his Development as an Artist.* 2d ed.; Cambridge: University Press, 1952.

Fiocco, Guiseppe. *Paintings by Mantegna.* New York: Henry N. Abrams, Inc., no date.

Goldscheider, Ludwig. *Donatello.* New York: Oxford University Press, 1941.

Gnudi, Cesare. *Giotto.* Translated by R. H. Boothroyd. Milan: Aldo Martello Editore, no date.

Leymarie, Jean. *Giotto Fresques.* Paris: Librairie Plon, 1950.

Panofsky, Erwin. *Albrecht Dürer*. 3d ed.; Princeton: Princeton University Press, 1948.

Tolnay, Charles de. *Michelangelo*. 5 vols. Princeton: University Press, 1943–1960.

Wescher, Paul. *Jean Fouquet and His Time*. New York: Reynal and Hitchcock, 1947.

Index

ACKNOWLEDGMENTS

The author wishes to thank the following publishers for permission to quote from their publications listed below:

Harvard University Press
Cambridge, Massachusetts

Early Netherlandish Painting
by Erwin Panofsky

Holt, Rinehart and Winston, Inc.
New York

History of Western Art
by John Ives Sewall

Western European Painting of the Renaissance
by Frank Jewett Mather, Jr.

Methuen & Co., Ltd., Publishers
London, England

English Literary Criticism: The Renaissance
by J. W. H. Atkins

Oxford University Press, Inc.
New York

English Literature at the Close of the Middle Ages, by Sir Edmund K. Chambers

Penguin Books, Ltd.
Harmondsworth, Middlesex, England

Art and Architecture in France 1500–1700
by Anthony Blunt

Philosophical Library Inc.
New York

The Flemish Masters
by Horace Shipp

Princeton University Press
Princeton, New Jersey

Albrecht Dürer
by Erwin Panofsky

Random House, Inc.
New York

Petrarch: Sonnets and Songs, trans.
Anna Maria Armi

Renaissance in Italy
by John Addington Symonds

Syracuse University Press
Syracuse, New York

The Age of Dante
by Domenico Vittorini

The University of Wisconsin Press
Madison, Wisconsin

Spain and the Western Tradition. The Castilian Mind in Literature from El Cid to Calderon
by Otis H. Green